MW01488694

Certified

macromedia®
FLASH™

Developer Study Guide

macromedia®
PRESS

This title is published by Macromedia Press in association with Que Publishing.

www.quepublishing.com

201 West 103rd Street, Indianapolis, Indiana 46290

Copyright © 2002 by Que

All rights reserved. No part of this book shall be reproduced, stored in a retrieval system, or transmitted by any means, electronic, mechanical, photocopying, recording, or otherwise, without written permission from the publisher. No patent liability is assumed with respect to the use of the information contained herein. Although every precaution has been taken in the preparation of this book, the publisher and author assume no responsibility for errors or omissions. Nor is any liability assumed for damages resulting from the use of the information contained herein.

International Standard Book Number: 0-7897-2717-X

Library of Congress Catalog Card Number: 2001098266

Printed in the United States of America

First Printing: January 2002

05   04   03   02   4   3   2   1

Trademarks

All terms mentioned in this book that are known to be trademarks or service marks have been appropriately capitalized. Que cannot attest to the accuracy of this information. Use of a term in this book should not be regarded as affecting the validity of any trademark or service mark.

Warning and Disclaimer

Every effort has been made to make this book as complete and as accurate as possible, but no warranty or fitness is implied. The information provided is on an "as is" basis. The author and the publisher shall have neither liability nor responsibility to any person or entity with respect to any loss or damages arising from the information contained in this book.

PUBLISHER
David Culverwell

EXECUTIVE EDITOR
Candace Hall

ACQUISITIONS EDITOR
Angela Kozlowski

DEVELOPMENT EDITOR
Mark Kozlowski

MANAGING EDITOR
Thomas F. Hayes

SENIOR EDITOR
Susan Ross Moore

COPY EDITOR
Candice Hightower

INDEXER
Kelly Castell

PROOFREADER
Bob LaRoche

TECHNICAL EDITOR
Matt Wobensmith

TEAM COORDINATOR
Cindy Teeters

INTERIOR DESIGNER
Anne Jones

COVER DESIGNER
Sandra Schroeder

PAGE LAYOUT
Rebecca Harmon
Cheryl Lynch

Overview

Introduction   **1**

PART I   **FLASH BASICS**   **7**

1   The Flash Environment   **9**

2   Drawing Tools   **19**

3   Flash Fundamentals   **33**

4   Actions   **49**

5   Using Variables   **59**

PART II   **FLASH DEVELOPMENT**   **65**

6   ActionScript   **67**

7   Events   **79**

8   Variables   **89**

9   Functions   **99**

10   Programming Basics   **107**

11   Code Reuse   **117**

PART III   **FLASH OBJECTS**   **123**

12   Using Objects   **125**

13   The MovieClip Object   **129**

14   Arrays   **139**

15   Color   **147**

16   Key   **151**

17   The Mouse Object   **155**

18   Sound   **157**

19   Other Objects   **171**

PART IV   **BUILDING APPLICATIONS**   **181**

20   External Data   **183**

21   Data-Driven Movies   **191**

22   Debugging   **195**

23   Error Handling   **201**

24   Profiling   **205**

PART V   APPENDIX   209

   A   Answers   **209**

   INDEX   217

Contents

INTRODUCTION   1

PART I   FLASH BASICS   7

1   THE FLASH ENVIRONMENT   9

What Is Flash? 9

The Flash Interface 10

Flash File Types 10

The Movie Explorer 11

The Library 14

The Library Window 14

Flash Symbol and Asset Types 16

Summary 17

Sample Questions 17

2   DRAWING TOOLS   19

Flash Drawing Tools 19

The Arrow, Subselect, and Lasso Tools 19

The Arrow Tool 19

The Subselect Tool 21

The Lasso Tool 21

Stroke and Fill Controls 22

The Color Section 22

The Stroke Panel 22

The Drawing Tools 24

The Line Tool 24

The Pencil Tool 24

The Pen Tool 25

The Oval and Rectangle Tools 27

The Brush Tool 27

The Painting Tools 29

The Dropper Tool 29

The Ink Bottle Tool 29

The Paint Bucket Tool 29

The Eraser Tool 30

Summary 31

Sample Questions 31

3   FLASH FUNDAMENTALS   33

Symbols and Instances of Symbols 33

Creating Symbols 34

Layers 35

Creating, Viewing, and Editing Layers 37

Using Guide Layers 38

Using Mask Layers 39

Timelines 39

Working with Frames 41

Keyframes 42

Frame Labels 42

Frame Rates 43

Nested and Multiple Timelines 43

Frame-by-Frame Animations 44

Tweening 45

Motion Tweening 45

Shape Tweening 46

Summary 47

Sample Questions 48

4   ACTIONS   **49**

Buttons 49

Creating a Button 49

Setting the Four Button States 50

Using a Button in a Movie 51

Changing a Button's Shape 52

Button Actions 52

Animating a Button 55

Invisible Buttons 55

Importing Graphics and Bitmaps 56

Summary 57

Sample Questions 57

5   USING VARIABLES   59

Variables 59

Flash Date Types and Data Operations 60

ActionScript Functions 61

Scope of a Variable 61

Summary 63

Sample Questions 63

PART II   FLASH DEVELOPMENT   65

6   ACTIONSCRIPT   **67**

What Is ActionScript? 67

Objects and Classes 68

ActionScript Programs 70

Writing Scripts 73

ActionScript Keywords 73

Comments 73

Semicolons 74

Parentheses and Curly Braces 74

Dot and Slash Syntax 75

ActionScript Terms 76

Summary 77

Sample Questions 77

7 EVENTS   79

Using Events 79

    Programming Events 80

    Mouse Button Events 80

    Frame Events 81

    Clip Events 86

Summary 87

Sample Questions 88

8 VARIABLES   89

Data Types 89

    Constants 90

    String Data Type 90

    Number Data Type 92

    Boolean Data Type 92

    Object Data Type 93

    Movie Clip Data Type 93

    The `typeof()` Function 94

Naming Variables 94

Working with Variables 95

Loading and Sending Variables 97

Summary 98

Sample Questions 98

9 FUNCTIONS   99

What Is a Function? 99

Predefined Flash Functions 100

Using Functions 101

    Writing Functions 101

Function Literals 103

Custom Classes 104

Summary 105

Sample Questions 105

10 PROGRAMMING BASICS   107

Flow Control 107

The `if` Statement 107

Loops 110

    The `for` Loop 110

    The `for...in` Loop 112

    The `while` Loop 112

    The `do while` Loop 113

Controlling Looping 114
Summary 116
Sample Questions 116

11   CODE REUSE   117

Includes 117
Smart Clips 118
    Smart Clip Button and Check Box Objects 119
    Smart Clip Menu Objects 119
Summary 121
Sample Questions 121

PART III   FLASH OBJECTS   123

12   USING OBJECTS   125

What Is an Object? 125
Creating Objects 126
Summary 127
Sample Questions 127

13   THE MovieClip OBJECT   129

MovieClip Object Methods 129
    The attachMovie Method 130
    The duplicateMovieClip Method 131
    The getBounds Method 132
    The getBytesLoaded and getBytesTotal Methods 132
    The globalToLocal and localToGlobal Methods 132
    The hitTest Method 133
    The loadMovie and unloadMovie Methods 134
    The startDrag and stopDrag Methods 134
    The swapDepths Method 134
    Using MovieClip Methods 135
MovieClip Properties 135
    The _alpha Property 136
    The _quality Property 136
Summary 137
Sample Questions 137

14   ARRAYS   139

Creating and Populating Arrays 140
Array Methods 141
Loops and Arrays 143
Summary 144
Sample Questions 145

15 COLOR 147

Color Object Methods 147

Summary 149

Sample Questions 149

16 KEY 151

Key Object Methods 151

Key Object Properties 152

Summary 153

Sample Questions 153

17 THE MOUSE OBJECT 155

Mouse Object Methods 155

Summary 156

Sample Questions 156

18 SOUND 157

Sound Sampling 158

Sampling Frequency 159

Bit Depth 161

File Sizes 162

Supported Sound File Formats 163

Flash and Sound 164

Importing Sound Files 164

Using Sounds in a Movie 164

Sounds and Buttons 166

Background Music 167

Linking Sounds 167

Sound Editing Controls 167

Exporting Sounds 168

Using Sounds Effectively 169

Summary 170

Sample Questions 170

19 OTHER OBJECTS 171

Math 171

Date and Time 172

Date Methods 173

Creating and Using a Date Variable 174

Using a Timer 178

String Object 178

Summary 180

Sample Questions 180

PART IV   BUILDING APPLICATIONS   181

20   EXTERNAL DATA   183

Sending Messages 183

Standalone Flash Player 184

Using Web-based Flash Players 185

Sending and Receiving Data 186

Flash and XML 187

Flash XML Object 188

Flash XMLSocket Object 189

Summary 190

Sample Questions 190

21   DATA-DRIVEN MOVIES   191

Flash and Middleware 191

Data Interaction with Middleware 192

Summary 193

Sample Questions 193

22   DEBUGGING   195

The Output Window 195

Using the trace Command 196

Examining the Debugger 197

Using the Debugger 198

Summary 199

Sample Questions 199

23   ERROR HANDLING   201

ActionScript Error Handling 201

Showing HTML Errors 203

Summary 203

Sample Questions 204

24   PROFILING   205

Previewing Movies 205

The Bandwidth Profiler 206

Summary 207

Sample Questions 207

PART V   APPENDIX   209

A   ANSWERS   211

INDEX   217

About the Author

Dr. Tim Parker has been writing about computers and programming for more than 20 years. In that time he's written over 2,500 feature articles and 60 books. He's served as columnist, Editor, and Technical Editor for a dozen magazines focusing on UNIX, Linux, and Windows. Dr. Parker has taught hundreds of classes in computer security, UNIX, and networking for Fortune 500 companies and the U.S. Navy. He currently resides in Ottawa, Canada with his dog and a network of far too many computers and devices. In his spare time he is a private pilot and scuba instructor.

Dedication

For Nancy, with love and appreciation.

Sentio me iam te novisse.

Acknowledgments

I've worked with Macromedia Flash (and before Flash, Shockwave) from the early days. In fact, with some amazement looking back a decade, I find that I've been designing sites and HTML pages almost from the rollout of the marvelous tool we call the World Wide Web. It's a remarkable journey from the days of WAIS and Gopher to the current World Wide Web, and from simple ASCII editors to complex tools like those offered by Macromedia. Perhaps the granddaddy of the plug-ins was Shockwave, now supplanted by Flash. With the release of Flash 5, Macromedia offers a tool that both beginner and veteran Web designers can work with, simplifying complex animation and movie production for the Web.

When approached with the idea of a Flash Study Guide I had mixed emotions. On one hand, Flash is a very simple tool to work with. For anyone with experience with high-level programming languages and GUI design tools, Flash is quick, sleek, and easy to work with. Why anyone would need a Study Guide to something so simple was surprising. However, a wealth of detail and possibilities are underneath the surface of Flash, especially when mixed with other tools like XML. Also, the ridiculous number of "Web design experts" who know only a few tags in HTML and pass themselves off at ridiculous per-hour rates to unsuspecting customers have been creating a bad market for us. Everyone puts Flash on their resume because it is a standard tool. Most of these experts seldom knew much more than the basics. Certification is a measure of the knowledge available to someone, and claiming to be a Flash Certified Developer differentiates the wannabe from the knowledgeable. That can only be a good thing for the industry. Sure, certification is an inconvenience because it requires a little studying and writing a test, but the benefits outweigh the inconvenience.

Over the last two decades of writing, I've lost count of the number of books that came from my keyboard. The number is well over 60, according to my bookshelves (I'm missing a few early books and the source is on CP/M diskettes, so a true count is difficult). One thing I do know is that no book is the result of one person. In this case, I wrote all the content, but there was an expert staff at Que who edited and formatted the text I wrote, making it look like a professional product. To all those at Que in production who make writers look good (and seldom get any kudos except a small mention on the credits page), my thanks for this and all the others. To the technical editors and the staff at Macromedia, thanks for making sure what I wrote was correct. My acquisitions editor at Que, Angela Kozlowski, helped put the idea for the book in my head and managed my submissions, providing feedback from the rest of the team professionally as always. I've worked on several books with Angela and the crew at Que, and each has been a pleasant experience.

Writing a book may seem like a simple life. Sit at your desk for a few minutes a day, crank out a few pages, and collect a check for the effort. The reality is very different (but I'd love to find out where to sign up for the fantasy). Long days, every day of the week, are usually necessary to get a computer-oriented book out on time, often with compressed deadlines and the inevitable problems cropping up to annoy your best laid plans. This all takes a toll on family and friends, as well as pets. To my family and friends, my appreciation for understanding why I had to work yet another long day. To my faithful and understanding dog, I promise we'll go for that run tomorrow. To my good friend Nancy, thanks for understanding why I couldn't be with you those nights, those weekends, and through the rough times you've seen this year. That's why this book is for you.

Dr. Tim Parker

October 2001

Tell Us What You Think!

As the reader of this book, *you* are our most important critic and commentator. We value your opinion and want to know what we're doing right, what we could do better, what areas you'd like to see us publish in, and any other words of wisdom you're willing to pass our way.

As an Associate Publisher for Que, I welcome your comments. You can fax, e-mail, or write me directly to let me know what you did or didn't like about this book—as well as what we can do to make our books stronger.

Please note that I cannot help you with technical problems related to the topic of this book, and that due to the high volume of mail I receive, I might not be able to reply to every message.

When you write, please be sure to include this book's title and author as well as your name and phone or fax number. I will carefully review your comments and share them with the author and editors who worked on the book.

Fax:	317-581-4666
E-mail:	feedback@quepublishing.com
Mail:	Angela Kozlowski
	Acquisitions Editor
	Que
	201 West 103rd Street
	Indianapolis, IN 46290 USA

Introduction

Macromedia's Web tools are well known and widely used. The idea of a certification method to ensure Web developers are confident and competent with these tools is a logical move, especially because many people now style themselves as Web design experts. Macromedia's Flash is one of the most widely used tools for the Web, and is a good candidate for a certification test.

With the ColdFusion certification process, a Study Guide to the subject and the ensuing test seemed sensible. With the development of the Flash certification, a similar Study Guide was inevitable. There are many important differences between ColdFusion and Flash, not the least of which is that ColdFusion is much more of a programming exercise than Flash. The content of this Study Guide took a while to develop, but includes everything you need to know about Flash to not only assure yourself that you are well versed in the subject, but also ready to move on to the certification process.

The subject of a Flash Study Guide was tackled looking at the overall Flash product first, and then delving into the details. In this book you do not find absolutely everything that is possible in Flash. You also do not find lots of tutorials and lengthy code examples. What you find is a concise summary of the salient features of Flash, arranged in order of increasing complexity, with short code samples to indicate many elements. You can learn how to use Flash from this book, but the idea is to reinforce and complement your experience with a summary of the features and capabilities.

As you read through the book, it may be tempting to skip certain chapters. While you may feel confident that you know all about a particular subject, though, you will find many tips and notes, as well as helpful information on limitations and platform dependencies, of which you may not be aware. These could crop up in the certification test, so starting from the beginning and taking time to go through the pages in order is recommended. Of course, you can jump about all you want, but you should skim each chapter for important points (tips, cautions, and notes) prior to writing the test.

I hope you find this book useful, encapsulating a wide variety of information in a succinct format. Good luck on the certification test!

What Is the *Certified Flash Developer* Exam?

The popularity of Macromedia's products continues to grow, and along with it, so has the demand for experienced developers. Once upon a time (Internet time, that is, and actually not that long ago in conventional time), claiming to be a Flash developer was easy; the product was simple enough that, with a minimal investment of time and energy, developers could realistically consider themselves experts.

This is not the case anymore. The product line has grown both in actual products and in their complexity, and the levels of expertise and experience among developers are diverse. Claiming to be an expert is not that easy, and recognizing legitimate expertise is even harder.

The Macromedia Certified Professional Program

This is where certification comes into play. Formal, official certification by Macromedia helps to mark a threshold that explicitly separates developers by their knowledge and experience, making it possible to identify who is who.

The *Certified Flash Developer* certification is one in a series of certification tracks from Macromedia—this one concentrating on developers using Macromedia's Flash. Other exams and certification programs being developed concentrate on other products and areas of expertise.

Reasons to Get Certified

There's really only one important reason for Flash developers to become certified (aside from the goodies you receive): Being able to call yourself a Macromedia *Certified Flash Developer* means that you can command the respect and recognition that goes along with being one of the best at what you do.

Just as has happened with other products and technologies in this space, certification is likely to become a prerequisite for employers—an additional barometer by which to measure the potential of candidates and applicants.

Whether being certified helps you find a new (or better) job, helps persuade your boss that the pay raise you want is justified, helps you find new clients, or gets you listed on Macromedia's Web site so that you can attract new work or prospects—whatever the reason—it will help you stick out from the crowd.

About the Exam

Becoming a *Certified Flash Developer* involves being examined on your knowledge of Flash and related technologies. As far as exams go, this one is not easy—nor should it be. In fact, more than a third of all examinees fail their first test. This is not a bad thing; on the contrary, this is a good thing because it means that you really have to know your stuff to pass. You do not merely receive a paper certificate; the exam and subsequent certification have real value and real significance. "Very challenging, but fair" is how many examinees describe the exam itself.

The Exam Itself

The exam is a set of multiple-choice or true-false questions you answer electronically. A computer application issues the test to you, and you know whether you passed immediately upon test completion.

In the test you are presented with each question and the possible answers. Some questions have a single correct answer while others have two or more (you are told how many answers to provide). If a question stumps you, you can skip it and come back to it later.

After you have answered all the questions you can review them to check your answers. After you are done (or the time is up; the test has a 60-minute time limit), you get your results. You need at least 70% correct to pass and achieve certification. Examinees who score at least 80% on the test are certified with an Advanced Flash Developer status. So to stand out from the crowd, you need to know your stuff, and know it well. If you do not pass, you need to wait at least 30 days before you can try taking the test again. You may take the test no more than three times in a single year, starting from the date of your first test.

What You'll Be Tested On

Being a Flash expert requires that you know more than just Flash. As such, the exam includes questions on related technologies. The subjects you are tested on are:

- Flash functionality
- Flash command usage and syntax
- Flash drawing tools
- Creating user interfaces for Flash movies
- Use of Flash objects, instances, and interactions between these items
- Integrating Flash with external data sources such as Structured Query Language (SQL) databases

Every question counts, and you cannot assume that one particular topic is more or less significant than others. You need to know it all, and you need to know it all well.

Preparing for the Exam

Obviously, the most important preparation for the exam is the use of Flash itself. If you do not use Flash regularly, or have not done so for an extended period, you probably will not pass the exam.

Having said that, we can tell you that many experienced Flash developers still find the exam challenging. Usually, they say it is so because they don't use some features and technologies, or because they have learned the product, but have never paid attention to changing language and feature details (and thus are not using the product as effectively as they could be).

And this is where this book fits in. This book is not a cheat-sheet. It does not teach you Flash from scratch, nor does it give you a list of things to remember to pass the test. What it does is help you systematically review every major (and not so major) feature and technology in the product—everything that you need to know to pass the test.

Where to Take the Exam

To offer the exams worldwide in as many locations as possible, Macromedia has partnered with a company called VUE. VUE offers exams and certification programs for a wide range of companies and products, and has more than 2,500 regional testing facilities in more than 100 countries.

You can take the Macromedia Flash 5 Developer exam in any VUE testing center. For a current list of locations, visit the Web site at `http://www.vue.com/macromedia/`.

How Much It Costs

The fee to take the exam in North America is $150 (U.S.). Pricing in other countries varies. The fee must be paid at the time you register for the exam. If you need to cancel, you must do so at least 24 hours before the exam, or the fee is not refunded.

As a special gift to readers of this book, and to encourage you to study appropriately for the test, Macromedia has sponsored a coupon that you can use for a discount off the exam fee. Refer to the coupon for details and usage information.

How to Use This Book

This book is designed to be used in two ways:

- To prepare for your exam, you should start at the beginning of the book and systematically work your way through it. The book flow, layout, and form-factor have all been especially designed to make reviewing content as pleasant an experience as possible. The content has been designed to be highly readable and digestible in small, bite-sized chunks so that it will feel more like reading than studying.
- After you have reviewed all content, reread the topics that you feel you need extra help brushing up on. Topics are all covered in highly focused and very manageable chapters so that you can easily drill-down to the exact content you need. Extensive cross-referencing enables you to read up on related topics as needed.

Even after the exam, you'll find that the style and design of this book make it an invaluable desktop reference tool as well.

Contents

The book is divided into four parts, each containing a set of highly focused chapters. Each chapter concludes with a summary and sample questions (the answers to which are in Appendix A).

Part I: Flash Basics

This part covers the basics of using the Flash environment, the drawing tools, and use of the Timeline. It includes chapters on the following topics:

- The Flash Environment
- The Flash drawing toolset
- Use of layers and the Timeline
- Flash Actions
- Flash use of variables

Part II: Flash Development

This part covers the use of Flash functions and variables, and the programming language built in to Flash. This part includes chapters on the following topics:

- ActionScript programming language
- Using Events to trigger ActionScript commands
- Flash Variables
- Writing functions
- Programming in the Flash language
- Smart Clips

Part III: Flash Objects

This part covers the objects built in to Flash, and includes chapters on the following topics:

- Using Objects
- The `MovieClip` Object
- The Color, Key, Mouse, and Sound objects
- The Math, Date, and String objects
- The use of Arrays

Part IV: Building Applications

This part covers a wide range of advanced development technologies and features, and includes chapters on the following topics:

- Importing data from external applications
- Debugging ActionScript programs
- Handling Errors
- Using the Bandwidth Profiler

Conventions Used in This Book

The people at Que Publishing have spent many years developing and publishing computer books designed for ease of use and containing the most up-to-date information available. With that experience, we've learned what features help you the most. Look for these features throughout the book to help enhance your learning experience and get the most out of Flash.

- Screen messages, code listings, and command samples appear in `monospace type`.
- Uniform Resource Locators (URLs) used to identify pages on the Web and values for Flash attributes also appear in `monospace type`.
- Terms that are defined in the text appear in *italics*. Italics are sometimes used for emphasis, too.

TIP

Tips give you advice on quick or overlooked procedures, including shortcuts.

NOTE

Notes present useful or interesting information that isn't necessarily essential to the current discussion, but might augment your understanding with background material or advice relating to the topic.

CAUTION

Cautions warn you about potential problems a procedure might cause, unexpected results, or mistakes that could prove costly.

Cross-references are designed to point you to other locations in this book that provide supplemental or supporting information. Cross-references appear as follows:

→ Events and variables are covered in detail in Chapter 7, "Events," and Chapter 8, "Variables."

The Accompanying Web Site

To further assist you in preparing for the exam, this book has an accompanying Web site. This site contains the following:

- Updated exam information (should there be any)
- Links to other exam-related sites
- Any book corrections or errata (should there be any)
- A sample interactive test that you can use to help gauge your own exam readiness

Where to Go from Here

Now you're ready to get started. If you think you're ready for the exam, start with the sample questions (in the book or online) to verify your skills. If you're not ready (or if the same questions indicate that you might not be as ready as you thought), pay attention to the topics that need more attention by reading the documentation and actually writing appropriate applications.

When you're ready, work through this book to review the content and prepare for the exam itself as described here.

And with that, we wish you good luck!

PART I

FLASH BASICS

1   The Flash Environment

2   Drawing Tools

3   Flash Fundamentals

4   Actions

5   Using Variables

CHAPTER 1

The Flash Environment

What Is Flash?

Macromedia Flash 5 is an application that has many purposes, but the primary role is to enable you to develop interactive multimedia programs, usually for use through a Web browser. A set of drawing and editing tools like those in Macromedia Freehand are built into Flash 5, as well as an animation utility like those in Macromedia's Director. In addition, Flash 5 (through its Generator component) is also a graphics engine for delivery of Web content.

> **NOTE**
>
> ActionScript is based on the same specifications as the JavaScript language and can integrate with HTML (Hypertext Markup Language) and XML (eXtensible Markup Language). If you are familiar with JavaScript, C, or C++, you will find ActionScript quite familiar.

The core of Flash is its multimedia authoring ability, and its ability to produce animation sequences called movies. With Flash, movies can be composed of any number of scenes arranged in any sequence and played based on a set of actions defined in the movie. Every scene in a Flash movie can have an almost unlimited number of layers, each layer laid one on top of the other (from back to front) to provide a stacked set of images of infinite complexity. In addition, every layer can have a stacked set of objects in it. To show a sequence of scenes, a set of frames are created and played by Flash. Frames may repeat the content of the previous frame (this is a static frame) or change the content (a keyframe). Frame-by-frame animation is how Flash movies are played.

> **NOTE**
>
> Flash movies can have an unlimited number of layers. In fact, there is a limit of 16,384. It is unlikely anyone will use this many layers in even the most complex movie, though.

The Flash Interface

When you launch Flash, the default settings display a number of dialogs and panels. These are familiar to developers, but it is worth quickly reviewing the formal names and tasks for each of these dialogs and panels for future reference. Flash's environment is fundamentally the same for both the Windows and Macintosh platforms, although some platform-dependent changes are of course necessary.

The Toolbox is where the drawing and painting tools reside by default. Normally the Toolbox is opened in the upper-left corner of the window (it can be opened, if not visible, using the Windows, Tools menu item). The Toolbox has four sections. The top panel contains the drawing and painting tool icons. Beneath those tools are the View tools (the Hand and Magnifier tools). The View tools are followed by the Color tray that enables choice of stroke and fill colors. The final section contains the Options tray where modifiers for the drawing and painting tools are displayed.

> **TIP**
>
> Under Windows, the Toolbox can be either a floating or a docked panel. Under Macintosh, the Toolbox can only be a floating panel. A docked panel resides at the edge of a window and becomes an integral part of the border. To drag the Toolbox to a border on a Windows machine and prevent it from docking, press the Ctrl key while dragging to the border.

Usually, the top of the Flash default window contains the Timeline. The Timeline shows the frames of a Flash movie and the relationships of elements to each other in the movie. Below the Timeline is usually the Stage (also called the work area) where most drawing and placement of elements in a movie occurs.

Depending on default settings and the resolution of the video display being used, another set of panels may appear either on the right side of the window or floating in various places on the window. These contain a wide variety of items, including panels for color control, sound editing, text entry, and many other possible choices. Each of these panels can be toggled for display through the Window, Panels or Window, Panel Sets menu items.

Flash File Types

Flash uses two different file types and file extensions. Within the authoring environment, Flash uses a work or project file that has a .FLA extension. FLA files enable movies to be organized into scenes, layers to be created, and timelines to be managed. FLA files are the basic file type used by all Flash development projects. The FLA file is also included in the Library with all imported bitmaps, sounds, and other elements stored within.

It would be impractical to use FLA files for playing movies on the Web or through a Flash player because of the sheer size and complexity of the FLA file. Instead, a smaller file is created from the FLA file using a Publish or Export option. This file, called a Shockwave Flash Movie File has the extension .SWF. (Macromedia now refers to SWF files as Small Web Files to avoid reference to the older Shockwave application). SWF files do not include details about the Library, timeline, and so on. The SWF file is a compressed delivery file for the Flash Player that contains the raw bytecode for the movie.

Although some other file formats can store parts of a Flash movie, only SWF files can store the entire interactive functionality of a Flash movie. The SWF format is open and available for any application support; details of the SWF format are downloadable from the Macromedia Web site. You can incorporate Flash SWF files into other movies by using the loadMovie action.

SWF files can be played by a number of applications that have the Flash Player incorporated either directly or as a plug-in. Current applications that can handle SWF files are:

- Netscape Navigator (equipped with the Flash plug-in)
- Internet Explorer (equipped with the Flash ActiveX control)
- Flash Xtra (part of Macromedia Director and Authorware)
- Microsoft Windows and applications such as the Microsoft Office suite (using the Flash ActiveX control)
- QuickTime
- Standalone Flash players

Flash SWF files can be generated from the Flash Publish feature. Alternate file formats, including GIF, JPEG, PNG, BMP, PICT, QuickTime, and AVI files (for single frame and movies depending on the format) can also be generated by Flash using the Export Movie or Publish options.

The Movie Explorer

The Movie Explorer is used to locate, arrange, and edit any media involved in your production. When you are working with many different files, the Movie Explorer is particularly useful as it enables you to see the organization and the flow of a Flash movie in a logical progression. Further, the Movie Explorer can be used to find problems with a movie, to search for particular text or variables in a movie, and to provide a shortcut editor. The Movie Explorer can be launched using the Movie Explorer icon at the bottom-right corner of the Stage, by using the Windows, Movie Explorer menu choice, or by using the Control+Alt+M (Windows) or Option+Command+M (Macintosh) shortcut.

The Movie Explorer updates itself automatically (in real time) as changes are made to a movie, which is both useful and also a drain on your system resources. If you do not need the Movie Explorer, it is best to close it and save the resources.

The Movie Explorer dialog is broken into a number of parts. Two tabs are built in to the Movie Explorer: the Movie Explorer itself and Actions Panel, which allows you to examine the actions of any objects or frames in a movie. The Movie Explorer has a set of six filtering icons across the top to control what is displayed in the Explorer window, followed by a Find text field underneath, and then the Display List below that. Changing the size of the Movie Explorer dialog enables the Display List to be sized appropriately to display the required items.

The Movie Explorer Display List is laid out in a hierarchical tree-like structure. The format of the Display List is similar to that used by Windows Explorer, allowing expansion and contraction of items using small plus or minus buttons in the display. These are used with the different Find icons at the top of the window. For example, selecting the Show Buttons, Movie Clips, and Graphics icon searches the movie for all scenes that include one of these items, and displays a plus sign next to any contracted scene that includes them. Clicking the plus sign expands the display for that scene to include all the items within it. When navigating through the Display List, the bottom of the dialog shows the complete path for any selected item.

What is shown in the Movie Explorer dialog is controlled either through the filtering icons at the top of the window, or for more control, by a set of preferences allowing individual selection of each type of item. You can change the preferences through the Movie Explorer's Customize Which Items To Show icon. This presents a dialog divided into two parts. The first enables you to select the items to be displayed in the Movie Explorer window (Text, Buttons, Movie Clips, and so on) and the second enables you to toggle context (Movie Elements and Symbol Definitions). All the items in the Movie Explorer Settings dialog are check boxes; when checked, the items are selected and are used by Movie Explorer.

> **TIP**
>
> Although it is often tempting to show all items in the Movie Explorer, the display can quickly become crowded and difficult to work with. The use of these filtering buttons to eliminate items you don't care to see can help you use the Movie Explorer more effectively.

Each item that is selected in the Display List has a contextual menu associated with it that can be displayed with a right mouse click or Control+click (Windows) or Command+click (Macintosh). The pop-up menu may have invalid selections grayed out. The first item on the menu, Goto Location, is used frequently to find an item (very useful when the item is in a masked or invisible layer). The same pop-up menu can be displayed by using the triangular arrow in the top-right corner of the Movie Explorer window. The options available in these menus are shown in Table 1.1.

Table 1.1   Movie Explorer Menu Options

Menu Option	Meaning
Goto Location	Jumps to the layer, scene or frame for the selected item
Goto Symbol Definition	Jumps to the definition for the selected symbol (Show Movie Elements and Show Symbol Definitions must both be checked in the Movie Explorer Settings dialog box)
Select Symbol Instance	Jumps to the scene containing an instance of the selected symbol (Show Movie Elements and Show Symbol Definitions must both be checked in the Movie Explorer Settings dialog box)
Find in Library	Highlights the selected item in the library; if the Library Window is not open, it is opened automatically
Panels	Opens all relevant panels for the selected item
Rename	Renames the selected item
Edit in Place	Edits the symbol in context of the Stage
Edit in New Window	Edits the symbol in the Symbol Editing Mode
Show Movie Elements	Shows all movie elements in the movie, organized by scene
Show Symbol Definitions	Shows all components related to a symbol (both Show Symbol Definitions and Show Movie Elements can be active at the same time)
Show All Scenes	Toggles Show Movie Elements between the selected scenes and all scenes
Copy Text to Clipboard	Copies selected text to the clipboard for use in other applications
Cut	Cuts the selected text
Copy	Copies the selected text
Paste	Pastes text
Clear	Clears the selected text
Expand Branch	Expands the selected item; the same as clicking the plus sign
Collapse Branch	Collapses the selected item; the same as clicking the minus sign
Collapse Others	Collapses all items in the tree except at the selected location
Print	Sends the tree to the printers with all context expanded and all types of content selected

The Print function can be a useful way of displaying everything involved in a movie for reference in complex work. Because the Print option expands all items and selects all content automatically, it provides an overall and exhaustive view of the movie.

To find any item in Movie Explorer, enter the name of the element in the Find field. Any elements that contain that name are shown in the Display List as you type (you do not need to press Enter when you're done). To edit any item, select it in the Display List. When you select an element in the Movie Explorer Display List, the Timeline and the Stage also shows the items as selected. If you select a scene or keyframe, the display moves to that point. Changes to an item can be performed through the pop-up menus or by simply double-clicking the item.

> **TIP**
>
> If you double-click a symbol, the item is opened in Symbol Editing Mode automatically.

The Library

The Library is used to store all assets and symbols (elements that recur) for use as instances in a Flash movie. Every movie has its own version of the Library. Although you don't have to use the Library to store elements, most developers find it convenient to place everything used in a movie within the Library. Buttons, movie clips, and many other elements you create are stored in the Library when you create them. When you import sound or bitmap files, they are automatically placed in the Library.

The Library Window

The Library is represented within Flash as a window not a panel. (The Library window is not to be confused with the six Common Libraries, which are panels used to store buttons, graphics, and so on. The Common Libraries are created during installation and are populated with a set of default elements. The Library is empty when Flash is installed, and is populated by symbols you create and move to the Library. The Library is accessed through Window, Library while the Common Libraries are accessed through Window, Common Library.) When a new document is created, the Library is initially empty. An existing Library from another movie can be opened using the FLA file to make that Library's contents available to the current movie.

The Library window has a preview pane at the top that shows a rendition of any item selected, and the list of library contents below in the Library Sort pane. The top right of the Library Sort pane has icons to change the sort order and toggle Wide and Narrow states. The Sort icon lets you change the sort order from ascending to descending alphanumerics. The Wide and Narrow icons control how wide the Library window is, and how much information is displayed. Usually, only a name is shown in the Narrow state, although a scrollbar along the bottom of the pane allows viewing of the other information. The Wide state shows the Name, Kind (type of element), Use Count (number of times the symbol is used), Linkage (a name assigned for use by ActionScript), and Date Modified (the last time the symbol was modified).

Items in the Sort window are listed in alphabetical order unless you change the sort order. Each item has an icon indicating the type of element it is, as well as the name of the element. Symbols inside the Library can be stored as a simple list, or you can organize them into folders that appear in the Sort window. Using folders lets you better control the symbols in the Library, but the way in which you use folders is up to you. Some developers organize by symbol type, others into smaller submovies of a larger movie. You can move elements into a folder either by dragging within the Sort window, or by using the Move to New Folder option.

TIP

When you select any animated symbol or sound from the library, a controller for that symbol appears in the top-right corner of the preview pane, enabling you to see or hear the element (useful for determining which is the symbol you really wanted).

The Options drop-down menu appears in the upper-right corner of the Library window and has many options, all listed in Table 1.2.

Table 1.2   Library Option Menu Items

Menu Item	Meaning
New Symbol	Creates a new symbol which is then stored at the root of the Library Sort window unless you have created a folder and selected that folder before choosing New Symbol
New Folder	Creates a new folder in the Library
New Font	Displays the Font Symbol properties dialog allowing you to eventually create a font symbol that can be used in a shared library
Rename	Renames the symbol
Move to New Folder	Opens the New Folder dialog
Duplicate	Duplicates the symbol
Delete	Deletes the symbol
Edit	Opens Symbol Editing Mode
Edit With	Launches external applications for editing based on the Properties dialog for that symbol type
Properties	Displays the Properties dialog for that symbol type
Linkage	Displays the Linkage Options menu, which enables an identifier string name to be used for access with ActionScript
Define Clip Parameters	Displays the Define Clip Parameters dialog used to assign variables with values to movie clips, creating a Smart Clip
Select Unused Items	Finds all unused items in the Library
Update	Used to update the Library when imported items have been edited after importing them
Play (Stop)	Plays or stops playing the symbol in the preview window

Table 1.2 Continued

Menu Item	Meaning
Expand Folder	Opens the selected folder
Collapse Folder	Closes the selected folder
Expand All Folders	Opens all folders
Collapse All Folders	Closes all folders
Shared Library Properties	Displays the Shared Properties dialog for use with shared libraries
Keep Use Counts Updated	Provides real-time updates of the Use Counts field
Update Use Counts Now	Updates the Use Counts field

To edit an item in the Sort window you can either use the Edit menu option to enter Symbol Editing Mode, or double-click the item to use Edit in place mode. The Keep Use Counts Updated option can impose a lot of overhead with complex movies, so the Update Use Counts Now should be used instead.

The bottom of the Library window has icons for the most commonly used tasks from the drop-down menu: New Symbol, New Folder, Item Properties, and Delete Item.

Flash Symbol and Asset Types

Flash has three basic symbol types: graphics, buttons, and movie clips. Every other item in the Library is an asset (with the exception of Font Symbols). The Library shows an icon next to each type of symbol or asset to indicate its type. Flash supports several types of symbols and assets, both native and imported. The symbol and asset types recognized by Flash 5 are shown in Table 1.3.

Table 1.3 Flash Symbols and Assets

Symbol or Asset	Use
Bitmaps	Imported bitmap
Buttons	Used for interactive events; buttons have four states (Up, Down, Over, and Hit) with each state defined using graphics, sounds, or other symbols
Graphics	Static images or simple animations (Flash ignores any sounds or actions within a Graphic symbol)
Movie Clips	A movie that is used inside a larger movie; they can contain actions, sounds, and other symbols
QuickTime	QuickTime assets are treated as a linked asset by Flash
Shared Font	A font that is a common library element
Smart Clip	A movie clip with parameters defined within itself
Sounds	An imported sound clip

Summary

Flash is a complex multimedia authoring environment with many different capabilities. The Library and Movie Explorer are two tools that help you organize and manage elements of a Flash movie, and should be used by anyone developing a complex project.

Sample Questions

1. What capability is required to allow Flash movies to play in Microsoft Office application software?
   A. DirectX
   B. ActiveX
   C. Cut-and-paste
   D. OLE

2. Which panel or window enables you to perform a find and replace operation?
   A. Movie Explorer
   B. Paragraph
   C. Character
   D. Color

3. Which filetype is used for the rendered file for playback in a Flash Player?
   A. SWF
   B. FLA
   C. PA
   D. EXE

CHAPTER 2

Drawing Tools

Flash Drawing Tools

Macromedia Flash incorporates a number of tools to help draw and paint objects, either freeform or by using some constraints to restrict the shapes created. Most of the tools provide modifiers appearing in the Options Tray that enable different behaviors of the drawing and painting tools. It is important to remember that the drawing and painting tools can affect other objects that may be on the same layer.

Prior to looking at the drawing tools, let's look at selecting items in a layer, as well as the stroke and fill controls that are available. More information on Flash's color controls can be found in Chapter 15, "Color," but for now let's take a quick look at how color applies to the drawing tools.

The Arrow, Subselect, and Lasso Tools

The Arrow, Subselect and Lasso tools are used to select any item in a layer. The Arrow tool selects specific items such as lines and fills, while the Subselect tool enables single items to be selected. The Lasso tool can select multiple items at once using a free-form selection method.

The Arrow Tool

The Arrow tool enables you to select one or more items on the Stage, as well as modify existing items by dragging their shapes using handles. (The Subselect Tool is similar, but can be used for selecting only single items, as well as dragging anchor points.) You can select the Arrow tool directly from the Toolbox, or invoke it at any time you are using any other tool by pressing down the Control key (Windows) or Command key (Macintosh). As long as the Control key or Command key is pressed, the tool toggles to the Arrow tool.

The Arrow tool has five modifiers available in the Toolbox Options area. Depending on what has been selected using the tool, some of the modifiers may be grayed out. The Magnet icon (called Snap to Objects) is a toggle that causes any dragged item to snap to any existing items on the Stage using a grid layout.

The Magnet option imposes a grid over the Stage to which all items moved must adhere. The Grid settings can be modified using View, Grid, Edit Grid. The dialog that appears enables you to set the grid size, horizontally and vertically independently, in pixels (which means these settings are relative to the movie size). A Snap Accuracy drop-down menu lets you decide how close to another item the dragged item must be to snap to it. The Show Grid option in the Grid dialog enables the grid to be imposed over the Stage. This can be useful for alignment purposes, as well as to see the effects of the grid on snapping items.

> **TIP**
>
> When the Magnet icon is active and a snap to an existing item is possible, a small circle appears in the lower-right corner of the Arrow icon. If the Magnet icon is active and you want to temporarily override the setting to disable snapping, press the Shift key as you drag the item.

The Smooth and Straighten icons in the Options panel of the Toolbox appear when a line has been selected. These can be used to perform smoothing and straightening of the selected line. The Rotate and Scale icons are used to enable you to change the rotation and the size of the selected items. When either of the icons is selected, a set of handles appears that enables manipulation of the item.

To select an item on the Stage using the Arrow tool, click it. Alternatively, you can select multiple items at once by dragging a rectangular marquee around them (called drag-select). Multiple items can be selected by pressing the Shift key and clicking the items to be added. Selected items appear in a hatched pattern to indicate they are selected. If you have selected a group or symbol, a colored thin border (called a Highlight) appears around the selection. (The Highlight color can be set in the Edit, Preferences, General dialog.) To deselect an item or items you can use the Edit, Deselect All menu item, press the Escape key, or click anywhere outside the selected items.

You can move any Flash element using the Arrow tool by dragging the item selected, as long as you are not dragging at an anchor point. The Arrow tool can be used to modify a line or shape by selecting end points, anchor points, or corner points, and dragging the point to the desired new shape or location.

To rotate a selected item with the Arrow tool select the Rotate modifier from the Options panel. Rotate enables you to rotate as well as skew and slant the selected items. When you click the Rotate icon, eight round handles appear over the item. To simply rotate the items, use a corner handle. To skew or slant the items, use the handles in the middle of a line.

To resize an item selected with the Arrow tool, select the Scale modifier from the Options panel. As with the Rotate modifier, eight handles appear, but they are square instead of round. To resize the item symmetrically use the corner handles. To resize asymmetrically, use the handles in the middle of a line.

The Subselect Tool

The Subselect tool is used similarly to the Arrow tool, but it usually selects a single item. The Subselect tool is usually used to drag and reshape items on the Stage using points.

The Subselect tool can be used to adjust straight lines or curves by selecting a line, and then dragging one of the anchor points to the new position. Curves can be adjusted by using the tangent handles that appear when the curve is selected with the Subselect tool. You can either drag the tangent handle or the anchor point on which the tangent resides.

The Lasso Tool

The Lasso tool is usually used to select a group of irregular areas of a drawing. By selecting a group of items using the Lasso tool, they can be moved or modified as a whole, even if not a formal group.

The Lasso tool has three options in the Toolbox. The Magic Wand option is used to select ranges of a bitmap that are of a similar color, usually after the bitmap has been broken apart. After selection, the parts can be recombined into a single group, or modified individually using selection tools.

The Magic Wand Properties icon has two settings: Threshold and Smoothing. These are chosen when the Magic Wand icon is selected. The Threshold setting enables you to set the range of colors that are treated as the same by the Magic Wand. Values for the Threshold value range from 0 to 200, and the higher the number the broader the selection of colors included in the Magic Wand.

> **NOTE**
> The number you enter is treated as a plus or minus value for the Threshold range, so entering 15 means that a color with a value of 40 is matched by the Magic Wand if its color value is between 25 and 55. Setting a value of 0 means that the colors have to be exact matches.

The Smoothing setting of the Magic Wand Properties icon determines how much smoothing is performed on the edges of a selection. The four options are Smooth, Pixels, Rough, and Normal. Smoothing is similar to antialiasing in that edges of a shape are dithered so they look smoother. (Antialiasing is a technique that smooths the edges of shapes, lines, and text to make them appear less jagged on the screen, but at the cost of using many more CPU cycles.)

Stroke and Fill Controls

The Stroke and Fill settings are used to specify drawing line thickness and paint fill colors, respectively. Stroke and fill can be set in two ways. The Toolbox has a Colors section that contains stroke and fill selections, and the Stroke Panel (Windows, Panels, Stroke) contains the same controls and more.

I examine the use of color with Flash in more detail in Chapter 16, "Key." For now, let's examine the basic controls as they apply to the drawing tools.

The Color Section

The Color section of the Toolbox enables you to quickly select stroke and fill colors using pop-up dialogs. When either Stroke or Fill icons are clicked, a dialog called the *swatches dialog* showing the standard color spectrum appears. The color for stroke or fill can be chosen in several ways. The chosen color square in the swatches dialog can be clicked or the hex code for the color can be entered in the text entry box above the mosaic. As the cursor moves over each small square in the swatches the upper-left corner box of the dialog shows a larger patch of that color and the corresponding hex code appears in the hex text field.

The icon in the upper-right corner of the swatches dialog contains a circular icon that opens another dialog enabling the choice of more colors, as well as specifying the characteristics of any color. This is useful for providing total control over a color instead of relying on the default colors provided.

The Fill color dialog also has several gradient options along the bottom of the dialog. These are used to select gradient fills in several colors. Samples of the gradient fill are shown in the upper-left corner.

Underneath the Stroke and Fill color options in the Toolbox are three buttons. These enable default colors, no fill color, and color swapping to be performed with a single click. The default color icon sets the stroke to black and the fill to white. The default color settings cannot be changed. The No Color icon turns fill off and performs no fill option when a closed shape is drawn. The Swap Colors icon swaps the stroke and fill colors with each other.

The Stroke Panel

The Stroke panel contains Stroke and Fill tabs that duplicate the functions of the Stroke and Fill Color controls in the Toolbox, and add more flexibility and control. The Stroke tab enables you to set the stroke style. A drop-down menu shows several options, from hairlines to dotted lines, that can be chosen for the stroke style. You can also set a custom style. The stroke's style is chosen from the pull-down menu and includes seven choices as shown in Table 2.1.

Table 2.1   Stroke Style Choices

Stroke Style	Meaning
Hairline	A solid line one pixel wide that does not scale with the zoom setting
Solid	A solid, unbroken line
Dashed	A solid line with regularly spaced gaps
Dotted	A dotted line with evenly spaced gaps
Ragged	A line with variously sized and spaced gaps
Stipple	A stippled line mimicking a hand-stippled line
Hatched	A hatched line mimicking a hand-hatched line

The Solid stroke style is the optimum style for use on a Web page because it requires few points to describe it, resulting in smaller files.

A slider underneath the stroke style item allows the height of the stroke to be set. The slider reads out the value in the text box next to the slider. You can enter a stroke height directly into the text box instead of using the slider, if you want. When using the Stroke Height slider it is important to remember that some heights may not be visible at all zoom levels. The lower part of the Stroke tab shows a preview of the current style and height settings. The Stroke color icon next to the height slider enables you to choose a color from the same dialog that appeared from the Toolbox Stroke Color option.

To create a custom stroke style choose one of the stroke styles in the drop-down list, click the triangular button in the upper right of the Stroke Panel, and choose Custom (the only option that appears). The Line Style dialog appears. This enables you to generate a custom stroke by choosing the properties of the stroke individually. A preview window to the left of the dialog lets you see the stroke as you customize its settings. The Zoom 4x check box underneath the preview window enables you to zoom the preview to see fine details of the stroke. The options available in the Line Style dialog depend on the type of stroke selected.

The Thickness setting appears in all the stroke styles as both a pull-down menu and a text entry field to set any stroke thickness that you want. The Sharp Corners check box changes the way the ends of a stroke are drawn. When Sharp Corners is checked the ends of a line extend to each corner resulting in a crisper appearance.

For most Stroke Styles, other customizable settings are in the Line Style dialog, such as the spacing and shape of dots in the Dotted style, or the dot size, spacing, and density for the Stippled style. The Hatched stroke style is the most complex with size parameters that can be adjusted.

TIP

Any of the settings in the Line Style dialog can be modified for any stroke type to create a custom stroke style.

Stroke styles that are created using the Custom option cannot be saved for future recall, although you can create a separate .FLA file that contains a library of your stroke styles. If using a .FLA file, you can open the file and use the Dropper tool and the Ink Bottle tool to move the styles to another file.

The Fill tab in the Stroke panel enables you to select a fill color, similar to the dialog in the Colors section of the Toolbox. A drop-down menu contains these five basic fill options:

- None: No fill
- Solid: A single color fill
- Linear Gradient: A gradient fill running horizontally or vertically
- Radial Gradient: A gradient fill running from a central point out
- Bitmap: A bitmap applied as a fill

For all the fill options an icon underneath the drop-down menu is used to present the color swatch dialog, enabling you to choose the color of the fill. The two gradient fill options present sliders that enable you to control the rate at which the gradient increases from nothing to full saturation. A preview panel to the left shows the result, while the right slider enables you to drag the hollow and empty sliders along to set the zero and full saturation points.

The Drawing Tools

Several drawing tools are used by Flash: the Line, Pencil, Pen, Oval, Rectangle and Brush tools. Let's look at each tool separately.

The Line Tool

The Line tool is used to draw a straight line between a starting and ending point. The line uses the current stroke color and line width settings. The Fill color setting has no effect for the Line tool. No modifiers are in the Options Tray for the Line tool.

Lines are drawn from the first click point to the point of release. To draw connected lines, release and re-press the mouse button without moving the mouse. The Line tool can be constrained to drawing at 45-degree multiples by depressing the Shift key when drawing the line. This constraint can be applied for any lines in a series.

The Pencil Tool

The Pencil tool is used to draw freeform shapes and lines, just like a pencil can be used in the real world. The Pencil tool follows the tip of the cursor, drawing a line using the stroke color, line weight, and style currently selected, when the left mouse button is pressed.

The Pencil tool has three modifiers: Straighten, Smooth, and Ink. As its name implies, the Straighten modifier creates straight lines drawn by the Pencil tool. The lines are a best approximation of the straightened lines created by the tool, and include angles as necessary to follow the shapes drawn. Separate lines produced with the Pencil tool while the Straighten modifier is active are connected to each other.

TIP

The Straighten modifier can also be used for circles and ovals by approximating these shapes with the cursor.

The Smooth modifier provides line smoothing, but does not smooth to the extent of the Straighten modifier. The Ink modifier does no smoothing at all. With the Ink modifier selected, the shapes drawn with the cursor are left unmodified. The Smooth modifier connects lines that are drawn close to each other automatically, while no attempt to connect lines is performed with the Ink modifier. Lines drawn with the Ink modifier are treated literally as drawn by Flash, involving no processing at all. These lines can become very complex and require a considerable amount of data to describe. The use of these lines causes file sizes to swell considerably. (You can smooth an Ink modified line by selecting the line with the Arrow tool, and then using Modify, Smooth; Modify, Straighten; or Modify, Optimize.)

The Straighten and Smooth options are also available through the Pencil tool's pop-up menu, enabling line-processing functions to be performed while a line is being drawn. Vertical and horizontal lines can be forced by pressing the Shift key while drawing a line with any of the three Pencil modifiers active.

The Pen Tool

The Pen tool is used to draw precise smooth or straight lines as opposed to free-form lines produced by the Pencil tool. The stroke and fill attributes are used to set colors for the Pen tool. The default appearance of the Pen tool is a small pen nib icon. This can be temporarily changed to a cross-hair icon for more precise control by pressing Caps Lock. To return to the Pen icon, use Caps Lock again. To use a cross-hair image as the default Pen tool icon, use the Preferences dialog.

The Pen tool behavior is customizable through the Edit, Preferences, Editing dialog, where three options are available. Show Pen Preview enables you to see the line segments as the cursor is moved. The line segment is fixed in place only when you create the end point with a mouse click. If Show Pen Preview is not selected, the line is not shown on the Stage until the end point is selected. The Show Solid Points option displays unselected anchor points for the lines to appear as solid boxes. Any anchor point that is selected is shown as a hollow box. This setting is the default behavior: Deselecting the Show Solid Points reverses the behavior, so selected points are solid boxes and unselected points are hollow boxes. The Show Precise Cursors option makes the Pen tool cursor appear as a cross-hair cursor instead of a pen icon. This is useful when precise control of points is necessary, usually with high zoom factors.

In normal use, the Pen tool is used to click a point, and then the cursor is dragged to create the end points for the line or curve. A series of points can be created to result in smooth straight lines or curves flowing one to another.

The Pen tool can be used in several ways for drawing lines and curves. The easiest task is to draw a set of connected straight lines. A mouse click creates the first anchor point.

Move the cursor to the end point of the line and click again. The line appears with two anchor points (called corner points to indicate they terminate a line). To draw more segments, click at the location of the next corner point, and continue until all lines have been drawn. To terminate the shape's last line, double-click for the end point, or Control+click (Windows) or Command+click (Macintosh) anywhere away from the shape. The shape can be closed if you are still drawing lines by clicking the first anchor point (a small circle appears at the lower right of the pen icon if clicking there closes the shape). Terminate the shape by double-clicking to close the shape, Control+click (Windows) or Command+click (Macintosh) away from the shape after placing the last point, choose a different drawing tool, or right-click away from the shape (Windows only).

> **TIP**
>
> You can constrain any line in a shape to a 45 degree multiple on the Stage by pressing the Shift key.

Curved shapes or lines can be drawn in a similar way with the Pen tool by using a click-and-drag motion instead of just clicking. Click the location of the first anchor point (where the curve begins) and press the mouse button. While the mouse button is pressed, the pen icon changes to an arrowhead shape. Drag the arrowhead in the direction the curve is to be drawn. On the Stage, a tangent line appears with tangent handles at the end. The angle and the length of the tangent line determine the shape of the curve that is produced. Releasing the mouse button changes the cursor back to the pen icon, removes the tangent line, and places the curved line on the Stage. As usual, the Shift key can be used to constrain the lines to 45 degree multiples.

Points on a shape that mark the change from curved to straight lines, and vice versa, are corner points. The default appearance is for curve points to appear as circles and corner points to appear as squares. To convert a curve point to a corner point, click the point with the Pen tool. To convert a corner point to a curve point use the Subselect tool with the Alt key (Windows) or Option key (Macintosh) to drag the point.

To move an anchor point, use the Subselection Tool and move the point to the desired location. To add an anchor point, click the line with the Pen tool. The pen or cross-hair icon has a small plus sign appear to its lower right if a point is to be added. To delete a corner point, you can use the Subselection tool to select the point, and then press Delete, or click the point with the Pen tool. When a point can be deleted a small minus sign appears in the lower right of the Pen icon. To delete a curve point, you can use the Subselection tool or double-click with the Pen tool.

> **TIP**
>
> You can often use the deletion of anchor points on a curve to smooth the curve as well as reduce the overall size of the saved file.

A number of different icons can appear in the lower-right corner of the Pen icon, depending on the actions possible at that cursor position. The icons available are shown in Table 2.2.

Table 2.2   Pen Icons

Icon	Meaning
+	Adds a point to the path in the current location
-	Removes the current point
^	Changes the point to a corner point
o	Indicates the point is an end point
X	Displays when the Pen is over the Stage
Filled box	Appears when the Control key (Windows) or Command key (Macintosh) is pressed and acts like the Subselect tool
Hollow box	Appears when the Control key (Windows) or Command key (Macintosh) is pressed and the icon is over a point; acts like the Subselect tool

The appearance of the lower-right symbol in the Pen tool can help you quickly determine what action is possible at the current cursor location.

The Oval and Rectangle Tools

The Oval and Rectangle Tools are used to create these basic shapes, either stroked, filled, or both stroked and filled. The Oval tool has no modifiers, while the Rectangle tool enables you to specify a corner radius in a pop-up dialog box. The Rectangle corner radius is measured in points. A corner radius of zero means square corners for the rectangle. The corner radius can be adjusted by using the up and down arrow keys while the rectangle is being drawn. This enables you to choose the corner radius dynamically, seeing the results onscreen. (The Rectangle tool with different corner radius settings is used to create buttons.)

If a fill color is chosen, the oval or rectangle automatically fills with that color. Gradients can be chosen at the bottom of the fill panel, or you can select no fill (the red diagonal slash through a rectangle icon in the upper-right corner of the fill panel). The stroke color and line width settings are used to color the line surrounding the oval or rectangle.

The Shift key can be used to constrain the shapes of both Oval and Rectangle tools. With the Oval tool, Shift constrains the shape to circles, while the Rectangle tool constrains to squares.

The Brush Tool

The Brush tool draws strokes like you would achieve with a paintbrush. This enables special effects with varying line widths that are especially useful for flourishes or calligraphy. Brush strokes are always filled and have zero thickness outlines, although when viewed as an Outline (View, Outline) the brush stroke is represented with an outline representing the thickness of the stroke. (You can think of a pencil stroke as a single vector with no fill while a brush stroke is a fill with no outline.) Using the Brush tool, you can paint areas of different sizes on the Stage. Brush tool fills can be solid, gradient, or bitmaps.

> **TIP**
>
> As with other tools, you can constrain the brush strokes to only horizontal and vertical directions by using the Shift key at the same time as dragging the tool.

Several modifiers appear in the Options Tray with the Brush Tool. The Brush Mode modifier has five settings that affect where the brush's stroke appears, and these are summarized in Table 2.3.

Table 2.3   Brush Mode Modifiers

Modifier	Meaning
Paint Normal	No special effect; anything created using the Brush tool paints over existing lines and fills on the same layer
Paint Fills	Paints any fills and background untouched areas, but not lines
Paint Behind	Paints in any blank areas behind the Stage's lines and fills, leaving other parts unaffected; this is not a fill, affecting only those areas behind the lines and fills that are touched by the Brush tool
Paint Selection	Paints a new fill where the Brush tool touches
Paint Inside	Paints the fill where the Brush tool starts, but doesn't paint over lines

The Brush Size and Brush Shape modifiers are drop-down menus that enable you to select the size and shape of the brush tool. There are 10 Brush Size options and nine Brush Shape options. The Brush Shapes provide several angles of stroke.

The Brush Size sizes always appear in the drop-down menu as circles, although the actual shape of the tool is dependent on the Brush Shape option. The width of the circle chosen in the Brush Size modifier is the width of the stroke of whatever shape is chosen in the Brush Shape menu (in other words, the Brush Size choices do not change shape to reflect the Brush Shape choice). The sizes chosen in the Brush Size menu are relative to the Zoom setting and do not change in the drop-down menu as zoom settings change.

The final standard modifier for the Brush tool is the Brush Lock Fill. The Lock Fill option is a toggle that controls how Flash handles gradient or bitmap fills. When the toggle is activated all subsequent areas that are painted with the Brush tool use the same gradient or bitmap. The Lock Fill function is applied automatically if the Dropper tool is used to pick up a gradient or fill.

A modifier called Brush Pressure appears in Flash if you are using a pressure-sensitive tablet (if you are not using such a device, this modifier is not visible). The Brush Pressure modifier is a toggle that is used to enable or disable the fine pressure sensitivity of the tablet so that with Brush Pressure enabled, the size of the brush stroke increases with increasing pressure on the tablet.

The Painting Tools

The painting tools used by Flash are the Dropper, Ink Bottle, and Paint Bucket. Let's look at each of these paint tools separately.

The Dropper Tool

The Dropper tool lets you pick up the color and style information from existing items. Modifiers are not used with the Dropper tool.

When the Dropper tool is not over an existing line or fill, the icon appears like the Dropper tool icon. However, when over a line or fill, the icon changes in the lower-right corner. Over a line, the Dropper tool adds a small pencil image to the icon, while a brush image appears when over a fill. When the icon has changed, a press of the Shift key changes the Dropper icon to an inverted U icon. When you click the mouse in this mode, the attributes of the line or fill are inherited by the Flash drawing tools (including color and styles).

When you have clicked the Dropper tool on a line, the tool is automatically changed to the Ink Bottle tool enabling you to apply the inherited attributes to lines on the Stage. When the clicked item is a fill, the Dropper tool changes to the Paint Bucket tool enabling you to apply the fill. If a bitmap was clicked, a thumbnail of the bitmap appears in the Fill Color option in the Toolbox.

The Ink Bottle Tool

The Ink Bottle Tool is used to change the color, style, and thickness for any line. The Ink Bottle can be employed after using the Dropper tool to apply an existing line style, but it can also be used at anytime to apply the current color and style settings. The Ink Bottle is also very useful for applying custom styles to multiple lines.

Remember that some lines may not appear properly, depending on the zoom level.

The Paint Bucket Tool

The Paint Bucket tool fills closed areas. After selecting the Paint Bucket icon and the color of the fill, click the area to be filled. The fill can be a solid color, gradient, or bitmap. The Paint Bucket can be used after using the Dropper tool to capture a fill, or independently using the default fill setting.

The Paint Bucket tool has one multiple-choice modifier, which contains the following four settings. These settings determine how gaps or broken-apart areas in a shape are handled by the fill:

- Don't Close Gaps: Gaps have no effect on the fill
- Close Small Gaps: Small gaps are closed
- Close Medium Gaps: Small and medium gaps are closed
- Close Large Gaps: Small, medium, and large gaps are closed

The size of the gap depends on the zoom level, so some gaps may be closed by the Paint Bucket tool with one of these options and yet left alone at a different zoom level. If gaps are too large, they may have to be closed manually.

Two icons at the bottom of the Modifier panel are also used with the Paint Bucket tool. The first is the Lock Fill option that is used with gradients and bitmaps. (When the Dropper tool is used to pick up a bitmap or gradient, the Lock Fill option is turned on by default.) The Lock Fill is a toggle that controls whether the size, angle, and point of origin of a gradient apply to all areas and shapes that are painted with the fill. In other words, all areas that are painted with a gradient or bitmap with the Lock Fill on appear like a single, continuously filled shape and not a set of individual fills, apart from each other.

The Transform Fill option enables you to adjust the size, angle, and center of a gradient or bitmap. When selected, the Paint Bucket icon changes to the Reshape Arrow. A set of adjustment handles appear around any selected fill, and the Reshape Arrow can be used to modify the appearance of the fill. Three functions are available with the Reshape Arrow: adjusting the rotation of the fill (to provide gradient directions other than horizontal), scaling and skewing the fill's size, and adjusting the center point of the fill (which alters the appearance of the gradient or bitmap).

To adjust the scale of a fill symmetrically, use the square corner handle located in the lower-left corner of the frame (assuming no rotation has been performed). To adjust asymmetrically, use the square handles on an edge, not the corners. To skew a fill horizontally, use the round handle on the right border (again assuming no rotation has occurred yet). To skew vertically, use the round handle on the top border.

> **NOTE**
>
> There are some anomalies with the Reshape Arrow. First, if you resize the gradient or bitmap to be smaller than the area to be filled, the fill tiles itself to occupy the area to be filled. This can produce undesirable effects. Second, while bitmaps can be skewed and scaled, gradients cannot be skewed (only scaled).

The Eraser Tool

Technically the Eraser tool is neither a drawing nor a painting tool, but it does belong as part of both. The Eraser tool is used to erase lines, fills, and anything else that has been drawn. The Eraser tool is an integral part of the toolset, because without it precision would be required for every drawn element.

It is important to remember that the Eraser tool removes elements, not just hides them or colors them the same as the background. Also, the Eraser tool only erases lines and fills in the current frame. It does not erase text, symbols, or groups. (To erase a part of a group, either ungroup the group or choose Edit Selected from the menu bar.)

The Eraser tool has three modifiers. The first is the Eraser mode, and this pull-down menu has five options, shown in Table 2.4.

Table 2.4 Eraser Tool Erase Modes

Mode	Meaning
Erase Normal	Erases all lines and fills it passes over as long as they are on the active layer
Erase Fills	Erases only fills and leaves lines unaffected
Erase Lines	Erases only lines and leaves fills unaffected
Erase Selected Fills	Erases only fills that are currently selected leaving unselected fills and all lines unaffected
Erase Inside	Erases the areas of fills that you initiate erasing on, leaving unselected fills and all lines unaffected.

The Erase Selected Fills and Erase Inside options are similar except Erase Inside selects only the fill that the erasure is initiated on with everything else left unaffected.

The Eraser Shape option lets you define the size and shape of the eraser from a drop-down menu. Two different shapes are available (circle and square) and each shape has five different sizes. The Eraser Faucet option toggles on or off and enables you to delete an entire line segment or an entire fill area by simply clicking anywhere on the line or fill.

Summary

Flash's Toolbox contains a considerable assortment of tools for drawing and painting items on the Stage. The Arrow, Subselect, and Lasso tools can be used to select items already placed on the Stage and used to modify their shape, remove them, or drag them to new locations. The drawing and painting tools usually have modifiers that enable their behaviors to be customized to suit your needs. Understanding the behavior and use of these modifiers is an important aspect of using Flash to its full capabilities.

Sample Questions

1. What does the Magnet option of the Arrow tool do?
   A. Changes the icon to a magnet to allow you to pick things up
   B. Imposes a grid over the Stage that all moved items must adhere to
   C. Lets you select a color and style from one object and apply it to other objects
   D. Forces the selected object to bend in the direction of the arrow

2. When using the pen tool, if you select an anchor point, what will the shape and fill of the point be?
   A. A hollow box
   B. A filled box
   C. A hollow circle
   D. A filled circle

3. If you have a pressure-sensitive tablet the Brush Pressure icon accomplishes what?
    A. Lets you change the size of the brush stroke by tapping on the tablet
    B. Lets you change the size of the brush stroke using pen pressure
    C. Lets you modify the color of the line by selecting areas of the tablet
    D. Lets you automatically fill shapes by tapping twice in the shape

CHAPTER 3

Flash Fundamentals

Symbols and Instances of Symbols

Macromedia Flash relies on the use of symbols and instances of symbols for its various tasks. A symbol is simply any object (buttons, graphics, or movie clips) that you create once and then reuse one or more times throughout your movie (and other movies, too). The Library tracks all symbols; when you create a symbol it is automatically registered with the Library.

An instance is a copy of the symbol that is used on the Stage. For example, if you create a generic button and store it as a symbol in the Library, when you need buttons in your movie you can create instances of the button symbol everywhere you need them. The advantage to using symbols and instances is that you need create the symbol only once and then you can have many instances created with no effort. Otherwise, you would have to create a new button object every time you needed a button. Another reason to use symbols and instances is that using symbols saves a considerable amount of file size in the final movie. The SWF file need only contain a description of the one button symbol and any specific parameters of each button instance (color, size, and so on) instead of having a complete set of button code for each button on the Stage throughout the movie.

> **TIP**
> Using symbols results in a slightly faster playback of movies than if you created the movie without symbols.

Instances can be different from symbols in many ways (color, size, animations, and so on), but the basic characteristics of the symbol (the button's four states, for example) are all inherited by each instance. When you edit an instance of a symbol on the Stage, no change is made to the symbol (only the instance is updated). On the other hand, if you edit the symbol, all the instances of that symbol are updated automatically.

All symbols in Flash are treated as unique objects and have both a timeline and a stage (with as many layers as you want) associated with them. Three basic types of symbols are native to Flash: graphics, buttons, and movie clips.

A graphic symbol is used for static (non-animated) images (although they can be built in to animation using the timeline, frame-by-frame). Graphic symbols do not have interactive controls or sounds.

A button symbol is used to create buttons that enable viewer interaction, and has several states that indicate whether the cursor is over the button, clicking it, or has clicked the button. For more information on buttons see Chapter 4, "Actions."

A movie clip symbol is animation with its own timeline, independent of any timeline of which the movie clip instance may be part. Movie clips can be instantiated as standalone movies, or as part of another symbol (for example, you could have a movie clip instance displaying inside a button instance). Movie clip symbols have one characteristic that button and graphic symbols lack: the ability to add variable to the movie to control its behavior. You use ActionScript to add these variables and their values, as you will see in Part II, "Flash Development." When variables (also called Clip Parameters) are added to a movie clip the result is called a "Smart Clip."

Creating Symbols

Symbols in Flash are created two ways: by converting an existing object on the stage to a symbol or by creating an empty symbol and defining it afterwards. Symbol characteristics are specified in symbol editing mode, a distinctly different mode from movie editing mode in Flash. Remember that because symbols have their own timelines, when you enter symbol editing mode your movie's timeline may be replaced by the symbol's timeline (until you exit symbol editing mode).

To convert an existing object into a symbol, select the object or objects on the Stage, and then use the pop-up menu and select Convert to Symbol or use the Insert, Convert to Symbol menu item. The Symbol Properties window appears. Enter the name of the symbol in the text window, choose whether the symbol is a graphic, button, or movie clip type. When you click OK, the symbol is added to your library and the selected objects on the Stage are now a symbol instance. When the objects become a symbol they cannot be edited directly on the Stage; instead, you have to enter Symbol Editing mode to modify the symbol and its instances.

To create a symbol from scratch, there should be nothing selected on the Stage. Then, either use the Insert, New Symbol menu item, click the New Symbol icon in the bottom-left corner of the Library window, or choose New Symbol from the Options menu in the upper-right corner of the Library window. The Symbol Properties window appears and you can enter the name and type of symbol in that window. When you click OK, Flash adds the symbol to the Library and changes to symbol editing mode. You can now create the symbol's contents on the Stage and Timeline. After creating the symbol's contents, exit symbol editing mode by choosing Edit, Edit Movie, clicking the Scene button in the upper-left corner of the document window, or clicking the Edit Scene button in the upper-right corner of the document window and choosing a scene from the drop-down menu.

If you have an animation sequence you want to convert to a movie clip symbol, the process is a little different from converting a selected object. In the timeline select every frame in the animation to become a movie clip symbol (including all layers that may be needed). Use the pop-up menu to select Copy Frames or use the Edit, Copy Frames menu item to copy those frames to the clipboard. Next, deselect all the frames in the timeline and choose Insert, New Symbol. In the Symbol Properties dialog provide a name for the movie clip symbol and choose the Movie Clip behavior. When symbol editing mode is ready select frame 1 in the symbol's timeline, and then choose Edit, Paste Frames. All the frames in the clipboard should now be copied into the object's timeline. After you exit symbol editing mode, the movie clip symbol is ready for use.

> **NOTE**
>
> Make sure you remove the frames from the movie timeline that now are represented by the symbol, or duplication can occur when you instantiate the symbol.

If you want to duplicate an existing symbol and modify its characteristics, select the source symbol in the Library and choose Duplicate from the Options menu. You have to rename the duplicate, as there can be only unique names for symbols in the Library.

Layers

Layers enable you to build up complex images, one part at a time, or isolate elements on separate layers for editing and reuse much like a cartoonist uses layers of acetate to build up finished frames in an animation. The same layered acetate principle applies to Flash, where layers are laid one on top of the other (from back to front), and anything showing through from lower layers to the front layer is visible to the viewer.

> **NOTE**
>
> Flash actually imposes a limit of 16,834 layers on a movie. Fortunately, because this limit is far beyond what any movie will use, it is of no consequence.

Layers are navigated using the Timeline window. The left side of the Timeline window is the Layers window. Here, each layer is displayed with a name and some characteristics, from the top of the screen to the bottom. The layers are displayed in a Flash frame from the bottom of the list to the top, so the topmost layer in the Layers window is the highest layer displayed.

Each layer in the Layer window has a name followed by four flags. The first flag is a pencil. Double-clicking the pencil or the layer name allows you to change the name of the layer. The next icon is either a dot or a red X positioned below an eye icon. This makes the layer visible on the stage (the dot) or hidden (the X). A layer that is not visible does not become part of the Stage's image. Hiding layers is a good way to work on a single layer at a time in the Stage, removing any distractions from other layer's contents. The next flag is either a dot or a padlock icon, positioned under another padlock icon. This indicates whether the layer is locked (the padlock) or not (the dot). A locked layer cannot be modified until the lock is removed (all elements on the layer are locked with this flag). The final flag is either a solid colored square or a colored outline around a gray square (the square colors change with each layer; blue is the default color for the first layer created). Above this flag is a black outline of a square. This flag toggles whether the layer is displayed in full (colored square) or in outline mode (colored outline around a gray square). Outlined layers are useful when aligning material, as well as providing a skeleton on which other layers can be edited or created.

Each layer has its own Properties window that can be displayed by selecting a layer, displaying the pop-up menu (right-click), and choosing Properties from the menu. Alternatively, the Properties window can be displayed by double-clicking the icon to the left of the layer name (it looks like a page with the bottom-right corner folded up).

Several parameters can be changed in the Layer Properties window. The top of the dialog enables you to change the layer name, which defaults to "Layer 1", "Layer 2", and so on. Using descriptive layer names is a good way to organize projects, especially large ones.

The layer name is followed by two check boxes to show or hide the layer (the same as clicking the Hide flag after the layer name in the Layer window). The Type section consists of five radio buttons (some most likely grayed out, depending) that enable you to specify the type of layer this is. The options and their meanings are shown in Table 3.1.

Table 3.1   The Type Options

Radio Button	Meaning
Normal	The default setting; this is not a guided or masked layer
Guide	Used for laying out elements on other layers; guide layers do not show in a published Flash movie
Guided	Indicates the layer is a guided layer, usually with a motion guide layer as the template for motion
Mask	A mask layer is used to mask or hide parts of a layer, enabling other parts to show through; mask layers contain only a single element
Masked	Indicates the layer is a masked layer, usually with a mask guide layer to indicate motion

Underneath the Type buttons is a color swatch to enable you to choose the outline color, changing the outline icon box flag on the Layer window from the default color to whatever color you choose. This color is also used to display the layer's contents in outline mode on the Stage. These colors help you differentiate which elements belong to which layer when looking at several layers at once on the Stage. The View Layer as Outline check box is the same as clicking the Outline flag in the Layer window, and displays the layer's contents in outline mode. Finally, the Layer Height has three values that enable you to expand the layer height to two or three times the normal value in the Layer window. Expanding the layer height can be useful when animations or sound files are involved.

You can resize the Layer window to display more layers than the default value by grabbing the border between the Timeline and the Stage windows, and moving it either up or down. To change the order of layers in the Layer window, select the layer to be moved and drag it up or down in the layer list to its new position. Layers can be reordered at any time.

> **TIP**
>
> You can select more than one layer at a time (although only one layer can be active) by using Shift+click the layer name for contiguous layers, or Control+click (Windows) or Command+click (Macintosh) for non-contiguous layers.

Multiple layers can be affected at once in some useful ways in the Layer window. For example, to hide several layers at once, click the flag below the eye icon for the first layer to be hidden, and then drag the cursor through all the layers you want to hide. Each layer changes to the locked icon as the cursor passes over. The reverse can be performed to reveal several layers at once. You can also use a shortcut to hide all the layers except one. Alt+click (Windows) or Option+click (Macintosh) the hide flag in the one layer you want to see and all other layers are hidden. To hide all layers at once, Control+click (Windows) or Command+click (Macintosh) the eye flag in the headers of the Layers window and all layers are hidden. Reversing the process reveals all the layers.

Creating, Viewing, and Editing Layers

Layers can be added to the Layer window by clicking the Add Layer button at the bottom of the Layer window, by using the Insert Layer option from the pop-up menu attached to any layer name, or by choosing the Insert, Layer menu item. Added layers appear above any selected layer. Whenever a layer is added, it automatically becomes the active layer.

Layers can be toggled between visible and hidden using the flag next to the layer's name. It is important to remember that hidden layers are incorporated into published SWF files even though they are not visible (except for Guide layers, which are never included in the SWF file).

To edit a layer, select its name in the Layer window. When a layer is active and editable, a pencil icon appears next to the layer name in the Layer window. You can have only one layer active at a time, although many layers can be displayed simultaneously. Layers can be copied in their entirety (except for their name, which must be unique) by using Edit, Copy to copy the layer's contents, creating a new layer with Add Layer or similar sequence, and then using Edit, Paste. The created layer is selected by default, so you do not need to choose it for the paste operation.

To delete a layer from the Layer window, select the layer and either click the Delete icon at the bottom of the Layer window, drag the layer to the Delete icon, or use the pop-up menu and select Delete.

Using Guide Layers

Guide layers are useful as a means of keeping the layout and positioning of elements in a movie, as well as providing a template for drawing elements of a consistent nature on other layers and frames. Guide layers can also be used as motion guides, enabling easier creation of complex motions in a frame-by-frame animation. Guide layers are visible in the Stage (unless hidden), but are not exported to a Flash movie using the Publish menu item. (Guide layers therefore do not add to the final size of an SWF movie and hence can be used liberally in a movie project.)

To set a layer as a guide layer, use the Properties window and select Guide in the Type area. Alternatively, you can designate a layer as a guide layer by using the pop-up menu and selecting the Guide item. Any layer can be designated as a guide layer, regardless of its position in the Layer window. When you make a layer a guide layer, the icon next to the name in the Layer window changes to show two crossed lines or guides. Any number of guide layers can exist. When a layer is designated as a guide layer, the icon before the layer name in the Layer window changes from a piece of paper with a folder in the lower-right corner to a pair of lines at right angles to each other (indicating a grid). Guided layers are layers that follow a guide and are so indicated in the Properties window.

> **TIP**
>
> Most developers lock a guide layer once it is created to avoid accidental modification.

Motion guide layers are used to specify a path for an element to move along. A motion guide layer has one or more guided layers associated with it; these guided layers follow the path specified in the motion guide layer. Motion guide layers, like guide layers, do not appear in an SWF file. To convert a guide layer to a motion guide layer, the easiest way is to drag a normal layer onto the guide layer, which executes the conversion. (Because it is easy to accidentally convert a guide layer to a motion guide layer when moving layers about in the Layer window, many developers keep the guide layers at the bottom of the layer order.) A motion guide layer has a different icon next to the layer name than a simple guide layer. The motion guide layer icon is an arching line with a round circle partway along. A guided layer does not have a special icon but is indented underneath the guide layer in the Layers window.

Using Mask Layers

Mask layers are used to either hide or reveal elements in other layers, and can also add motion to the mask. A mask layer allows underlying layers to appear through the areas that are filled on the layer, and hides any underlying items that are in the unfilled area of the mask layer. (This is a little counterintuitive, as you might expect the unfilled areas of the mask layer to be transparent, but in practice it is easy to work with this convention.) A static mask is a layer that has no motion in it. Animated masks have a mask layer (to define the mask and a motion path) and one or more masked layers. Mask layers are above the layer that is to be masked in the Timeline (otherwise they don't mask the contents of that layer). You cannot mask the inside of buttons, although buttons themselves can be masked.

To define mask layers, set the Type of a layer to Mask in the Properties window and define the mask itself. The icon before the name of the mask layer in the Layer window changes to a circle inside a square, with a downward-pointing area inside. A masked layer has an icon that looks like a filled circle with a right-facing arrow inside it. Masked layers are indented in the Layer window underneath the mask layer. The mask is a single filled shape on the mask layer, such as a circle or more complex shape. Only a single shape can be on a mask layer, although that shape can be complex. The fill of that shape does not matter; all mask fills are interpreted as opaque in the final movie, although it is often convenient to use a transparent fill to allow proper positioning of the mask and underlying masks on the Stage. If motion of the mask is to be involved, a layer below the mask layer contains the motion path. Below the motion layer, if one exists, is the layer that contains the elements to be masked.

If you want to apply a mask to more than one layer, you need to indicate that the layer is masked. Normally, only the layer underneath a mask layer is masked. To create more masked layers, drag them under the mask layer in the layer order, and choose Masked in the Properties window or in the pop-up menu. To unmask a layer, change its type to Normal.

Timelines

The Timeline allows you to organize and view the progress of a Flash movie in conjunction with the Layer window. By default, the Timeline window (including the Layers window) is docked at the top of the Flash window. It can be moved to the bottom or either side of the Flash window by dragging it, or it can be displayed as a floating window. You can also hide it from view.

The Timeline itself is the right side of the Timeline window (the left side is the Layer information). To expand or contract the display of the Timeline or Layers panes, grab the dividing line between the two panes and move it back or forth. The Timeline itself can be expanded or contracted to show more layers by moving the dividing line between the Timeline and Stage windows.

The top of the Timeline has a list of frames increasing from left to right, numbered every five frames by default. On this list of frames is a rectangle called the Playhead, which shows which frame is currently being displayed. Underneath the frame numbers is a set of rectangles, one set for each layer in the Layer window, and one rectangle for each frame. Some of the frames are darker than others; dark frames are keyframes. By default, every fifth frame is a keyframe.

At the top-right corner of the Timeline, after the frame numbers, is an icon that displays a pop-up menu called the Frame View menu. The top five items on this menu change the number of frames displayed in the window by compressing or expanding the frame display. To decrease the height of the rows of layers shown in the Timeline, choose the Short menu item. The Tinted Frames option tints the frames a light color to clearly show where the frame starts and stops running, while turning off Tinted Frames removes the color and leaves the duration of the layer the same color as the background.

The last two menu options, Preview and Preview in Context, control how the frames are scaled to fit the Timeline. To scale thumbnails of each frame to fit the Timeline, choose Preview. If you want to see frames changing as an animation progresses, select Preview in Context. Both Preview and Preview in Context override the size options at the top of the menu, and expand the size of the timeline considerably. Using either Preview or Preview in Context can limit the amount of information you can see in the Timeline, but can be useful for seeing the actual content of a frame.

The bottom of the Timeline has a list of icons in the lower-left corner, followed by a display of the current frame number (the frame the Playhead is currently over), the frame rate (in frames per second), and the elapsed time from the start of the movie. The icons at the bottom of the Timeline are (from left to right):

- Center Frame: Positions the currently played frame in the middle of the Timeline (used when the Playhead has moved out of the window)
- Onion Skin: Displays surrounding frames as dimmed images on the Stage
- Onion Skin Outlines: Acts like Onion Skin, but displays only outlines of surrounding frames
- Edit Multiple Frames: Enables editing of all frames on the Stage, including dimmed (onion skin) frames
- Modify Onion Markers: Controls the way Onion Skinning is displayed on the Stage

Onion skinning is one way of showing more than one frame at a time on the Stage. This is useful when you have to handle frame-by-frame animation and align objects that are moving across or around the Stage. To see more than one frame of animation at a time, click the Onion Skin icon at the bottom of the Timeline window. The frame that is underneath the Playhead displays in full color, while frames surrounding the Playhead frame appear dimmed (as though seen through onion skin paper, hence the name). Each frame around the Playhead frame appears on the Stage, but only the current frame can be edited unless Edit Multiple Frames mode is selected. The Onion Skin Outlines option is the same as Onion Skin, except the images of surrounding frames are displayed as dimmed outlines.

> **NOTE**
>
> When using one of the Onion Skin modes, you can select any frame on the Stage using the Playhead. As you move through the animation, the selected frame becomes the highlighted frame on the Stage and the surrounding frames are dimmed.

There will be times when you want to edit more than the highlighted frame when in Onion Skin mode. To edit all the frames between a Start and End marker, you can use the Edit Multiple Frames icon. (Any layer that is locked isn't displayed in Onion Skin mode. This can be a useful way of hiding some layers in a sequence to prevent confusion when modifying frames in Onion Skin mode.) When using the Edit Multiple Frames mode, the onion skinning dimmed frame effect is turned off and all the frames in the sequence are displayed normally. Using the Edit Multiple Frames mode is a good way to reposition an element in all the frames displayed on the Stage at the same time, simply by grouping them all and moving them as a unit. Each individual frame is updated properly.

The Modify Onion Markers button leads to several options in a pull-down menu. The Always Show Markers item lets you always display the markers that indicate onion skins, whether Onion Skin mode is on or not. The Anchor Onion Skin Marks locks the onion skin markers to their current frame numbers instead of enabling them to move.

The Onion 2, Onion 5, and Onion All options tell Flash to display two, five, or all frames on either side of the current frame when displaying frames in Onion Skin mode. When you are displaying frames on the Stage in Onion Skin mode, dragging the timeline header's onion skin markers temporarily adjusts the number of frames that are displayed on the Stage. If the Playhead moves, the markers return to their original location. This can be a handy way of cutting down or expanding the number of frames visible on the Stage temporarily without worrying about changing the Onion Skin frame count.

Working with Frames

Each frame in the timeline (whether a regular frame or a keyframe) can be managed in the same way. You can add, delete, move, and perform other functions to each frame. You can also cut and paste frames.

To insert a new frame in the timeline, choose the Insert, Frame menu item after highlighting where in the timeline you want the new frame to go, or you can use the pop-up menu Insert Frame option. Use the right-click (Windows) or Control+click (Macintosh) to display the pop-up menu. To delete a frame, select the frame in the timeline and use the Insert, Remove Frame menu item or the Remove Frame option from the pop-up menu.

You can move a frame to another location in the timeline by selecting the frame or frames to be moved with the mouse, and then dragging them to their new location. You can extend the duration of a frame by selecting the final frame of the sequence and using Alt+click (Windows) or Option+click (Macintosh) to drag the frame to the new duration. If the frame is part of a tweened sequence (animation), you can drag either the first or last keyframes (because a keyframe is at either end) to the new duration.

Keyframes

A keyframe is simply a frame where a change in the animation occurs, or where there is some frame action that modifies the playback of the movie. Whenever you are working with tweened animations, keyframes are important as they indicate changes. Other than indicating a change in the behavior, frames are treated like normal frames, including the way they are deleted, moved, cut and pasted, and so on.

You can create a keyframe at any point in a timeline by choosing where you want the keyframe to reside and using Insert, Keyframe or using a right-click (Windows) or Control+click (Macintosh) to display the pop-up menu and then choosing Insert Keyframe. This converts an existing frame to a keyframe. To insert a new blank keyframe, use the Insert Blank Keyframe option from the pop-up menu or use the Insert, Blank Keyframe menu item.

If you want to convert a keyframe to a regular frame, select the keyframe and then choose the Clear Keyframe option from the pop-up menu, or use the Insert, Clear Keyframe menu item. When you convert a keyframe, that frame and all frames up to the next keyframe (if one exists) are replaced with the contents of the frame just before the keyframe you converted (because keyframes indicate changes in a frame, there can be no changes until a keyframe is encountered on the timeline).

Frame Labels

Frame labels are useful for identifying particular frames in a movie by something other than a frame number. A frame label lets you assign a name to a keyframe, usually used with the goto command for jumping to a particular place in the timeline. To add a frame label (and hence create a keyframe) select the frame and use the Window, Panel, Frame menu item to display the Frame panel (if it is not already open). At the top of the Frame panel is a text entry field with the current name of the frame displayed (or the default name if a name is not yet assigned). Enter the new frame name in this field. The drop-down menu underneath the frame label entry enables you to select tweening from None, Motion, or Shape.

Frame labels are exported with a movie, so long frame label names should be avoided to keep exported file sizes short. If you need to provide a fair bit of information for the keyframe, instead of using a frame label you can use a comment. Comments are not exported with movie data. To create a comment, precede the text with two slashes (//). You can have multiple lines of comment in a frame label and because they are not exported you can use them to provide verbose explanations of keyframes.

> **NOTE**
>
> When you add or remove frames from a layer, the label moves relative to the other frames before or after the new or removed frames. The frame name is thus preserved, even though the frame number has changed. Because of this, frame labels are much better than frame numbers when you modify the timeline and use the goto command.

Frame Rates

The bottom of the Timeline window displays the current frame and the frame rate, as well as the elapsed time. The frame rate used for Flash movies can be set to any value you want between 0.01fps and 120fps, but you usually have to balance the factors of jerkiness of the frames against the total number of frames (and hence file size) to find a balance. A frame rate of 24fps (frames per second) is used for projected movies in a cinema, as this rate was determined to be the rate at which movement from one frame to the next blurs to the extent it is perceived as continual movement. Setting too low a frame rate results in each individual frame registering to the viewer's eye, and looks jerky and fake. The usual setting for movies being sent over the Web or from a server is 12fps.

> **NOTE**
>
> Frame rates can be set over a wide range, but only one frame rate can be used for an entire movie (although you can vary effective frame rates for particular animations). This frame rate is set in the Movie Properties dialog (Modify, Movie). You can also display the Movie Properties dialog by double-clicking the frame rate box in the Timeline.

If you want to change the frame rate for an individual part of the timeline, such as a particular animation sequence, you can do so by adding or removing frames (remember that real frame rates can be set to only one value for the whole Flash movie, so a trick like this is necessary). For example, to lengthen an animation and make it seem to last longer than it really does and hence slow the animation down, you could add either keyframes or in-between frames. In-between frames are better than keyframes, as keyframes increase the size of the SWF file. However, in-between frames should show some movement of any elements in motion, and therefore require more work to set up. To shorten an animation (and hence make it faster), you can remove frames, but make sure that the overall effect is not disjointed motion.

Nested and Multiple Timelines

You usually have a single timeline attached to your Flash movie. Using ActionScript, you can use multiple timelines, nesting them within other movie timelines. This is possible because each movie can have its own timeline. When you have a timeline that incorporates other movie clips, those timelines are invoked by the master timeline, and the two timelines communicate events (such as starting and stopping) with each other.

One timeline can call several other movie clips each with its own timeline, which themselves can call other movie clips with associated timelines, and so on. Any action normally used on a timeline (for example, `play`, `stop`, and `goto`) can be used in any other timeline.

Nesting of timelines is made possible because movie clips (and their timelines) are both an object and a symbol in Flash terms. As an object, you can use methods to control playback of the clip and properties to control the way the clip appears. As an instance of a symbol a movie clip can be used for animated loops and buttons.

> **NOTE**
>
> Because a movie clip is a symbol it can be stored in the Library, and an instantiation of that symbol can be used in a timeline of another movie clip.

To nest or use multiple clips and timelines, the symbol needs to be in the Library and an instantiation of the symbol is created. To instantiate the movie clip, it needs to be both placed on the Stage and also named as an instance (the process is the same as using a creator function for any Flash object). Place an instance of the symbol on the Stage by dragging it from the Library to the Stage, and then select the instance and in the Instance panel enter a unique name of the clip instance. Because the instance now has a unique name ActionScript can use it.

To incorporate one movie instance into another timeline use a target path. The target path is really just an object name that lets Flash find the object. For movie clip timelines, you need to provide both a target path and an action for the clip (the target path tells Flash where the object is and the action tells Flash what to do with it). The actions possible with a movie clip are GoTo, Stop, and Play. For more information on ActionScript see Part II, but the command you need to use an instance and play to a particular frame number is:

```
InstanceName.gotoAndStop(endframe);
```

Where `InstanceName` is the name of the instance and `endframe` is the frame number where you want to stop playing the movie clip.

Frame-by-Frame Animations

With frame-by-frame animations you create each frame in an animation sequence manually, instead of letting Flash generate intermediate frames for you (such as with tweening). Frame-by-frame animation is best when you have complex animations to perform that tweening could not easily perform for you. Because of the sheer number of frames involved, frame-by-frame animation results in a larger SWF file size than tweening the intermediate frames.

To create frame-by-frame animation you need to set a keyframe in a layer, draw the shapes on the Stage, and then move to the next frame. Each frame should be a keyframe, so the keyframe can be inserted or changed from a normal frame. Every time you add a new keyframe, the contents of the previous keyframe appear and you can then modify them to show the next frame in animation. Continue this process adding new keyframes and changing the animation, one frame at a time, until finished.

> **TIP**
>
> To test a frame-by-frame animation, press the Enter key, use the Control, Play menu item, or click the Play button on the Controller. It is usually a good idea to use the Play function continually to ensure the flow of movement is fluid as you create each frame.

Tweening

Tweening is a method of creating frames in between keyframes. This is necessary because of the huge size of an SWF file if you define each frame of an animation individually, whether there is movement in the frame or not. Tweening produces a set of incremental frame change information that enables Flash to mathematically determine interim frames between keyframes, saving file size and enabling a computer's CPU to render the in-between frames instead of reading them from the file.

Flash uses two kinds of tweening: motion tweening and shape tweening. With both types of tweening, you provide a starting and ending keyframe and let Flash determine the changes necessary to draw each in-between frame, based on the number of frames that are to be created between the two.

There are some differences between the way motion and shape tweening are handled by Flash, and choosing the correct type of tweening requires a little understanding of the underlying processes. Motion tweening only works on symbols and groups. If you are working on a frame that has multiple objects, some or all in motion, the objects must be made into a group for motion tweening to be used. If you have a symbol that is to be in motion, only motion tweening can be used. Shape tweening only works on a shape that is editable. If you have a shape that you want to morph into something else, shape tweening must be used.

> **TIP**
>
> Essentially, if the change that is to be performed cannot be done without redrawing the entire subject, shape tweening is used. Motion tweening is used when the change in the object could be performed using standard Flash dialogs, panels, or property windows.

Motion Tweening

You can use motion tweening with motion to make changes to an object's position, size, rotation, and other effects. You can also use tweening for subtle or drastic color changes, making an objects color throb, change, or drift in and out of the background color. As mentioned, for motion tweening to work you need to use symbols or groups.

To create a motion tween you can use one of two methods. The first involves creating starting and ending keyframes for the motion to be tweened, and then using the Motion Tweening option in the Frame panel. The second method is to create the first keyframe, and then use Insert, Create Motion Tween, moving the objects on the Stage to their target location and letting Flash create the ending keyframe. Both methods work equally well and require about the same amount of effort.

Using either method of tweening, you can use a few options in the Frame panel. After choosing Motion tweening, you can specify the Easing value directly or use the pop-up slider. Easing values dictate the rate of motion change from frame to frame and indicates whether the motion should be constant (an easing value of 0), speed up towards the end of the animation (a negative easing value), or slow down towards the end (a positive easing value). Using easing enables you to make the motion appear smoother as acceleration effects (positive or negative) are imposed. The Rotate value enables you to specify no rotation (the default), Auto (which rotates the object once either clockwise or counterclockwise, depending on which direction requires the least motion of the object), and both clockwise (CW) or counterclockwise (CCW) with a number indicating the total number of rotations the object is to perform as it moves. The check boxes at the bottom of the panel provide more flexibility. If you are using a motion path, click the Orient to Path box to set the baseline of the motion tweening along the path. The Synchronization check box lets you ensure that the instance being tweened is looping properly (this is often necessary if the number of frames in the animation is not an even multiple of the number of frames available in the timeline). Finally, the Snap box can be used to attach the tweened objects to the motion path using the registration point.

You can use a motion guide layer with tweening, linking more than one object to the guide layer if you want. To do this, create a tweened sequence as usual, selecting the Orient to Path option in the Frame Properties window to enable the tweening to follow the motion guide you use. Next add a motion guide (either through Insert, Motion Guide or using the pop-up menu's Add Motion Guide). The new motion guide layer appears above the layer with the object to be guided (assuming you did not deselect that layer at some point). To create the path the tweening is to follow, use the drawing tools to draw the path on the motion guide layer, snapping the beginning of the path to the first frame and the end of the path to the last frame of animation. When you play the animation, the motion should now follow the path (which you can hide using the Eye column in the Layer window).

Shape Tweening

Shape tweening is usually used for morphing effects, where one shape gradually flows into another shape as the animation proceeds. As with motion tweening, shape tweening can also affect location, color, and size of the shapes. Keep in mind that shape tweening cannot work with groups or symbols. If you need to tween shapes in a group, you need to break the group apart (Modify, Break Apart) first, and then tween the shapes individually or together. If you have multiple shapes to be tweened at the same time, you'll find it faster to tween them individually instead of all at once. If you do need to tween multiple shapes at the same time, they have to be on the same layer.

The process for tweening a shape is to create or select an empty keyframe to hold the start of the animation on the layer with the shapes. In this keyframe create or copy the image for the starting shape of the tween. Then create a second keyframe further down the timeline, leaving the number of frames between the two keyframes that the animation is to last. On this second keyframe draw the end shape. In the Frame panel (Window, Panel, and Frame) set the Tweening option to Shape. As with motion tweening you can enter values for Easing. The Blend option lets you handle changes in edges as one shape tweens to another. Distributive blending has intermediate shapes, which are smooth (and potentially irregular in shape), while Angular blending preserves straight lines and corners. The Angular blend mode is intended for shapes that have sharp corners.

Shape hints are a way to control shape changes that are complex and that you want to control in the way they morph from one shape to another. Shape hints can prevent intermediate shapes from being unidentifiable blobs, preserving some semblance of the original and destination shapes as the morphing proceeds. Shape hints use a circle with a letter ("a" through "z") to identify points that are to correspond on both the starting and ending shapes (there can be only 26 shape hints).

To place a shape hint use the Modify, Transform, Shape Hint menu item. The circle with a letter in it appears on the shape and can be positioned at the proper point. Do this for each shape hint on the starting and ending frames. Shape hint markers are yellow in the first keyframe and green in the last keyframe. A red shape hint indicates the point is on a straight line. Using shape hints effectively takes a bit of practice and a logical approach, as you want to make sure the correlation between starting and ending points is consistent and does not require complex manipulations for Flash to adhere to them. Often for complex shape morphing you will find it easier to draw some intermediate shapes manually and produce shape tweening as a series of animations, instead of one animation sequence. If you want to remove a shape hint, simply drag it off the Stage. To remove all shape hints use the Modify, Transform, Remove All Hints menu item.

Summary

In this chapter I've discussed symbols and instances, the use of timelines and layers, as well as some subjects closely allied to them both such as keyframes and tweening. The ability to nest timelines is a useful feature of Flash, but requires the use of ActionScript which is examined in Part II.

Sample Questions

1. Which of the following statements is *not* true about symbols?

    A. Symbols are treated as unique objects and have both a timeline and a stage.

    B. All symbols have a unique name.

    C. Symbols are all tracked by the Library.

    D. Symbols are always a movie clip data type.

2. When creating a mask, which statement is true?

    A. The mask can be any shape and complexity.

    B. Masks contain only a single element.

    C. Masks must be a transparent color.

    D. Masks can have only one masked layer beneath them.

3. What is the usual frame rate for a Web-based animation?

    A. 9fps

    B. 12fps

    C. 18fps

    D. 24fps

CHAPTER 4

Actions

Buttons

Buttons are used to provide some interactive features to your Macromedia Flash movie and enable the viewer to cause actions to occur by selecting different buttons. Buttons range in appearance drastically and can be of any shape and color, and can have animations embedded on them.

Buttons in Flash have four states, and are labeled in the Timeline for each state. The four states are:

- Up: The cursor is not over the button and hence it is not selected
- Over: The cursor is over the button but it has not been selected yet
- Down: The cursor is over the button and it has just been selected with a mouse click
- Hit: An invisible state that defines the active area of a button

Although all four states could look the same, it is common that each state looks a little different. This gives the viewer positive feedback that a button is positioned correctly for selecting (Over), has been clicked (Down), and is below the active area (Hit). Normally you use different graphics for each state, although you could use other techniques to differentiate the states.

Creating a Button

In Flash, buttons are symbols. To create a button on a frame, you need to create the button symbol and assign it a button's behavior (the four states are the behaviors). Whenever you create a button instance the timeline shows the four states. The first three keyframes dictate the appearance of the button while the fourth keyframe shows the active area of the button.

The process for creating a button symbol is to use Insert, New Symbol to open the Symbol Properties dialog. The top of the Symbol Properties dialog enables you to enter a name for the symbol, while the bottom of the dialog has three different behaviors for the symbol (Movie Clip, Button, and Graphic). Choose Button for the behavior. The Library now shows the new symbol and the timeline shows the four button states. Flash puts a keyframe in the Up state automatically, but not in the other three states. You have to add keyframes there manually.

> **TIP**
>
> An important point is that the viewer sees only the first three states of the button. Because the Hit state defines the area of the button, it is not visible to the viewer.

Setting the Four Button States

After a button has been created in the library and timeline, you can create the four states. I go through the four states in order, but you can work on them in any order you want.

In the timeline you select the Up state, and then create a graphic (or place a graphic symbol from the Library) on the Stage. A crosshair appears in the middle of the Stage to act as a central point for the symbol, but you can place the graphic anywhere on the Stage. The graphic can be simple (an oval or rectangle, for example) or complex (with text, graphics, or animation in the body of the graphic). After drawing or placing the graphic, it is now a button (and the Library shows a preview of the button if the symbol is selected).

For the Over state you need to select the Over frame in the timeline, and then create a keyframe there (Insert, Keyframe). This frame is a duplicate of the Up state frame. You should make some change to the button to indicate the change in state. This could be as simple as slightly changing the fill color using the Color palette, enlarging some item inside the button, or changing animations. The idea, of course, is to show the user that the cursor is now over this button, and any visual indicator is useful.

For the Down state, select the Down frame in the timeline and again create a keyframe (Insert, Keyframe). The Stage contains a copy of the Over frame. Again, you should make some change to the button to show that it has been selected. Typically, this may be a noticeable change in color, reversing the color scheme of part or all the contents of the button, or using some shading to indicate an indented look.

As mentioned earlier, the first three keyframes (Up, Over, and Down) are used to indicate the three states for the button. The fourth frame (Hit) is used to define the active area of the button. To do this select the Hit frame from the timeline and again insert a keyframe (which duplicates the Hit frame on the Stage). Any area that is filled on the Stage is a trigger for the button.

NOTE

Normally you have the active area for a button the same as the graphic image, but some interfaces work better with larger or smaller active areas than the actual button. A larger active area for a button gives more flexibility for the viewer to interact with the button and works well when only a few buttons are used on the screen, or when the viewer is not likely to be very dexterous. Smaller active areas are useful when many buttons are crammed closely together and you want to ensure that the button press is intentional.

If your button is a funny shape (such as a wiggly line or fancy shaped image) make the active area a normal shape over that button, such as an oval or rectangle. Because the viewer does not see the Hit keyframe, you can do anything you want to the image on the Stage. Many developers choose to simply color the button in a solid fill as a reminder that the image is not viewed, although you could just as easily leave the Down image the way it is for the Hit frame.

If you are using buttons frequently in your projects, you can create a single project with an assortment of button symbols defined in it. These buttons can then be used in any other project. This ensures you have consistent button shapes and actions, as well as saves you the trouble of defining the four button states over and over.

The button's four states are now recorded in the Library. You can use this button anywhere in your movie that you want, and as many times as you want because each is an instance of the symbol. You can preview the four states of the button at any time by selecting the object in the Library (the Up image appears in the Preview window at the top of the Library) and selecting the Play (right arrow) button in the upper-right corner. All three visible states of the button will be shown one after another.

TIP

There may be times when you want to use more than one area for the Hit state. This may occur when you have two or more areas on a frame with the same button, or several buttons with the same actions attached to them. You can accomplish this task easily by copying and pasting the Down frame graphics to the Hit keyframe.

Using a Button in a Movie

After all four states have been defined you can use the button symbol. In Movie Editing mode (Edit, Edit Movie), drag a copy of the button symbol from the Library to the Stage. You can still modify the button's color, size, and orientation any way you want on the stage without affecting the original symbol.

Flash automatically deactivates the rollover capabilities of a button when it is in movie editing mode. (The reason for this is simple: If the button was active, you could never work on it with the cursor, as it would be considered Over or Down.) To preview a button's action on the Stage, you need to enable the buttons. This is easily done from the

Control, Enable Simple Buttons menu item. All buttons on the Stage are now considered active and display their proper behavior when the mouse moves over them or they are hit. Naturally, you should turn off Enable Simple Buttons when you want to work on the Stage. (Not all button behaviors are shown with Enable Simple Buttons; if there are complex behaviors, you do not see them in this mode. Instead, you have to enter test mode through Control, Test Movie or Control, Test Scene and try the buttons.)

Changing a Button's Shape

Not all buttons are simple geometric shapes. You may want a button that changes shape when the Over or Down states are active. Or, more likely, you may want to hide the button as part of a larger image and have the button change in that image (such as a door opening when the mouse is Over, or a mouth smile when Down, and so on). The creation of the three visible states (Up, Over, and Down) is accomplished using the drawing and painting tools in the normal manner, but the Hit state may require special handling as the active area could be a complex shape, or even change shape with each of the other states.

After you have created the graphics for the three visible states, the Hit state can be drawn using one of two fairly simple methods. The first involves opening the three visible frames one at a time and using the Edit, Copy command to copy the button shape in that frame, and then go to the Hit frame and use Edit, Paste in Place to place that shape on the Hit frame. When all three visible frames have had their shape pasted on the Hit frame you have a composite shape of all three shapes that defines the active area (assuming you want all three shapes to be active, of course). The second approach uses onion skinning. Draw a simple geometric shape on the stage that is large enough to cover all three button shapes, and then turn on onion skin mode so you can see the precise shape you need to cover (the three shapes appear in outline within the larger shape you drew. You can then use the drawing tools to modify the shape to suit the active area, using the outlines as a guide.

> **TIP**
>
> If you use the onion skin mode, you should use a transparent color for the Hit fill to enable the other graphics outlines to show through clearly.

Button Actions

Buttons have some actions built in when they are created (the movement from Up to Over, Over to Down, and so on are all actions common to buttons). If you want to add more actions to a button, or modify a behavior for some reason, you can attach ActionScript commands to a button instance. To do this the Object Actions panel must be open. Select the button or a movie clip on the Stage and display the Actions panel using Windows, Actions or use the Show Actions button at the bottom of the Stage.

The best way to show the use of a button action is to use a simple example. We create one button that simply jumps to another frame when it is pressed. Open a new Flash document and create two keyframes in frames 1 and 2. For each frame, place some identifying text on the Stage (such as "Frame 1" and "Frame 2"). For each frame use the Actions panel to add a Stop action (double-click Stop in the Actions toolbox). This prevents the frames from continually looping and ensures a stop after each frame has been run (you'll see why in a moment).

After selecting the first frame in the timeline either use a button from the Library and create an instance of it, or create a new button on the Stage. Select the button. The Object Actions panel shows no commands in the list for this button. Choose whatever commands you want the button to execute from the Object actions panel, making sure you fill in any parameters in the lower part of the window necessary for the command to run (such as Frame 2 for the goto command). After all the commands are entered you can test the button through Enable Simple Buttons. If you entered goto with Frame 2 as the jump frame, whenever you click the button with the text for the first frame visible, you should see the second frame's text appear right away (and the button disappears unless you copied it to the second frame). Using this method you can define simple or complex ActionScript commands to a button in any state.

More than one action can be attached to a button using ActionScript. To do this, it is useful to understand the way Flash handles buttons using ActionScript. One ActionScript command, On Mouse Event, is available only for buttons and this command handles all decisions about ActionScript commands attached to the button. This command is called a button handler and may be present as the first line of any ActionScript command list for a button. When the mouse button is clicked, the handler bases its actions on the commands that follow.

When using On Mouse Event in ActionScript, it is converted in the Actions panel to on (). The parentheses are then filled in by the proper parameter. The mouse handler uses the command on (release) to indicate that releasing the mouse button (after a click) triggers actions that follow in curly braces. The mouse handler automatically adds the on (release) command to the ActionScript whenever you select an action attached to a mouse in the Actions panel. The following is the ActionScript:

```
on (release) {
        gotoAndPlay (2);
}
```

This tells the handler when the mouse button is released, the movie jumps to frame 2 and continues playing from there.

The commands attached to on (release) are executed only when the mouse button is released as part of the click, and that's usually where you want to attach ActionScript commands. However, you can attach commands to any of the mouse actions, such as when the Over state is triggered by the cursor moving over the button. This is easily done in the Object Actions panel by selecting the On Mouse Event command in the Basic Actions list. The bottom part of the Object Actions panel shows check boxes that reflect the state of the mouse. By default, Release is checked. To trigger an action when the cursor is over the button, select Roll Over instead and the ActionScript command changes to On (rollover). Any of the states listed in the Object Actions panel can have ActionScript commands attached to them, enabling a button to perform all types of behaviors as the mouse maneuvers around.

A few of the mouse events listed in the Object Actions panel need a little explanation, as the behavior may be unexpected. The events and their triggering actions are shown in Table 4.1.

Table 4.1   Mouse Events

Event	Meaning
Press	When the mouse button has been pressed down in the hit area of the button
Release	When the mouse button is released after a press in the hit area of the button
Release Outside	When the mouse button is released outside the hit area of the button, even though the press was within the hit area (enables a user to change his or her mind about clicking a button)
Key Press	When the user presses a specific keyboard key while the mouse button is prevented (to enable keyboard triggering instead of mouse clicks)
Roll Over	Whenever the cursor is over the button's hit area
Roll Out	Whenever the cursor moves away from the button's hit area after being over it
Drag Over	When the mouse button is pressed inside the button's hit area, the cursor is then moved outside the hit area with the button still pressed, and then the cursor moves back into the hit area
Drag Out	When the mouse button is pressed inside the button's hit area, and then the cursor is moved outside the hit area with the button still pressed

Using these mouse events, you can have several different behaviors attached to a single button. The ActionScript is built up the same way, but uses different triggering statements such as:

```
on (release) {
       gotoAndPlay (2);
}
on (keyPress "P") {
       gotoAndPlay (2);
}
on (rollOver) {
       gotoAndPlay (10);
}
```

When more than one ActionScript command is attached to a button it joins the commands in the curly braces. For example, when a button is selected and released you can have ActionScript stop playing some background music or sounds, and then jump to frame 10 of the animation and continue playing from there. This ActionScript would look like this:

```
on (release) {
        stopAllSounds ();
        gotoAndPlay (10);
}
```

You can add as many ActionScript commands from the Object Actions panel as you want.

Animating a Button

You can use animations within a button and you can also animate the button itself. For example, when the button is Down you might want it to expand or shrink in size, and then quickly return to normal, you might want the button to glow and change color intensity before or after being pressed, or you might want to have the button perform some motion such as spinning in place when Down. You can accomplish all these effects by animating the button, not the contents of the button.

To animate a button, create the button symbol normally and set up keyframes for all the states. (Instead of doing these one at a time you can select the three non-keyframe states and use Modify, Frames, Convert to Keyframes and convert all three at once.) All the keyframes are blank at this point.

After the keyframes are created, select the frames that are to be animated and create a movie clip symbol, or import an existing movie. In the Hit state, create a graphic that covers the areas of the three states.

> **TIP**
>
> You can use a movie clip in the Hit state of a button, but only the first frame of the movie clip determines the active area and not the overall area the movie moves during the animation.

Buttons are symbols and hence can be tweened for motion. To do so, select the instance of the button to be moved and add an action to the button as you normally would through the Actions panel. Then create a motion tween as you normally would. If you want the animation of the motion to loop continually, add the following action to the ActionScript command:

```
gotoAndPlay (1);
```

Invisible Buttons

A button can be invisible and still be a button. Because three frames have graphics to indicate the appearance of a button and one frame that indicates the hit area, only the Hit state needs to be defined with an invisible button. You can, of course, still define graphics for some or all the other states, enabling visible feedback to the user for Over and Down states for example.

TIP

Invisible buttons have a number of uses, but the most common is to simply tell the user to click anywhere in the frame to cause an action such as moving to the next frame.

To define an invisible button, the easiest way is to create a visible button as usual, and then delete one or more of the first three visible frames, but leave the fourth frame (the Hit frame) alone to indicate the now invisible active area. It is useful when doing a full frame Hit area to make the area slightly larger than the frame size.

Another common use for invisible buttons is to combine them with the Over state to display a tooltip-like pop-up that can be clicked. For example, if you have text on a frame and the user positions the mouse over an uncommon word, a small text message such as Click for definition can appear. When the user clicks the message, the definition for that term appears. The same can be used for a graphic item that can be expanded, for example. To perform these button tasks you need both an invisible button as well as an Over state graphic to hold the pop-up message. In the Over keyframe, draw the pop-up message (such as in text balloons used in cartoons). The hit area in the Hit stage is defined as the word or graphic that you want the user to click. The process is surprisingly easy to accomplish and adds considerably to a user's experience.

Importing Graphics and Bitmaps

Instead of drawing your own graphics you can import from other applications. Many different file formats can be imported into Flash, including most file formats generated by drawing tools (including Macromedia's FreeHand and Fireworks). Because most design tools available enable flexible file formats to be saved there are likely several choices that can be used to enable importation into Flash. If QuickTime is installed on your machine (either Windows or Macintosh) even more file formats can be imported. Images that provide animation or sequences can be imported as separate frames in a movie, as well.

To import a file into a Flash movie use the File, Import menu option (or, if the image is on the clipboard, simply use Edit, Paste). If the filename to be imported ends with a number and other files have numbers in sequence in the same location, Flash gives you the option of importing them all as a sequence of frames.

Flash bitmaps have a properties window in the Library associated with them that enables you to perform smoothing and compression operations on the bitmap. The Bitmap Properties window has a text area for the name of the bitmap, followed by a statement of the current size of the bitmap in pixels, as well as the density of the bitmap. The Allow Smoothing check box lets you turn on antialiasing to smooth the edges of a bitmap. The Compression drop-down menu enables you to select the types of compression applied to the bitmap based on common file formats.

Underneath the Compression box is a Use document default quality box, which applies standard compression settings to the bitmap based on the compression algorithm you selected. If you want to override the default value, uncheck this box and new fields appear enabling you to enter a quality value (between 1 and 100; the higher the setting the higher the quality and larger the file size). The Compression box enables you to perform loss-less compression (no loss of data in the image) using PNG/GIF algorithms, or standard photo JPEG compression (some compression, but good retention of image despite losses).

> **NOTE**
>
> The Test button enables you to see the results of the selected file compression before you execute it, enabling you to compress to the point where visibility is affected yet you manage to lower the file size.

You can do several things with imported bitmaps, including leaving them as they are. You can convert bitmaps to vector graphics, edit them as a bitmap, or break them apart for modification with Flash drawing tools.

To convert a bitmap to a vector graphic use the Modify, Trace Bitmap command. The Color Threshold setting in the Trace Bitmap window asks for a value between 1 and 500. This determines the threshold color values between adjacent pixels; if they are within the threshold range, they are treated as the same color. The Minimum Area value is between 1 and 1000 and is used to set the number of pixels around each subject pixel when considering the color to be assigned to the subject pixel. The Curve Fit pop-up menu lets you select the way outlines are drawn around areas, and the Corner Threshold pop-up menu lets you decide whether to retain sharp edges or smooth them. Trace Bitmap converts the bitmap into a vector graphic with areas of color.

To break a bitmap apart into discrete areas that can be modified using drawing tools, use the Modify, Break Apart menu item. You can then use any of the Flash drawing or painting tools on each area. The Lasso tool is useful with the Magic Wand modifier for selecting areas in the broken apart bitmap.

Summary

In this chapter I've discussed the use of buttons and the many ways you can handle buttons in Flash, as well as techniques for making invisible and animated buttons. I also discussed how you can handle bitmaps inside Flash.

Sample Questions

1. Which button state does the viewer never see?
    A. Up
    B. Over
    C. Down
    D. Hit

2. What does the button Roll Out event mean?
   A. The cursor has clicked the button and moved away from the hit area.
   B. The cursor has moved over the hit area without clicking it.
   C. The cursor has been click-dragged over the button hit area.
   D. The cursor has moved over and off the button more than once in less than two seconds.

3. If you are creating an invisible button, which one state do you need to define?
   A. Up
   B. Over
   C. Down
   D. Hit

CHAPTER 5

Using Variables

Variables

Variables are used to hold values and are referenced by an alphanumeric name. The variable name is unique, but the contents can change to any value, at any time. Macromedia Flash uses variables for many purposes, including as part of ActionScript (which I discuss in more detail in Part II, "Flash Development").

> **TIP**
>
> Variables can be used to reference parts of a movie clip, as well as to control parameters for a movie clip that can change as the movie plays, usually based on interaction from the viewer.

Variables in Flash can hold any type of data, numeric and strong. Even more flexible, a Flash variable can hold an object or a movie clip instance (actually, it holds a reference to them, not the object or movie clip instance). Flash variables can also hold Boolean values (`true` and `false`). Variables in Flash can be named anything you want with the following restrictions:

- The variable name cannot be a Flash keyword
- The variable name cannot be either of the values `true` or `false` because these are Boolean values
- The variable name must be unique within the scope of the variable (I discuss scope later in this chapter)

Although I discuss Flash variables in more detail in Chapter 8, "Variables," in this chapter I look at the basics of declaring and defining variables, as well as deal with the scope of variables.

Flash Date Types and Data Operations

Unlike many high-level languages, Flash variables do not have to be explicitly declared, but instead are dynamically typed by Flash. In other words, you do not need to tell Flash whether a variable is a number or a string, and what kinds of values are held. Flash can figure out the type of storage a variable needs based on its definition. For example, if you have a variable called FrameRate and define the value like this:

```
FrameRate = 12;
```

Flash knows to declare a variable called FrameRate and assigns it a numeric value of 12. This example shows the simplest way to create a variable in Flash, and to define an initial value for it. The equal sign tells Flash to assign the value 12 to the variable FrameRate. If there is no existing variable called FrameRate, Flash creates one. The semicolon is necessary to tell Flash the statement is completed. The only restriction is that you declare or define a variable before you use it in an expression.

> **NOTE**
>
> If you attempt to use a variable before defining it, the variable value is set to undefined and the script produces a logic error.

Flash enables you to change the type of a variable using an assignment operator. For example, you could reassign the value of FrameRate to be a string by using quotation marks to enclose the new value:

```
FrameRate = "Unknown";
```

In this case, the variable FrameRate has had the value of 12 (a number) replaced with the string Unknown. You can convert data types in Flash any time you want, and Flash handles the conversion automatically. This can create problems, though, as the variable value may be expected to be of a particular type for use in an upcoming calculation.

> **TIP**
>
> Care should be taken when using variables to make sure you do not inadvertently convert a variable's type, causing undesirable results.

Flash enables mixtures of numbers and strings, resulting in a string (the most flexible data type is the result of mixed data type operations). So, the statement:

```
FrameName = "Window " + 1;
```

results in a string "Window 1" assigned to the variable FrameName (note the value 1 was not added to any existing variable in this statement, but simply used as a numeric value which is converted to a string).

To determine a variable's data type, Flash supports the typeof() function which is used like this:

```
Result = typeof(FrameRate);
```

In this statement, the type of data stored in the FrameRate variable is determines by the typeof() function, and the result is assigned to the variable Result. In this case, the value of Result will be "number." This type of statement is frequently used with the trace() function which enables you to debug scripts by following changes in variable values.

> **NOTE**
>
> The trace() function triggers an output window that displays the value of the variable whenever the function is run.

Type conversions can be forced in Flash. For example, if you have a variable that currently holds a string value and you want to convert it to a numeric value (the string "7" and the number 7 are two different values to Flash), you can use the Number() function. Similarly, to convert a numeric value to a string value, you can use the String() function. I don't use either of these functions in this chapter, but you will see them later in this book.

ActionScript Functions

Although I discuss the ActionScript functions later in this book I need to mention the basic structure of ActionScript functions, as well as ActionScript code, here. Most ActionScript programs are made up of a set of statements that either define or manipulate a variable value, call a function that is part of ActionScript, or defined by the user.

In ActionScript, all functions use a pair of parentheses after the function name. These parentheses indicate that this is a function. Sometimes a value (or values) is within the parentheses, but many functions do not have value in the parentheses. The previous examples all had a value in the parentheses, but many functions have no values.

If you are defining a new function to be used by ActionScript, you need to add code to define the way the function works. This is done in a set of curly braces. For example, if you were defining a function called ShowTemperature, the function in ActionScript code may look like this:

```
function ShowTemperature(){
        statements defining the function...
        }
```

Between the curly braces, all the commands that are to be part of the ShowTemperature function are provided. Any set of curly braces in ActionScript code is called a code block, and this is important for defining a variable's scope.

Scope of a Variable

All variables in Flash (and all other high-level languages for that matter) have scope. Scope means where the variable has some meaning and hence can be used. Flash has two types of ActionScript variables, both with different scopes. A global variable has scope everywhere, and hence can be referenced at any time, by anything, in Flash. A local variable, on the other hand, has scope only in a certain block of code. Outside of that block of code, the variable is not defined and has no meaning.

If you are defining a new function and use a variable in that function that is local, only within that code block (the two curly braces after the function name) would there be a meaning for the local variable. If you tried to reference that variable outside the function, it would have no value.

> **NOTE**
>
> When you use a variable in ActionScript you do not need to precede the name with any symbol, like in some high-level languages, but simply use the name as is.

Global variables are the easiest to use and declare. Any time you make an assignment in a block of code such as:

```
FrameRate = 12;
```

the variable is set as a global variable. If you want to declare a global variable and not assign a value at the present time, you need to specify the setVariables action.

To declare a local variable inside a code block, you can use the keyword var anywhere inside the block, as long as the declaration comes before the use of the variable. For example:

```
function ShowTemperature(){
        var degrees_C;
        var degrees_F;
        more statements defining the function...
        }
```

In this code block for the function ShowTemperature two local variables are declared using the var keyword. If you tried to use the variables degrees_C or degrees_F anywhere outside this function they would have no meaning. Inside the function, however, they can be used at any time.

Local variables may seem like more trouble than global variables, but using local variables has several advantages. For one, name collisions are much less likely. A name collision occurs when the same variable name is used for different purposes. For example, if you created the function shown previously with both degrees_C and degrees_F as global variables, and then you had another function using the same variable names, there could be confusion as to which values should be used. Although this doesn't seem likely with these two variable names, many developers use variable names like i (for loops) and temp (for temporary values) frequently. Local variables remove the possibility of using the wrong variable value in an ActionScript program.

Another important reason to use local variables is to prevent accidental modification of a value. For example, if I again use the previous example and declare both variables as global, there is the possibility that another function or code block would change the values of either variable, and when the ShowTemperature() function is called, you would be using a value you cannot be sure of. Accidental modification of a variable value occurs quite often and can be difficult to diagnose and debug. By using local variables, you limit the extent of the problem to a single code block.

> **TIP**
>
> There is a savings in both speed and filesize using local variables instead of global variables, as they do not have to be handled for the entire movie. The effect is small, granted, but when you are working with complex ActionScript programs, every few bytes can add up!

Summary

In this chapter I've taken a quick look at the basics of using variables, their scope, and mentioned the basic operators that are supported by Flash's ActionScript language. These operators are discussed in more detail in Part I.

Sample Questions

1. What value is returned if you try to use a variable before you have defined it?
    A. You get an undefined value.
    B. You get a zero value.
    C. You get a NULL character.
    D. No value is returned.

2. Which keyword do you use to ensure a variable is defined as a local variable in a function?
    A. number
    B. local
    C. var
    D. No keyword is needed as it will have scope only inside the function anyway.

3. Which function is used to determine whether a variable is local?
    A. typeof()
    B. Number()
    C. trace()
    D. There is no function to determine if a variable is local.

PART II

FLASH DEVELOPMENT

6   ActionScript

7   Events

8   Variables

9   Functions

10   Programming Basics

11   Code Reuse

CHAPTER 6

ActionScript

What Is ActionScript?

ActionScript is the scripting language built in to Macromedia Flash. ActionScript can be used for many purposes—some simple and easy to work with and some complex involving creating your own programs. ActionScript is used to control interactive features on a Flash movie (such as the behavior of buttons and movie playing controls) as well as to control navigation (jumping back and forth along a movie's timeline).

> **NOTE**
>
> Any movie clip that has ActionScript commands associated with it is called a "Smart Clip," a term you saw in earlier chapters.

ActionScript is based on the same language specification as the JavaScript language, which itself is based in Java, C, and C++. If you have programmed in any of these languages, you will find many similarities with ActionScript, although ActionScript is easier to work with. If you know any other high-level programming language, you will find ActionScript easy to learn. If you've never programmed before, don't worry: ActionScript is not only easy to learn, but you don't have to do a lot of coding to accomplish useful tasks. Many of the steps you have to go through can be performed through selections in a dialog, instead of manually coding in an editor.

ActionScript is an object-oriented programming language, like JavaScript, Java, and C++. In earlier chapters you read that symbols are reusable items stored in the Library, and that when you use a symbol you create an instance of it. Symbols are objects. The fact that ActionScript is an object-oriented language means that it is designed to control these objects using commands that influence the object's (and instance's) behavior directly.

> **NOTE**
>
> While object-oriented programming has a lot more complexity (especially in more complex languages like C++), most of those complexities are hidden for you by ActionScript's interfaces and dialogs.

You can work with ActionScript in two different modes. The simplest is through the windows, panels, and dialogs with which you are familiar. Flash's interface enables you to perform many of ActionScript's commands without knowing anything about programming. (If you remember Chapter 4, "Actions," I associated ActionScript commands with the behaviors to be performed when a button was pressed. I simply selected the correct action from a list of actions, and then added the parameters—in that case a frame number—that was needed. The dialog wrote the code for me and associated it with the button.) The second way to write ActionScript programs is expert mode, which is the more traditional edit-debug cycle using a traditional text editor and writing the ActionScript commands line by line, testing as you go.

Objects and Classes

You have seen that Flash uses symbols (general items in the Library) to create specific instances of those symbols on the Stage or Timeline. Flash uses an organizational level (and all object-oriented systems, for that matter), called a class. A class is a term used to describe the high-level structure from which objects are created.

A class has two components: properties and methods. A class property is the description of the item and all its characteristics. For example, a class for an automobile would have things like "four wheels," "steering wheel," "engine," and so on. Every instance created from this class has all these characteristics. Using object-oriented terminology, each instance inherits the characteristics of the class. You can think of class as a high-level description (such as an automobile) and instances as the specific description (such as Porsche Boxster, Volkswagen Beetle, and so on). The level of complexity increases from class through to instance. At each level, more details can be added to completely describe the instance, which is the most detailed.

The other component of a class is its methods. Methods are simply the way the class behaves. In programming terms, methods are the functions and procedures that are attached to the class. For example, if we have a class dealing with making windows appear on your computer, the methods involved would be things such as drawing the window on the screen, adding the title bar, completing the background colors, and so on. The methods of a class are inherited by the instances that are created from it. At each stage, just as with properties, the level of complexity can increase. For example, the class for making windows appear on your computer has generic routines for drawing a window on your screen and the instance is very specific about the type of window and the appearance it has.

If you think back to creating symbols in the Library in earlier chapters, you assigned some characteristics to those symbols. When you created an instance of the symbol on the Stage, though, you could resize the instance, change its colors, and perform many different changes to the object. The Library's symbol (class) didn't change at all, only the instance. In this case, the instance still had the overall characteristics of the class (such as its general oval shape for a button, and its four states), but the exact details of the size, color, and behavior of the four button states were more detailed and specific to the instance. The instance inherited the basic properties (button shape, four stages, and so on) and the methods (basic behavior of the button when a cursor is over it, clicking it, and so on) from the class. Classes simply add another level to the structure and permit more flexibility in designing objects.

> **NOTE**
>
> The advantage to using classes is that you can create reusable generic classes for use in many different movies, saving you from recoding the same routines every time. Properly designed classes have both properties and methods that enable the instances that derive from it to have most of the characteristics necessary, requiring only a little tweaking to get the proper behavior. The time saving in using properly designed classes can be enormous when you do a lot of Flash development. (The real problem, of course, is to properly design the classes in the first place!)

You have been working with classes all along when you use Flash, whether you realize it or not. All movie clips, for example, are instances of a class called MovieClip. The MovieClip class has a number of properties and methods that describe what a movie clip should look like and what it should do. It has properties like the number of frames, size, and so on. It has methods such as playing and stopping the movie. When you create a movie clip, you create an instance of the MovieClip class, which has these properties and methods, and you can refine the behavior and set the properties any way you want in the instance. (Imagine how complex Flash would be if you had to manually code all the properties and methods every time you wanted to create a movie!)

In Chapter 4 you read how to create symbols in the Library using simple menu choices. You also read how you can create instances of those symbol by dragging the symbol (class) from the Library to the Stage. Creating a class from scratch, assuming the default classes are not suitable, is a little more complex. Creating a class is done through a special function called a constructor. The constructor is a template that explains what the class's properties and methods are. ActionScript then examines the constructor and creates the class.

> **NOTE**
>
> This is very similar to defining a function in a high-level programming language, including ActionScript. You write the code for the function inside curly braces, and the compiler or interpreter then creates the function with the code you have written.

In true object-oriented fashion, classes do not have to create instances from themselves. One class can be made from another class. In this case, the class that acts as the template for the other classes is called a superclass, and the one created is called a subclass. A subclass can then act as a superclass for another subclass. The number of classes (superclass and subclass) that can be created is limitless, and there can be any number of levels of classes inside Flash, although often you do not need super- and subclasses.

Classes (and hence instances) can communicate with each other using a set of methods. One class may need to obtain data from another class, so a set of interfaces are defined as methods that enable one class to signal to another class that it needs (or is ready to send) data, and the method also defines the format of the data and what to do with it after it is received (or sent).

If this all sounds overly complicated, don't get too worried. In practice, Flash makes working with classes and instances remarkably easy. In fact, you can happily use Flash without really knowing anything at all about these subjects, but if you want to get into ActionScript and advanced Web design, you should understand the basics of Flash's object-oriented design. As you go through this part of the study guide, you'll see lots of examples of using ActionScript to build classes and objects.

ActionScript Programs

An ActionScript program has a particular layout and flow. An ActionScript program is simply a list of valid ActionScript commands, one line after another, stored in a file, objects, or other place within Flash. The program may be short (one or two lines, for example) or very long (many pages of commands).

Without anything to tell it otherwise, Flash starts reading the ActionScript program at the top and continues executing line by line until it reaches the bottom. There may be commands within the program that tell Flash to stop executing, or to jump to another line in the program, in which case Flash follows these instructions. There may also be conditional statements that tell Flash to do specific things if some condition is met (or not met). Flash simply follows the instructions, line by line, which build up the flow of the program. Flow control is discussed later in Chapter 10, "Programming Basics."

As mentioned earlier, ActionScript programs can be built in two ways: expert mode and normal mode. You can toggle between expert and normal modes by using the Window, Action menu item to display the Actions window, and then using the Export Mode or Normal Mode selections from the Options pop-up menu. If you want to automatically enter one particular mode every time you launch the Actions window, you can use the Edit, Preferences menu item to set the default mode. There are several differences between normal mode and expert mode:

- Expert mode doesn't display the parameter fields at the bottom of the Actions window
- Only the add (+) button works in Expert mode; the delete button is inactive because you can manually delete lines in the action list panel

- The up and down arrow buttons are inactive in Expert mode because you can manually alter the order of statements in the action list panel
- Normal mode includes a special grouping of actions in the Actions toolbox called Basic Actions which is useful for new users. This grouping does not appear in Expert mode.
- When you select an item in the Toolbox using Expert mode, it is placed in the action list panel automatically and leaves you to manually add any parameters and complete the syntax properly

Normal mode is when you select ActionScript commands from a list in the Toolbox part of the Actions panel. An Actions panel for each object is on the Stage or Timeline, and it can be displayed using Window, Actions or the pop-up menu for a selected object.

> **TIP**
>
> Normal mode is ideal for when you want to attach simple behaviors to objects like buttons or control frames.

The Actions panel has a list of ActionScript commands in the left pane (called the Toolbox), a pane for the generated ActionScript code in the right pane (called the actions list), and a pane for providing controls for each command at the bottom of the window (called the parameter panel). In the Toolbox, all available ActionScript commands are broken down into categories of basic actions, actions, operators, functions, properties, or objects. Normal mode usually shows only the most commonly required ActionScript commands associated with buttons, movie clips, and graphics. As you select the commands from the list in the Toolbox, the ActionScript code is built in the right part of the window.

Expert mode is for developers who want or need to enter commands in an editor window. To use Expert mode, toggle the mode in the Actions window Options pop-up menu. The right panel is the window where you type the commands you want to use, or you can select from the different categories displayed in the left window. Expert mode is used to enable editing of scripts and is more flexible than normal mode.

Expert mode does enable you to use an external editor if you do not want to use the Actions panel's edit area. (The Actions panel editor is somewhat limited in ability and space, but does have some automatic features that can be useful for ActionScript coding.) To use an external editor write your ActionScript code in the external editor as normal, and then tell Flash to incorporate the file you saved as part of the ActionScript script. This is done with the `include` directive followed by the filename (and fully qualified pathname if not in the current directory). Alternatives to using the `#include` directive are to simply cut-and-paste the script code into the action list panel or import the file using the Options pop-up menu Import from File item.

> **CAUTION**
>
> If you are importing a script that has errors in it, you will not be able to import it in normal mode; expert mode enables scripts with errors to be imported.

The `include` directive is placed in the action list by using the `include` directive in the Toolbox. By convention, ActionScript scripts have a .as file extension. To include a file called `MyMovie.as` as part of the current movie you would enter the action:

```
#include "MyMovie.as"
```

in the action panel of the Actions window. In this case, because no path is specified, the .as file should be in the same directory as the current .FLA file.

If you toggle between expert and normal modes during an editing section, Flash does the following:

- When switching to normal mode from expert mode Flash reformats all the statements in the action list panel and removes any whitespace and indenting; when switching from expert mode to normal mode and then back to expert mode, Flash leaves the code in the action list panel as it would appear in normal mode.
- When switching from expert mode to normal mode, any scripts with errors in them cannot be converted without correction of the error (Flash displays error messages when you try to convert to normal mode).

You can have the Actions window perform a simple syntax check on your ActionScript code as you write it by using identifying colors. When syntax highlighting is active, the following colors are used to identify words:

- Blue: Keywords and predefined identifiers
- Green: Properties
- Pink: Comments
- Gray: Strings enclosed in quotation marks

You can use these colors to help avoid common syntax errors such as capitalization errors (for example, if you type "Include" instead of "include", the fact that the entry is not blue would indicate a syntax error was made. To turn syntax highlighting on or off use the Colored Syntax menu item in the Options pop-up menu.

In addition to syntax highlighting, the Options pop-up menu Check Syntax item performs a quick check of the syntax of the ActionScript script and displays any error messages. Any syntax errors are highlighted in red in the actions list (in normal mode only). When you move the cursor over the red item a tooltip shows the correct syntax or other help. Any ActionScript script statements that cannot be exported to another file are highlighted in yellow (this can occur when exporting a Flash 5 movie to a Flash 4 file, for example). Finally, green highlight is used to indicate deprecated syntax.

Writing Scripts

As you have just seen you can use either expert or normal mode to write ActionScript scripts. While using normal mode is easy and quick, most developers find they need to use expert mode for many tasks. Before we look at the way you write scripts, we need to take a quick look at the way ActionScript handles comments, curly braces, and other miscellaneous subjects.

One point that should be borne in mind throughout this Part II of this study guide is that ActionScript does not differentiate between upper- and lowercase except for keywords. In other words, case is not important to ActionScript and you can write in upper- or lowercase as it suits you. For the most part, developers tend to write in lowercase, as this is the convention for most high-level languages where case is important.

ActionScript Keywords

ActionScript keywords are reserved and cannot be used for variable or function names, or any other purpose than their intended scripting purpose. The list of ActionScript keywords is relatively short compared to many high-level languages. The following keywords are reserved by ActionScript:

- `break`
- `continue`
- `delete`
- `else`
- `for`
- `function`
- `if`
- `in`
- `new`
- `return`
- `this`
- `typeof`
- `var`
- `void`
- `while`
- `with`

You can use any other words for variable or function names. Remember that case is not important to ActionScript except for keywords, which are always lowercase. This means the names "`break`" and "`Break`" are different as far as ActionScript is concerned. Although this would enable you to use a capitalized version of a keyword for a variable or function name, this practice is highly discouraged.

Comments

Comments can reside anywhere inside an ActionScript script. When you choose the comment command in the Action window Toolbox, Flash inserts the characters "`//`"

into your program in the left pane. If you are in expert mode and are writing scripts manually, you can embed comments anywhere as long as they are preceded by the two slashes.

Comments may be placed anywhere on a line, and when the ActionScript parser reads two slashes it ignores anything from those two characters to the end of the line. Multiline comments must have each line preceded by the two slashes (ActionScript does support multiline comments using the traditional */ and /* block syntax). When you write comments, they appear in pink if the syntax highlighting option is turned on.

> **TIP**
>
> You should use comments liberally to describe your scripts, especially larger ones, to help you understand complex statements later. It is a good idea to document all variables and their usage, although like many good programming practices this is frequently ignored.

Semicolons

All ActionScript statements should end with a semicolon. This tells the parser that the statement is finished and can be executed. Some statements do not have to have semicolons, such as function definitions. However, usually a set of curly braces indicates the end of the statement anyway.

Having said that ActionScript statements should end with a semicolon does not mean they have to have one. Flash compiles ActionScript statements quite well without the semicolon, as it usually can figure out where the statement ends.

> **TIP**
>
> So why bother using semicolons at all? Simply because it is the convention and they have long been used by the languages ActionScript is based on. It's also good programming practice and helps avoid problems in the future with the code.

Parentheses and Curly Braces

Parentheses are used to pass arguments (also known as parameters) to a function, and are used even when there are no arguments to pass. Functions always have a pair of parentheses after the function name, and it is inside these that the argument resides. All built-in Flash functions have parentheses, as will all custom functions. Whether arguments are expected depends on the function.

Curly braces are used to hold the body of the function. The body holds all the statements that are to be executed when the function is called. Although you can have a function with no statements in the body, you still need the curly braces.

A typical function call with no arguments looks like this:

```
function clearWindow () {
        statements...
        }
```

In this case, the statements inside the curly braces are executed whenever the clearWindow function is called. Note that the parentheses after the function name are empty; this function has no arguments. An example of a function using arguments is:

```
funtion calcTemp (degrees_c, windchill) {
        statements...
        }
```

In this case, two arguments are being passed. Both are given placeholder names (see Chapter 9, "Functions," for more information) and contain values when the function is called. When the calcTemp function is executed, all the statements between the curly braces are executed.

One quick observation is the naming convention of all the functions you have seen so far. Normally, function names consist of a verb and a noun, such as calcTemp (calc is the verb, short for calculate, and Temp is the noun, short for Temperature). The convention is to have the verb before the noun, and to have the verb start with lowercase and the noun start with uppercase. For those who are familiar with Java or C++, it is worth noting that function names are not case-sensitive as they are in those languages. The function name does not depend on the signature of the function (which refers to the number or type of parameters used by the function). In Flash, a function is known only by its name, which makes working with functions much easier.

TIP

This convention arose years ago when a series of functions for working with GUIs was developed and the habit has been carried on since then.

Dot and Slash Syntax

You often need to clarify which object a particular property or method belongs to. For example, if you have two objects both with a clearWindow method, and you call clearWindow in your script, Flash has to know which object's clearWindow method you are referring to. The way this is indicated is with "dot syntax." Dot syntax is easy to use, You specify the name of the object, a period, and then the property or method name. For example, if your two objects are called object1 and object2, you would specify either object1.clearWindow or object2.clearWindow to help Flash determine which method to execute.

Flash uses dot syntax for objects as well as for movie clips, so you can reference items in a clip using dot syntax as well. For example, if you have a movie clip called dogRunning, you could call dogRunning.play() to invoke the play function for that movie clip.

The advantage to dot syntax is that it makes it explicitly clear which object a method or property call applies to, and enables you to easily manipulate many objects at once. For example, if you have movie clips called dogRunning, dogSleeping, and dogFrisbee, you could call dogRunning.play() and dogSleeping.stop() at the same time, and even throw in some method from `dogFrisbee` as well. Flash can keep track of everything through the use of the object name.

If the object you are dealing with has methods that involve properties, you can use two dots. The reference `dogSleeping.dogStopping.dogSize` means to use the `dogSleeping` movie clip, which has `dogStopping` as part of the timeline and the `dogSize` property (variable value) of `dogStopping`.

Dot syntax uses two special terms called _root and _parent. The _root alias refers to whatever is in the main timeline. The _parent alias refers to an object in which the current object is nested. In real terms this means that if you have `dogRunning` in the timeline and it has a movie clip called `dogStopping` embedded in it, you could use _root to refer to `dogRunning` and _parent to refer to `dogStopping`.

> **NOTE**
>
> Why bother using these two aliases? Because you don't have to use specific names for the _root and _parent parts in dot syntax, enabling for more generic usage regardless of the clips involved. This is also known as a relative path.

Slash syntax is a hold-over from Flash versions 3 and 4, but is still supported in Flash 5, although it is not recommended for use. Slash syntax used slashes instead of dots. Although you may still see slash syntax in older scripts, for the most part the format has disappeared, so I won't discuss it here.

ActionScript Terms

Several terms are going to be used throughout this section, so it's worth looking at their definitions now. Some of these terms have been introduced already, and some need to be defined and explained. The terms used by ActionScript are summarized in Table 6.1.

Table 6.1 *ActionScript Terms*

Term	Meaning
Action	An action is any statement that tells Flash what to do (for example, start playing a movie clip)
Argument	A value or variable passed to a function (also called a parameter)
Class	A data type used to create objects; classes are created with a constructor
Constructor	A function used to define a new class, including both properties and methods
Data type	A definition of the contents enabled in a variable, such as numeric, string, Boolean, movie clip, and so on
Event	An action that occurs during playback of a movie (such as a user clicking a button or the playhead entering a new frame)
Expression	A part of an ActionScript statement that produces a value (such as `Num1 * Num2`)

Table 6.1   Continued

Term	Meaning
Function	Reusable code block that may have arguments and may return a value when called; Flash has many built-in functions and you can define functions any time you need to
Handler	A special action that manages an event (such as loading a move clip or detecting the click of a mouse button)
Identifier	A name used for a variable, class, object, property, function, and so on; Flash requires that all identifiers start with a character, an underscore, or a dollar sign
Instance	An object that belongs to a class and inherits the properties and methods of the class
Instance name	Each instance of a class has a unique name enabling it to be referenced in ActionScript scripts
Keywords	Reserved words with special meaning, such as all ActionScript commands, which cannot be used for variable names
Methods	The functions that are part of a class or instance
Objects	Collections of properties (attributes) with a unique name and value
Operators	A term that performs some calculation to result in a new value, such as adding two numbers together
Target path	The hierarchical address of an instance
Property	Attributes that are part of a class or instance
Variable	An identifier that holds a value

I use these terms throughout the rest of this book, so this list can be used for reference. It is important to understand the proper terminology to avoid confusion.

Summary

In this chapter I discussed what ActionScript is, what it does, and the basics of using it. You've seen the general syntax rules (including the use of curly braces, parentheses, semicolons, comments, and so on), as well as the keywords that are used by ActionScript. I rounded out the chapter with a look at terms that are used throughout the rest of this book.

Sample Questions

1. What do you call the functions that are attached to an object?
   A. Properties
   B. Methods
   C. Identifiers
   D. Keywords

2. What is a Smart Clip?

    A. A movie clip that loops automatically.

    B. A movie clip that has keyframes every fifth frame.

    C. A movie clip that has user-configurable parameters associated with it.

    D. A movie clip that has other movies embedded in the Timeline.

3. If you have one object called `class1`, which has another object called `class2` as an instance, and that object has a variable called `var1` associated with it, what is the correct dot syntax to access the variable value?

    A. `var1.class2.class1`

    B. `class1.class2.var1`

    C. `class2.var1`

    D. `class1.var1`

CHAPTER 7

Events

Using Events

An event is any action that occurs while a movie is playing (not necessarily a movie clip). Examples of events are the playhead moving into a new frame, a movie clip being loaded upon instruction from the Timeline, or a button being pressed by the user. Events are managed by an event handler, which takes care of finding out what event has happened and what to do about it.

You saw an example of using events and a handler in Chapter 4, "Actions," when we looked at assigning behaviors to a wide variety of button interactions. An event handler, in this case a mouse handler because it is the mouse that changes the states of the button, knows about the states. The handler has both built-in instructions (changing the color, size, or animation as defined by the different images for each state), as well as user-supplied instructions assigned with the Actions panel (if any were specified). You can also assign events to a frame in the Timeline as you will see.

The handler for a button event is called On Mouse Event. This handler is used only for buttons and nothing else. For events in a movie clip, the handler is called On Clip Event. Each of these handler's ActionScript statements start with the words on onMouseEvent or onClipEvent. These handlers appear as simply on() in ActionScript until fully fleshed out. The statements to be executed when the handler responds to the events then follow. The event code can be created in either normal or expert mode in the Actions panel.

For most simple events, normal mode works well and quickly, but expert mode is sometimes required when complex combinations of events are involved. For now, we'll look at simple events and use normal mode in the Actions panel.

Programming Events

The easiest way to look at programming for an event is to take a simple example. In this case, we'll assign an action to an object, which can be either a button or a movie clip.

Start by selecting the object (button or movie clip) on the Stage, and then choose Window, actions. As long as the object selected is legal for handler events, the window appears normally. If the object is illegal, the window appears, but is dimmed.

In the Toolbox on the left side of the Actions panel choose the action to be performed (it will be in Basic Actions, the only section active in normal mode). You can select the action to be performed in several ways, such as double-clicking the action, highlighting the action and clicking with Add (+) button, or dragging the action to the actions list in the left side of the window. Either way, Flash automatically inserts the "on," On Clip Event or On Mouse Event handler code as the first line to trigger the actions.

If the action you are choosing requires arguments for the function, the parameter pane can be filled in normal mode or you can manually add the parameters in expert mode. You can keep adding actions to the action list until all the statements you want to execute when the event triggers are completed.

TIP

When you complete a set of actions for an event you should always test them carefully. You can use the Control, Test Movie menu item to enable all the buttons and other events on the Stage and to see how they behave for each state. Careful testing of events is an important part of developing a Flash movie.

Mouse Button Events

The mouse event handler manages the different interactions of the button and the handler code starts with the word "on" followed by the event. For example, to respond to the event of a user click a button and release the mouse. The following event is triggered:

```
on (release)
```

Each event has its own section of script that shows what to do when the event occurs. In Chapter 4 we briefly looked at the events that a mouse (or keyboard shortcut) can trigger. These are summarized in Table 7.1.

Table 7.1   Mouse Events

Event	Occurs When...
Press	The cursor is over a button and the mouse click is pressed.
Release	The cursor is over a button and the mouse click is pressed and released (the default action if no event is specified).
Release Outside	The mouse click is released outside the button's hit area.
Key Press	A keyboard key is pressed.
Roll Over	The cursor moves over the button's hit area.

Table 7.1   Continued

Event	Occurs When...
Roll Out	The cursor moves outside the button's hit area after being over it.
Drag Over	The mouse click is pressed over the button's hit area, and then dragged outside the hit area, then back over the hit area again.
Drag Out	The mouse click is pressed over the button's hit area then dragged outside the hit area.

Frame Events

Most movies have keyframes in their Timeline. You can set an event to occur when a keyframe is reached. This is called a *frame action*. One of the simplest frame actions causes the movie to loop continually. In the last keyframe there is an instruction telling the movie to go to and play the first frame of the movie.

> **NOTE**
>
> When you place a frame action, the Timeline shows a small letter "a" in the upper corner. Many developers who set frame actions find it easiest to place all the actions in a separate and single layer in the Timeline to make it simple to observe where events occur (and to simplify locating them). Most developers call this layer "Actions" to indicate what it held in that layer.

To assign an action to a frame in a movie, select a keyframe in the Timeline and choose Window, Actions. If you selected a frame that is not a keyframe, the previous keyframe is selected automatically. If there is no keyframe or you select multiple frames, the Actions panel displays, but is dimmed.

As with button events, the Toolbox is used to select the actions in the Basic Actions category. The parameters panel can be used to provide arguments, and the left side of the window shows the completed ActionScript code. The basic actions that you can add to a movie are summarized in Table 7.2.

Table 7.2   Movie Actions

Action	Meaning
Go To	Jumps to a frame number or a scene
Play	Plays the movie
Stop	Stops playing the movie
Toggle High Quality	Adjusts the display quality higher
Stop All Sounds	Suppresses all audio in the movie
Get URL	Jumps to a URL
FSCommand	Sends a message to the hosting environment, which is usually a browser
Load Movie	Loads an additional Flash SWF movie

Table 7.2   Continued

Action	Meaning
Unload Movie	Unloads (removes from memory) a loaded movie
Tell Target	Controls other movies or clips
If Frame Loaded	Checks whether a frame is loaded
Print	Prints the frames of a movie (if printable)

We can look at some of these movie events individually because they are useful and important to Flash development.

The Go To Command

The Go To action enables you to jump to a specific scene or frame in a movie. After performing the jump you can either play the movie from that frame or scene onwards, or tell the player to stop playback at that point (the Go To and Play and Go To and Stop commands, respectively).

To use the Go To command select Go To from the Toolbox window. In normal mode the parameter pane at the bottom of the window displays the available arguments. The Scene field can be Current (for the current scene), or Next or Previous for the first frame of the next or previous scene, respectively.

The Type pop-up menu enables you to choose a destination frame, including Next or Previous or a specific frame number, frame label, or an expression to calculate the frame number (as long as the expression resolves to a number). For frame number, frame label or expression settings in the Type field you need to enter the value in the Frame field. The bottom check box in the parameters pane enables you to go to the frame or scene and play from there. If the box is not checked, the Go To and Stop action is performed.

The Play and Stop Commands

The Play and Stop actions are used to control the movement through a movie. Flash's default action is that when a movie starts playing, it continues playing until told to stop or the movie ends. The Play and Stop commands can be used to control the playback through the movie and can be tied to frames or other events. For example, you can tell a movie to play through to the end of a particular scene, and then stop and wait for the user to click anywhere on the frame (using an invisible button to trigger the Play action). Normally, the Play and Stop actions are tied to buttons, although they don't have to be. To use the Play or Stop commands, click the action in the Toolbox. The script in the left pane of the Actions window uses the movie clip handler with the command you selected after, like this:

```
onClipEvent (load) {
        play ();
        }
```

This code tells Flash that when it loads a movie clip the onClipEvent handler should trigger the Play action. You can tie the playing or stopping of a movie to a button using the mouse event handler. For example, if you want to have a mouse click stop the playback of the movie, you would use the Stop action in the Toolbox. The following script tells Flash to stop the playback of the current movie when the mouse button has been clicked and released:

```
on (release) {
        stop ();
        }
```

The Toggle High Quality Command

The Toggle High Quality command causes a little confusion with some developers. The reason for this command is to help improve the quality of some clips. The problem with clip quality arises because of the antialiasing that is necessary to render and smooth the image on each frame of a movie during playback, which can be a very processor-intensive operation for complex frames. The Toggle High Quality command toggles the antialiasing calculations on and off. With antialiasing on, the movie will have a smoother, higher quality appearance at the potential expense of frame rate. With antialiasing turned off, frame rates can be maintained albeit at the expense of smoother frame images. This toggle affects all movies played by Flash, not just the current movie.

> **TIP**
>
> Some developers like to leave the control of this setting up to the viewer by placing a button on the scene that toggles the high-quality setting on or off. The viewer is then left with the responsibility of choosing the compromise between frame rate and frame quality. This really depends on the speed of the processor involved in the playback, so it is hard for a developer to make assumptions in advance.

To use the Toggle High Quality command, select the movie clip, button, or frame that will be toggled in the Timeline. (If you select a button, you can toggle the antialiasing setting on or off; if you select a frame, you can adjust the movie clip playback speed directly.) In the Toolbox select the Toggle High Quality action. The action window shows the `toggleHighQuality()` command.

The Stop All Sounds Command

Stop All Sounds is used to suppress the audio track completely without affecting the playback of the video. As with Toggle High Quality, many developers like to incorporate a button so all the viewers can toggle sounds on or off during playback. The Stop All Sounds is not a volume control, but a complete suppression of all sounds.

The behavior of Stop All Sounds changes a little depending on whether attached or streaming sound is used. Attached sounds will be completely suppressed for the duration of the movie when Stop All Sounds is executed. With streaming sounds, though, the sound resumes as soon as the sound's Timeline advances to the next frame. To use Stop All Sounds, select it from the Toolbox. There are no parameters to choose with this command.

The Get URL Command

The Get URL command enables you to load a file from a specific URL (Uniform Resource Locator) into a browser window. You can also use Get URL to pass variables to another application at the target URL. (This is handy for passing data to a CGI script.) Most developers use the Get URL command to load a Web page. To use the Get URL command, select it from the Toolbox. In the parameters pane, enter the URL using either absolute paths or a relative path (which can be properly resolved when the movie is played). If you want to have the target URL depend on an expression, select the Expression parameter and enter the expression that can evaluate to a URL. If you want the URL to open in a window, specify the window or HTML frame using one of these target names:

- _self: The current frame in the current window
- _blank: A new window
- _parent: The parent of the current frame
- _top: The top-level frame in the current window

If you want to send a variable to the target URL, use the Variable setting and choose the method for sending the variable:

- Don't Send: Do not pass any variables
- Send Using Get: Appends variables to the end of the URL
- Send Using Post: Sends variables separate from the URL

The Send Using Post is used when you want to send variables to a CGI script. This method sends the variables as a separate header instead of as part of the URL. Send Using Get includes the variables as part of the URL and can be used with short lists of variables. Send Using Get is often used with server-side scripts.

The FSCommand Command

The FSCommand command is used to send messages to whatever application is hosting the Flash player (such as any program that can host ActiveX controls). You can use several FSCommand commands for communication between the projector and the host environment (such as Windows or another application).

In the Toolbox, select FSCommand. In the parameters panel choose the option to control the stand-alone player from the Commands for Standalone Player menu. This has several options you can select to affect the projector:

- Quit: Close the projector
- Exec: Start running an application from within the projector
- Fullscreen: Set to True if fullscreen, or False for normal
- Allowscale: Set to True to enable scaling of the movie, False to prevent scaling
- Showmenu: Set to True to display the full set of right-click menu items; False to suppress the menu

The three True/False options can only have one of the two values, obviously. You can mix the settings, though, to produce the effects you need. Remember that these commands are used exclusively to enable the projector to communicate with the host environment.

The Load and Unload Commands

The Load and Unload commands enable you to control the playing of movies without closing the Flash player. It also lets you switch movies in the player without changing documents.

To load a new movie at a particular point in an existing movie, select the frame or button that launches the new movie. In the Toolbox, select the Load Movie action. The parameters pane asks for the URL of the SWF file to load. You can provide either absolute or relative addresses to the SWF file attached to the new movie.

> **CAUTION**
>
> The Flash player does not require all SWF files to be stored in the same folder, but it is a good practice to enable easier portability from platform to platform.

Before discussing the Location parameter, we need to quickly look at levels used by the Flash player. When a movie is loaded into the Flash player it is loaded in level zero. Other movies can then be stacked on top, in levels 1, 2, and so on. Whatever movie is in level zero dictates the frame rate, frame size, and background color for all the movies in the different levels. The Location parameter has two values: Level or Target. Level is used to load the new movie in addition to the existing movies and you need to specify a level number not currently used or a level number containing a movie that you want to replace with the new movie. If you want to replace the original movie and unload all the levels, enter the level number as zero. Entering Target for the Location parameter is used for loading into a movie clip instance. The loading movie inherits the attributes of the existing movie (including position and size, as well as scaling properties). The Variable parameter can be used to specify a method for sending variables to the URL as discussed earlier.

To unload a movie from a Flash player window select the frame, movie clip, or button that contains the unload action. In the Toolbox choose the Unload Movie action. In the parameters section you can use the Location field to specify the level of the movie you want to unload, or select Target and specify the path of the movie to be unloaded. You can also use an expression to determine which level is unloaded as long as it evaluates to a number.

The Tell Target Command

The Tell Target command can be used to control a movie or a movie clip. The movie or movie clip must have been loaded. To use the Tell Target command, there must be a Timeline that the action can be attached to. A movie clip to be targeted must have an instance name (a unique name set using Windows, Panels, Instance). Finally, the movie that is to hold the command must be on the Stage.

To use Tell Target, select the frame, movie clip, or button that holds the action and selects the Tell Target command in the Toolbox. Use the Insert Target Path button in the lower-right corner of the Actions window to specify the movie clip to be controlled. A movie clip hierarchy appears, and you can select the movie clip to be controlled from the list, which appears in the Target field automatically.

The Notation parameter enables you to specify how the movie clip target path is delimited (either dot syntax or slash syntax). The default is Dots, but you can also use Slash notation (which was used in Flash 3 and Flash 4, as discussed in Chapter 6, "ActionScript"), although slash notation is discouraged by Macromedia for use in Flash 5. The Mode lets you specify absolute or relative modes. Relative mode means to display only instances of movie clips that exist in the current frame of the current Timeline (and any children of it) and can use the prefix this to refer to the current Timeline. Absolute mode means that every movie clip instance in every frame of every scene in the movie is to be displayed. Absolute mode uses the prefix root or level to insert target paths.

The If Frame Is Loaded Command

You can use the If Frame Is Loaded command to check that a large file (a sound file, large movie clip, or bitmap, for example) has been loaded and is ready for use. This is useful so you don't trigger an event before the content is ready to be used.

> **TIP**
>
> Normally, the If Frame Is Loaded command is used associated with a frame, but it could be tied to a button as well.

To use this command, select the button, frame, or movie clip to be used as the event trigger and use the Toolbox to select the If Frame Is Loaded command. In the parameters pane use the Scene field to specify the scene containing the frame to be checked (you can use Current Scene for the loaded scene, or name any other scene). For Type, choose Frame Number, Frame Label or Expression as needed, as you saw in an earlier command. Also specify the frame to be loaded in the Frame field; this is the frame number that has to be loaded before the event is triggered. Finally, select the action that is to occur if the particular frame is loaded (such as Play).

Clip Events

The onClipEvent handler is similar to the button handler in that specific events trigger the handler. Nine events can be used with the onClipEvent handler. Table 7.3 shows the event and a description of when the event is triggered.

Table 7.3   Clip Events

Event	Description
data	Triggered when the loadMovie action loads an external SWF and when the data from a file or script using loadVariables is finished loading
enterFrame	Triggered when each frame on the Timeline is played
keyDown	Triggered when the user presses a key
keyUp	Triggered when the user releases a key

Table 7.3 Continued

Event	Description
load	Triggered when a movie clip instance appears on the Stage for the first time, when a new instance is added (using either attachMovie or duplicateMovieClip), or when an external SWF is loaded
mouseDown	Triggered when the left mouse button is pressed
mouseMove	Triggered each time the mouse moves
mouseUp	Triggered when the left mouse button is released
unload	Triggered when a movie clip instance exits the Stage after the last frame has been played, when an external SWF file is unloaded

The event is usually used to indicate new data has been received by the movie, either because a new movie has been loaded or variables have been received during an action. The event is used like this:

```
OnClipEvent ( data ) {
    // code here to handle new data
    trace("New data has been received...";
}
```

The keyDown and keyUp events are used to monitor the keyboard. When a user presses any key on the keyboard down, the keyDown event is triggered. When the key is released, the keyUp event is triggered. The reason for the two states is some keys, such as the arrow keys, are used held down for navigation. In these cases, a keyDown event should produce continual movement of the cursor. For normal key use, the keyUp event is used to trigger an action, such as pressing "q" to quit.

The mouseDown and mouseUp events are used to monitor the left mouse button. When first depressed, the mouseDown event is triggered. The button can be held down as long as the user likes, but when released it triggers a mouseUp event. The mouseMove event is triggered whenever the mouse is moved anywhere on the Stage. The mouseMove event can easily be combined with the hitTest method to detect mouse movements over movie clip instances.

The load and unload events are triggered in several conditions, but their actions are easy to understand. The enterFrame event is similarly obvious in its trigger.

Summary

In this chapter we've looked at events and how you can set events using movie clip, button, or frame triggers. You have seen how handlers are used, as well as the Actions panel. We've looked in some detail at the mouse and movie clip actions, and you know how to set the proper actions using the Toolbox and ActionScript in normal mode.

Sample Questions

1. What happens when you place a frame event on the Timeline?
   A. A small letter "a" appears in the frame.
   B. The frame turns gray to indicate it is a keyframe.
   C. A new layer for frame events is automatically created.
   D. The Timeline branches into two parts.

2. What does the Toggle High Quality event do?
   A. Increases the playback window resolution.
   B. Resizes the playback window to optimum dpi setting.
   C. Dithers pixels to show intermediate shades.
   D. Turns antialiasing on or off.

3. When using relative addressing which prefix refers to the current Timeline?
   A. `this`
   B. `root`
   C. `level`
   D. `next`

CHAPTER 8

Variables

Data Types

Chapter 5, "Using Variables," discussed the basics of using variables with Macromedia Flash. You saw that variables do not need to be explicitly declared as to type because Flash can figure out (and convert if necessary) the type that is to be used for the data to be stored in a variable. This doesn't mean that Flash does not have specific data types. It does, but you don't have to know too much about them for most simple ActionScript or expression usage. We should take a look at the different data types supported by Flash, though.

Data types are defined in two categories by Flash—*primitive* and *reference*. A primitive data type has a constant size and type and can hold the data value directly. Strings, numbers, and Booleans are all primitive data types. Reference data types have sizes that can change and instead of containing the data directly have a reference to the data instead. The reference data types used by Flash are movie clip and object.

> **TIP**
>
> You can think of Flash's reference data types like pointers in C and C++. Reference data types hold a memory address where the actual item begins in memory, or a reference to a disk file or URL.

Variables can be defined (and hence declared) in several ways with Flash. The most common is to create them explicitly using ActionScript, but you can also load variables and their values from a text file or from a CGI script. You can also obtain variables and their values from HTML tags. You have seen several examples of using ActionScript to define variables so far in this book, and many more examples follow. We'll look at loading variables from files, CGI scripts, or HTML tags later in this chapter.

Constants

Although constants are not really a separate data type, we do need to mention them and this is as good a place as any. A constant is a variable whose value never changes. Once a variable has been defined, its value is locked and all attempts to change it will result in errors.

Constants are named like any other variable (and have to adhere to the variable naming rules), but the convention is to place constant names in uppercase. Keep in mind that this is a convention, not a requirement because ActionScript identifiers are not case-sensitive. Flash has a defined set of constants that can be used for many purposes; these constants are all listed in the Toolbox. An example of a Flash constant is MATH.PI, which equates to the value of pi.

String Data Type

The string data type is used to hold a series of characters. Any other data type that refers to a string data type through an operation or function is also a string data type. Strings are defined in ActionScript by enclosing the string in quotation marks (either single or double, as long as they are a matched pair). For example, the following command defines a variable of data type string that has the value "This is a string".

```
str1 = "This is a string";
```

When you are declaring a string's contents, the contents are case-sensitive. The two strings "String" and "string" are not the same.

Anytime a string is declared it cannot be used as a number. For example, the following command creates a string data type with the string value "67".

```
num1 = "67";
```

This is not the same as a number data type with the value 67. (The ASCII values for the string and number are different even though they appear superficially the same.)

> **NOTE**
>
> All Flash input text fields, as well as all dynamic text fields, have a data type of string. To perform a numeric calculation using one of these text fields you must convert the string to a number first.

Although strings cannot be treated as numbers, you can perform a concatenation operation on strings using the plus sign. For example, the following results in the string Str3 having the string value "Strings can be added together".

```
str1 = "Strings can ";
str2 = "be added together.";
str3 = str1 + str2;
```

The string data type has a number of escape characters that can be used to embed a character in a string (and prevent it being interpreted as a control character of some sort). Table 8.1 shows the valid escape characters for the string data type.

Table 8.1   Valid Escape Characters for the String Data Type

Escape Sequence	Meaning
\b	Backspace
\f	Form-feed
\n	Line-feed
\r	Return
\t	Tab
\"	Double quotation mark
\'	Single quotation mark
\\	Backslash
\000	Octal value
\x00	Hexadecimal value
\u0000	Unicode character in hexadecimal (16-bit only)

There are several Flash functions that work to convert string data types. The functions `toUpperCase()` and `toLowerCase()` convert a string's case to all upper- or lowercase, respectively. For example, the following statements result in `str2` having the value `"THIS IS A STRING"`.

```
str1 = "This is a string";
str2 = str1.toUpperCase();
```

Only alphabetic characters are affected by the case conversion function. (Note the use of the dot syntax to indicate the object and then the function or function to be invoked.)

To convert a string to a number, you can use the `Number()` function. This is done with the string data type as an argument in the parentheses of the following function call, which converts the value in `str1` to a number and stores it in `num1`.

```
num1 = Number(str1);
```

If the value in the string does not convert properly to a number, then no conversion is performed.

You can use the `indexOf()` function to find the location of the first occurrence of a specific character inside a string. For example, to find the occurrence of the first space:

```
str1 = "This is a string";
num1 = str1.indexOf(" ");
```

This code finds the index (position) of the first space in the string. This returns a number, which in this case is 4.

> **TIP**
>
> The `indexOf()` function starts numbering characters at the first character with an index of 0.

The `slice()` function can be used to extract a substring from a larger string. The function requires the starting character number and a length of substring to extract. The special value of –1 for the length of substring means to extract to the end of the string. For example, the following code assigns the string to the variable `str1`, and then determines where the first space occurs and stores that value in the number variable `num1` (which is 5 in this case):

```
str1 = "This is a string";
num1 = str1.indexOf(" ");
str2 = str1.slice(num1+1, -1);
```

The string variable `str2` is then assigned the substring from the first space plus one (so from the sixth position) on to the end of the string (the –1 means to end of string). Therefore, `str2` has the value `"is a string"`.

Number Data Type

The number data type is used to hold numeric values. For mathematical operations, the values to be used must be numbers. Flash handles numbers as double-precision floating point data types (like a double float in other languages). This data type is used for all numbers, integer and floating point alike.

> **NOTE**
>
> The use of double precision floating point format is a compromise for storing information, as most numbers will not require this amount of precision, but it saves having to use multiple data types to handle integers and floats. Because there usually are not a high number of variables used in ActionScript programs, the overhead involved in using double floats is not excessive.

Flash supports all the standard mathematical operators on the number data type, as you will see later in this chapter. Flash includes a set of predefined Math objects, as well. These are a collection of functions that are designed to provide typical mathematical capabilities such as taking the square root of a number.

Boolean Data Type

The boolean data type can have only two values: `true` or `false`. The booleans are mostly used when performing logic flow controls, usually with an `if` statement, but they are also used as a flag for operations.

You can use the boolean values in standard comparisons, like this:

```
if (flag1 == true) {
        statements;
        }
```

> **NOTE**
>
> Internally, Flash stores boolean values as an integer value. Flash stores `true` as a 1 and `false` as a 0. You can use these values in comparison operations similar to those performed in high-level languages like C++ and Java.

Object Data Type

The object data type is a reference type used to refer to any ActionScript-based objects you create. Object data types store a collection of properties (including functions), each property with a unique name and a value. Any data types can be used for the properties, including object types themselves.

To access properties and their values inside an object data type, you use the dot notation, which uses the name of the object followed by a period followed by the property name. For example if you have an object called `movie1` and it has a property called `framerate`, you would access the value in that property using:

```
movie1.framerate
```

If there are nested objects (an object contained inside another object), you need to specify all the levels using dot notation. For example, if the object `movie1` mentioned earlier was itself a part of a larger object called `bigmovie`, you would access the variable like this:

```
bigmovie.movie1.framerate
```

If there is a function that is part of an object, you access the function in the same way using dot notation. For example, the built-in `Math` object has a square root function called `sqrt()` that you access like this:

```
Math.sqrt(var1);
```

`var1` is the variable you want the square root of. You have already seen examples of using this notation when you saw the `MovieClip` object. This object has functions for playing and stopping a movie clip, as well as several other functions. These would be accessed using the name of the instance of the movie clip, like this:

```
movie1.play();
movie1.stop();
```

Movie Clip Data Type

The movie clip data type is the only Flash data type that supports a graphical component. The movie clip data type is included (instead of using the object data type for the same purpose) to enable more control over movie clip playback. This is accomplished through a set of functions that are part of the data type.

> **NOTE**
>
> Flash supports the specific movie clip data type instead of using the more generic object data type so that it is easier to detect movie clip objects in code.

As with the object data type, you call the movie clip's functions with dot notation. To define a movie clip data type, you need to refer to an existing movie clip in the main Timeline like this:

```
objtype = _root.dogRunning;
```

If dogRunning is a movie clip in the Timeline, the variable is set to the value of movieclip. If dogRunning does not exist, the value is set to undefined.

The typeof() Function

You can use the Flash typeof() function to determine the data type of any variable (or any ActionScript element, for that matter). This function uses the variable's name as an option. You can display the results of the typeof() function with the trace() function like this:

```
str1 = "This is a string.";
trace("str1 is of data type " + typeof(str1));
```

This will display the following output:

```
str1 is of data type string
```

You can use the typeof() function at any time to determine a data type. It can be nested inside loops to display all the variables currently defined.

Naming Variables

As you saw in Chapter 5, Flash variables must have unique names within the variable's scope. This means that Timeline variables (those available anywhere in the Timeline) have to be unique in the movie, while local variables (those with a scope only inside a set of curly braces) must be unique only where they have scope. This does mean you can use the same variable name many times in a movie, as long as they are local variable instances and do not conflict with each other's scope.

The rules for naming variables in Flash are:

- The name must be unique within its scope.
- The name must be a valid identifier.
- The name cannot be a Flash keyword or a Boolean literal (true or false).

Normally you want your variable names to be as descriptive as possible.

Working with Variables

Variables can be used anywhere you would normally use a number, string, or Boolean value. You can use a variable to assign another variable a value, and you can manipulate variable values with standard arithmetic operators. For example, the following code defines two variables, and then creates more variables using those values and standard operators:

```
Num1 = 5;
Num2 = 6;
Num3 = Num5 + 9;
Num4 = Num2 + Num3;
Num5 = Num4;
Num6 = Num 4 - Num3 + Num1 * Num2;
```

The last statement brings up the subject of order of precedence (or which operations are performed first). Flash relies on the usual order of precedence for arithmetic operations, so in the last case, the multiplication (Num1 * Num2) is performed first, and then the subtraction and addition are performed. Multiplication and division are always executed before addition and subtraction unless parentheses are used to group operations, like this:

```
Num6 = (Num 4 - Num3 + Num1) * Num2;
```

In this case, the subtraction and addition are performed first, and then the multiplication occurs on the result.

Flash's ActionScript is based on the same standard as JavaScript, and as such inherits a lot of the basic language features similar to Java, C, and C++. If you have worked in any high-level language, you find ActionScript relatively easy to work with and adjust to. If you are a Java, JavaScript, C, or C++ programmer, you find the adjustment even easier, as most of the ActionScript operators and functions are similar. We can look at the basic Flash operators now so we can reference them in Part III, "Flash Objects."

The basic Flash numeric operators are:

- +: Addition
- -: Subtraction
- *: Multiplication
- /: Division
- %: Modulus
- ++: Autoincrement
- --: Autodecrement

The modulus is the result of dividing one number by another as many times as possible, and then using whatever is left over as the result. For example, 10%3 means to divide 3 into 10 as many times as possible (which would be three times) and take the remainder as the result (in this case it would be 1, as 10–9 leaves 1). The result of 11%4 is 3, and the result of 8%2 is 0.

Autoincrement and autodecrement are automatically increasing or decreasing (respectively) the value these operators appear after. For example, the following statement takes the current value of Num1 and adds one to it.

```
Num1++;
```

This is a simpler function of writing:

```
Num1 = Num1 + 1;
```

The arithmetic operators can be used for simple string manipulation in Flash, adding two strings to produce a new string, for example:

```
Str1 = "Flash ";
Str2 = "Study Guide";
Str3 = Str1 + Str2;
```

This results in the variable Str3 having the value "Flash Study Guide".

Flash supports the usual comparison operators for comparing values. The syntax used is familiar to programmers in other high-level languages:

- ==: Equal to
- !=: Not equal to
- <: Less than
- >: Greater than
- <=: Less than or equal to
- >=: Greater than or equal to

Logical operators supported by Flash are the usual logical AND, OR, and NOT, using the almost-universal syntax:

- &&: AND
- ||: OR
- !: NOT

Flash also supports bitwise operators. Flash automatically converts floating point numbers to 32-bit integers for bitwise manipulation. The bitwise operators supported by Flash are:

- <<: Shift left
- >>: Shift right
- >>>: Shift right with zero fill
- &: Bitwise AND
- |: Bitwise OR
- ^: Bitwise XOR
- ~: Bitwise NOT

Any of the operators mentioned previously can be used with the assignment operator to perform a compound assignment operation. For example, the following statement takes the current value of Num1 and adds 10 to it, then assigns the result back to Num1.

```
Num1 += 10;
```

It is the same as writing:

```
Num1 = Num1 + 10;
```

These compound operators support the modulus and bitwise operators, as well as the standard arithmetic operations.

Loading and Sending Variables

At the start of this chapter we mentioned that you can define variables either through ActionScript statements (the most common approach) or you can read the variables and the values in from a text file, a database query, a CGI script, or HTML tags. This is accomplished using the `loadVariables` command accessible through the Actions panel Toolbox. You can also send variables and their values to a specific location in a similar way using the `getURL` command.

The `loadVariables` command has three parameters in the pane at the bottom of the Actions panel (in normal mode). The first parameter enables you to specify a URL for the source of the variables. This can be a fully qualified path or a simple filename, either absolute or relative. If the file is elsewhere on the Internet, you can provide a full DNS path to the file, like this:

```
http://www.tpci.com/cgi-bin/flash/vars.pl
```

> **NOTE**
>
> You can use expressions with variables in them to provide a URL for the variable location, if you want, as long as the expanded expression resolves to a proper path name.

The Location parameter uses a pull-down menu to determine where the variables are to be loaded (such as a specific level or the entire Timeline). If you want the variables to be accessible throughout the Timeline, specify the `_root` or `_level0` setting (the two mean the same thing). You can also specify an explicit movie clip target. For example, to load the variables into the current movie clip you would use the `this` target.

The final parameter in the pane is Variables. This drop-down menu lets you specify whether you are loading or sending data. If you are importing variables from a file, you choose the Don't Send setting. If you are querying a data source such as an SQL database indirectly through middleware, you need to specify the GET or POST setting.

> **NOTE**
>
> Using GET and POST with `loadVariables` means you are sending variables declared on the active Timeline to the URL. This in turn sends back variable names and values to the Timeline.

The formatting of variable names and values is the same as standard URL text that has name and value pairs joined by an ampersand. This is known as query string format. For example, the following statements are how three variables and their values would be formatted for URL text:

```
num1=6.8&str1="Hello"&num2=5
```

You can send variables to Flash movies using HTML tags. This uses the `<EMBED>` and `<OBJECT>` HTML tags for this purpose. Variable names and value pairs are separated by a question mark and placed inside the `<EMBED>` tag using the SRC attribute like this:

```
<OBJECT...>
<PARAM NAME=movie VALUE="movie1.swf">
<EMBED SRC="movie1.swf?var1=5?var2=5.6">
```

To send variables and their values to a URL use the `getURL` command. This sends any variable names and values on the active Timeline to the URL when the GET and POST functions are chosen in the parameters pane. Despite the name's implied reception ability, `getURL` does not import or retrieve data, but only sends it to the URL. Also, the `getURL` command loads a new page, while `loadVariables` does not.

Summary

In this chapter we've looked at the different data types supported by Flash and some of the functions that support them. We also looked at the basic operators supported by Flash. Examples of using these operators are in future chapters.

Sample Questions

1. Which of the following is not a primitive data type?
   A. `number`
   B. `string`
   C. `object`
   D. `boolean`

2. Which of the following data types can use the "+" operator?
   A. `string`
   B. `object`
   C. `MovieClip`
   D. `boolean`

3. If you set a variable using a movie clip name and the clip is not in the current Timeline, what is the variable set to?
   A. `false`
   B. `undefined`
   C. `zero`
   D. An error message is displayed

CHAPTER 9

Functions

What Is a Function?

You saw functions briefly in earlier chapters, and now we can look at both the Macromedia Flash predefined functions and the functions you can write yourself. Functions greatly extend the functionality of Flash by enabling you to custom design a subroutine to complete necessary tasks, even if the Flash designers did not think of them.

Briefly put, a function is a code block of ActionScript commands that is called by a single name. Many inexperienced programmers think of functions as black boxes (something that takes an input, does something to the input, and generates output without having to show you what's going on inside) that have a name. You execute the black box name and pass in any parameters, and get back a result. Experienced programmers know that functions are a block of code that executes according to normal programming rules, but are reusable and callable by using the function name. Flash functions behave and are called in the same way as functions in other high-level languages like C and C++ and Java methods (which are very similar to functions). Functions can be called at any time by a command embedded in either an object or a Timeline. Functions are callable by anything that has a Timeline, including loaded movies.

Any parameters that need to be passed to the function are sent as arguments in the parentheses following the function name, and some functions return a value that can be assigned to a variable or used directly (as you will see later in this chapter). If you pass a function more parameters than it expects, it simply ignores the extra parameters. If you don't provide enough parameters, errors can result because Flash assigns the value `undefined` to those parameters.

> **NOTE**
>
> More developers use the words argument and parameter interchangeably. Whenever we refer to an argument or to a function it is the same as referring to a parameter or to a function.

There are a couple of basic rules for when you should create a function, and when you can leave the code as part of a larger ActionScript program (not as a function). The main decision to make is whether the piece of code will be reused, either inside this Timeline (and any called by it), or in other movies. If the code will be used again, you should consider making it a function. Also, if you have some complex mathematical operation to perform, you should also consider making the code a function because it can be more easily debugged as a function.

Predefined Flash Functions

Flash includes a number of predefined functions, some of which you have seen earlier in this book. The functions included with Flash 5 are listed in Table 9.1.

Table 9.1   Flash 5 Predefined Functions

Function	Use
boolean	Converts the argument to a Boolean data type
escape	Converts the argument to a string and encodes in it URL format
eval	Accesses objects, movie clips, variables, and properties by name based on the argument
false	Evaluates to False
getProperty	Returns the value of the argument for the movie clip instance
getTimer	Returns the number of milliseconds that have elapsed since the movie started playing
getVersion	Returns a string showing the Flash Player version and some platform information
globalToLocal	Converts a global variable to a local variable
hitTest	Tests to see if a hit event has occurred
int	Converts a decimal number to the closest integer
isFinite	Tests to see if the argument is finite and returns True if it is
isNaN	Tests the argument to see if the value is not a number and returns True if it is not
localToGlobal	Converts a local variable to a global variable
maxscroll	Read-only value that works with the scroll property to show the amount of information in a text field
Newline	Inserts a carriage return into the code
number	Converts a string to a number data type
parseFloat	Converts a string to a floating point number
parseInt	Converts a string to an integer number
random	Returns a random number between 0 and the integer argument

Table 9.1   Continued

Function	Use
scroll	Controls the display in a text fields; defines where the field begins displaying content
string	Converts a number to a string data type
TargetPath	Returns a strlng containing the target path in dot notation
true	Evaluates to True
unescape	Decodes the argument from URL format and returns a string

There are many other predefined Flash functions, but these are part of libraries of functions such as the Math or Key objects. These are all summarized in the *Macromedia ActionScript Reference Guide*, so we won't bother reviewing them all here.

Using Functions

You can use any function, both predefined and custom-written, by using its name followed by parentheses. Any parameters that are sent to the function must be enclosed in the parentheses. If no parameters are being sent to the function, leave the parentheses empty.

If you are using normal mode with the Actions dialog, you can attach a function to an object by selecting the command evaluate in the Toolbox. Then fill in any parameters in the parameter pane, including the function name and any arguments, and the completed function call will appear in the Actions List in the right side of the window.

> **TIP**
>
> You can call a function on another Timeline by specifying a target path using dot notation.

If you are using expert mode with the Actions dialog, you can enter the function name and any parameters that need to be passed directly into the code in the Actions List pane. If you are using an external editor, and then importing, the same procedure is used.

Writing Functions

To write a custom function you need to write the code block that will be executed when the function is called. You also need to determine what if any parameters are to be passed to the function, and whether any value is to be returned from the function when called. Functions are attached to the movie clip that defines them, and can be used by that clip and any other clips (and their Timelines) that are called from that clip. If you redefine a function that already exists, then the new function code block replaces the old function completely.

> **CAUTION**
>
> The ability to overwrite an existing custom or predefined Flash function means you should be careful in naming your functions. Avoid any function name that resembles a JavaScript or Flash function name, preferably by starting custom functions with a unique character. Many developers start all function names with "my", for example, to indicate it is a custom function.

Functions are defined by using the keyword `function` as part of the definition. This keyword is followed by the name of the function as well as the placeholder name for any parameters to be passed to the function. This is followed by the code for the function inside curly braces. If you are returning a value from the function, you need to use the keyword `return` followed by the value that you are returning. This can be either a variable name or an expression.

The following is a simple example of defining a function to convert miles to kilometers:

```
function convertToKilometers(miles){
        return miles * 8 / 5;
}
```

In this function, called `convertToKilometers`, one parameter that is assigned to the placeholder variable `miles` is passed. Inside the function is a single line of code that returns the value of the variable miles multiplied by 8 and divided by 5. In this case, we've sent the result (which is the number of kilometers that `miles` represents) back to the function call as an expression.

> **NOTE**
>
> The parameters supplied in the parentheses after a function definition are created as local variables when the function is called. These variables exist only while the function is running and have scope only inside the function curly braces. This is also called *block scope*.

We could just as easily have assigned the converted value to a variable and used the variable name in the `return` statement, like this:

```
function convertToKilometers(miles){
        var kilos;
        kilos = miles * 8 / 5;
        return kilos;
}
```

In this version of the script we defined a local variable called `kilos` (the `var` keyword indicates a local variable and uses that to hold the calculation, and then returns that value by calling the variable itself. Both versions of the function work the same way and the choice of which version to use depends on both your programming style and whether you want to perform more calculations inside the function at a later date that will need a local variable holding the converted value. The first version has a slight performance advantage, but the effect is minimal.

You could use variables within a function, of course, but the advantage to local variables is that they have limited scope (only within the function) and hence cannot conflict with any other variables defined in the Timeline. If you use non-local variables within a function you should be aware of all possible changes to the variable's values elsewhere in the Timeline. As a general rule, use local variables as much as possible.

> **NOTE**
>
> Naturally, you should document any custom written functions by using comments. Your comments should include any parameters that are to be passed in (including restrictions on data types, values, and so on) as well as any return value information. Comments should also identify and explain any complex or unusual code in your functions. Many developers also tag all functions with the developer's name, date, and reasons for writing the function.

If you do want to return a value from a function call, you have to use the `return` statement. ActionScript returns an undefined value if there is no `return` statement and the closing curly brace has been encountered. Not all functions return values, of course.

When you are passing more than one argument to a function, you simply specify them all in the parentheses of the function call, as well as in the definition of the function. For example, this function simply determines the modulus of the two numbers passed as parameters and returns the result:

```
function sendModulus(num1, num2){
        return num1%num2;
}
```

When the function is called inside some ActionScript code, the two parameters are specified on the function call line, like this:

```
myModulus = sendModulus( 78, 7);
```

This uses the values 78 and 7 for the two variables, respectively. (Of course, you could have done the modulus calculation more easily directly, but this shows the use of two arguments.)

> **TIP**
>
> Functions are normally defined at the start of a Timeline so that they are loaded with the first frame of the movie. As a general rule, place all functions on keyframes in the Timeline.

Function Literals

A function literal is a function that is defined in an expression instead of as a stand-alone function. Function literals do not have a name and are not reusable. To write a function literal for the miles to kilometers conversion we looked at previously, we would write the code like this:

```
kilos = function(miles){ return this.miles * 8 / 5; };
```

With this function literal we have defined the function (although it is unnamed), passed a parameter (you can also perform a function literal with no parameters, of course), and returned the calculated value assigning it to a variable in one line of code.

Custom Classes

Functions can be used to define properties and methods in a class, so being able to define new classes (and using custom functions to define the methods of that class) is a useful feature of Flash. Many developers never bother defining their own custom classes, but this can be a handy way of creating new libraries or objects for use in a series of movies.

To create a new class, use the new operator with a constructor function. This lets you instantiate objects of your new class. For example, you can create a constructor function called newframe that has two properties like this:

```
function newframe( num1, num2) {
        this.horiz = num1;
        this.vert = num2;
}
```

This defines a new class called newframe with the two properties horiz and vert. To instantiate an object of class newframe use the constructor function with the keyword new:

```
mynewframe = new newframe ( 50, 25);
```

When executed, this creates a new object called mynewframe, which has the properties horiz set to 50 and vert set to 25.

To attach a method (function) to the class newframe you need another function to do whatever the method is supposed to achieve, such as setting the parameters sent to the method. First you need to create the function:

```
function setframesize( dimen, dimensize ){
    set ("this.dimen" + dimen + "this.dimensize" + dimensize);
}
```

This function lets you pass the dimension (horiz or vert) plus a value, and then uses the set command to set the values. After you have created the function, you want to associate it with the class. You do this with the prototype property.

> **NOTE**
> The prototype property associates all new objects made from a class, which inherit the methods and properties.

To assign the setframeSize function as a method in the newframe class use the prototype property (which is already part of the newframe class):

```
newframe.prototype.setframe = setframesize;
```

This command sets the `setframeSize` function as a method in `newframe`. The method is called `setframe` inside `newframe`. (In this case we changed the name of the method to avoid confusion with the stand-alone function, but the name could be kept the same.) Finally, to use the method, call it like this:

```
newframe.setframe ( horiz, 50 );
```

This process of creating a custom class is best done in expert mode, although normal mode can be used.

Summary

In this chapter we've looked at functions, both intrinsic primitive functions provided by Flash, as well as custom written functions. You also briefly saw function literals. The proper use of functions can help reduce the amount of code you need to write to support your ActionScript events, and can result in less debugging and testing time after your functions are solid. Although you can write any Flash movie without the use of functions, developers find code easier to write and maintain when you properly use this feature.

Sample Questions

1. If you do not provide enough arguments in a function call, what value does Flash assign to the leftover parameters?
   A. `undefined`
   B. `null`
   C. `zero`
   D. `empty string`

2. If you do not have a `return` statement at the end of your function, what value is returned?
   A. `none`
   B. `null`
   C. `undefined`
   D. `empty string`

3. Which of the following is not true?
   A. Functions should be defined in keyframes.
   B. Functions can overwrite primitive Flash functions.
   C. Functions can refer to movie clip events not loaded in the Timeline.
   D. Functions should always have parentheses and curly brace pairs.

CHAPTER 10

Programming Basics

Flow Control

Many programs simply execute statements from start to finish, moving through each line of code one at a time. Sometimes, though, you want to repeat a number of statements more than once. To do this, you can use a loop, which essentially tells Flash to execute statements inside the loop a specific number of times. Also, you may want to have statements executed only under certain circumstances, such as a number being a particular value or some variable set to a particular string. To do this, you can use a conditional statement. Macromedia Flash provides both conditional and loop statements, as you will see in this chapter.

In addition to the basic statements for conditions and looping, Flash also provides a statement for breaking out of a loop, and another statement for forcing a loop to restart. We look at those statements after we look at the conditional and looping statements.

The `if` Statement

As with most programming languages, Flash ActionScript has a conditional operator, the `if-else`. This is used to test whether a condition is `true`, and if it is, a set of commands can be executed. If the condition is not `true`, another set of commands may be executed if they are present. The basic syntax of the `if` statement is:

```
if (condition) {
    statements if condition is true
} else {
    statements if condition is false
}
```

The logic flow is easy to see: The condition is tested. If the condition is `true`, the statements in the curly braces immediately following the condition are executed. If the condition is `false`, the statements after the condition are ignored completely. If an `else` statement follows the set of curly braces after the condition, and the condition is `false`, the statements in the curly braces that follow the `else` statement are executed. The `else` block of code is optional and can be left out completely. Of course, you'll be using a valid ActionScript statement inside the curly braces.

The following is an example of an `if-else` statement with code for both `true` and `false` condition evaluations:

```
if (num1 == 5){
    str1 = "It is five.";
    num2 = num1 * 2;
    } else {
    str1 = "It is not five.";
    num2 = num1 / 2;
    }
```

Although this is a contrived simple example, it does show the proper layout for the conditional statements. The statement starts with the keyword `if` followed by the condition to be tested. The condition is enclosed in parentheses and is always constructed so it can evaluate to a `true` or `false` value. (Note that we use the two equal signs as a comparison, checking to see if `num1` is equal to 5. If we had used a single equal sign, we would have assigned the value 5 to `num1`. This would have changed the meaning of the condition, even though it may superficially appear as though the loop is working properly.)

A code block in a set of curly braces follows the condition. This contains the code to execute if the condition is `true`. There can be any number of statements in the curly braces and they are executed one after another until the closing curly brace. After the closing curly brace, Flash detects the `else` statement followed by another set of curly braces. If the condition is `false`, these statements are executed. Both sets of curly braces are never executed as the condition cannot be both `true` and `false` at the same time (although it could be undefined, which is not the same).

Flash enables you to nest `if-else` statements for even more control of a program. For example, you can have an `if-else` inside one set of curly braces and Flash handles the code properly:

```
if (num1 == 5){
    str1 = "It is five.";
    if (num2 <= 5){
        num2 = num1 * 2;
    }} else {
    str1 = "It is not five.";
    num2 = num1 / 2;
    }
```

In this code, a second if-else has been placed inside the first set of curly braces. This test is only executed if the condition at the top is true, causing the statements in the first curly brace pair to be executed. After assigning a string to str1, the second if statement is executed. If the condition is true, the statements inside the following curly brace pair are executed. In this case, there is no else statement, so if the condition is false, nothing happens. Note that the curly braces are properly paired up.

You can write another if statement as part of the else statement (which many languages write as else if or elif). You can use the else if format with Flash, like this:

```
if (num1 == 5){
    str1 = "It is five.";
    num2 = num1 * 2;
    } else if (num1 > 10){
    str1 = "It is not five.";
    num2 = num1 / 2;
  }
```

In this case, the else if is used to test the variable only if the first condition is false (otherwise, the else statement is never executed). else is not in the else if in this example, but you can have one if you needed it, like this:

```
if (num1 == 5){
    str1 = "It is five.";
    num2 = num1 * 2;
    } else if (num1 > 10){
    str1 = "It is not five.";
    num2 = num1 / 2;
    } else {
      str1 = "It is greater than ten.";
    }
```

> **TIP**
>
> You can nest if statements many levels deep. For efficient processing of your code, place the most likely conditions at the top of the tree. This prevents your code from having to delve down many levels and test many conditions. Often, writing separate if statements instead of nested statements is a better approach (as well as more readable).

You can use Booleans with your if statements to apply and (&&), or (||), and not (!) conditions, like this:

```
if ( num1 > 5 && num1 < 10 ){
    str1 = "It is between 5 and 10";
} else if (num1 < 6){
        str1 = "It is less than 5";
        } else {
        str1 = "It is greater than 9";
        }
}
```

> **CAUTION**
>
> Make sure curly braces are properly paired and in the right place for the logic flow. Any misplacement could result in either errors or unintended execution of statements.

To add an `if` statement to your code you can use the Actions panel. In normal mode, select the `if` statement from the list of actions. In the condition field in the parameter pane, enter the expression to be used for the condition after the `if`. If you want to use an `else` or an `else if` statement as part of the logic flow, select the correct statement from the action list. If you are using expert mode, you can simply type the code into the action list making sure the syntax is correctly applied.

Loops

Like many other high-level languages, Flash has several types of constructs for enabling code blocks to be executed over and over, as long as some condition is met. These are loops. Flash supports the same loop structures as Java, C, C++, and some other languages. The four loop types are:

- `for`
- `for...in`
- `while`
- `do...while`

Each of these loop constructs has its own purpose and advantage, so we look at each of the loop commands, one at a time.

> **TIP**
>
> Do not use looping statements to monitor the value of variables in real time. An `if` statement is much more efficient. This is for a simple reason: When Flash enters a loop the display is frozen. Also, when executing a loop statement keyboard and mouse inputs are ignored.

The `for` Loop

The `for` loop is normally used for executing a series of statements in a code block a specific number of times, or until some condition is met. As you will see later, the `for` loop can also be used to process a list of arguments using a slightly different syntax. However, the `for` loop is for forcing a loop a specific number of times using a counter. The syntax of the Flash `for` loop is the same as the languages C, C++, and Java, as well as some others. The general syntax is:

```
for (initial; condition; loop){
    statements
}
```

The loop has a pair of parentheses after the `for` keyword, followed by the code to execute in curly braces. Inside the parentheses are always three pieces of information, separated by a semicolon. The initial component is a command or set of commands that are to be executed prior to the loop being performed. These initial statements are executed only once, when the loop is ready to execute, and are usually used to initialize variables used as loop counters or inside the statement block. The condition is an expression that tells Flash when to loop and when to stop looping. As with all other conditions, this must evaluate to `true` or `false`. If the condition is `true`, the statements in the curly braces are executed. If the condition is `false`, the statements in the curly braces are not executed and the `for` loop terminates. The third part of the parenthetical component is the loop statement or statements. These are executed after the statements inside the curly braces are executed, and before the condition is checked.

A simple walk-through of the logic will help make this clear. When the `for` statement is encountered, Flash runs the initial statements. Then, the condition is checked. If the condition is `false`, the statements in the curly braces are not executed and the program continues running after the closing curly brace. If the condition is `true`, the statements in the curly braces are executed, and then the loop statements are executed. Finally, the condition is checked again, and if `true` the curly brace statements followed by the loop statements are run all over again, repeating the process until the condition is `false`. As soon as the condition is `false`, the loop terminates and execution proceeds past the closing curly brace.

> **TIP**
>
> Any valid expression can be used in the three parts in the `for` loop's parentheses, as long as they conform to normal Flash rules.

Normally, the `for` loop is used when you want to execute the statements in the curly braces a specific number of times, either hard coded or supplied through a variable. If you wanted to execute the statements 10 times, for example, you would write the `for` loop like this:

```
for (i = 1; i <= 10; i++){
    statements
}
```

In this case we declared a variable `i` that is set to 1, then test to see if the value is less than or equal to 10. If it is, we loop through the statements in the curly braces, increment the variable, and then test the condition again. You can see this loops 10 times. You could have made this more flexible by supplying the number of times to loop through a variable, instead of hard-coding the value:

```
for (i = 1; i <= num1; i++){
    statements
}
```

In this case, when the counter i is greater than the value stored in num1, the loop terminates.

The for...in Loop

The other form of the for loop, which has been adopted from languages like UNIX shell programming, is used to process a list. This loop is called the for...in loop. There are few equivalents to this syntax in other high-level languages, but it is a useful syntax when you need to move one item at a time though many arguments. The syntax for this kind of for loop is:

```
for (variable in list){
    statements;
}
```

The variable is simply any variable that is used to act as a placeholder throughout the list to be processed. It holds each value in the list, one at a time. The keyword in must be in the parentheses, and this is followed by the name of the list or object that is to be processed.

The logic flow of the loop is quite simple. The list or object is analyzed to see how many items are in it and an internal pointer is set to the top of the list. The value there is stored in the variable and the statements in the curly braces are executed. After that, the list pointer is moved down one value, the new value stored in the variable, and the statements again executed. This continues until the end of the list. When no more items are in the list, the loop terminates and execution continues past the closing curly brace.

> **NOTE**
>
> In Flash, the for...in loop can only be used with objects and arrays, although some object properties cannot be used in this loop. The loop can also be used to examine the main Timeline and movie clip Timelines.

Normally, this format for the for loop is used to process a set of attributes in an object, but it can be used with a physical list of values as well. When processing object properties, you have to specify the object name. For example, you can set a bunch of properties for the current Timeline like this:

```
for (tempvar in _root){
    statements to set properties;
}
```

The _root indicates the current Timeline, while tempvar is a temporary variable that holds attributes.

The while Loop

The while loop is the simplest loop supported by Flash. It uses the while statement followed by a condition. As long as the condition is true, the contents of the curly braces are executed. The syntax is:

```
while ( condition ) {
    statements;
}
```

The condition is any valid Flash expression that evaluates to `true` or `false`. The following is a simple example of a `while` loop:

```
while ( num1 != 10 ) {
    statements;
    if ( condition) {
        num1 = 10;
    }
    statements;
}
```

The condition in this loop checks the variable `num1` for a value (it must have been predefined for this expression to be valid). If the value is not equal to 10, the condition is `true` and the statements in the loop are executed. Inside the loop, we've placed an `if` condition that sets the value of `num1` to `10` when the condition is `true`. This would then cause the `while` condition to be `false` the next time it is executed. This `if` statement is called an exit condition because it causes an exit of the loop the next time the `while` statement is executed.

You can use `while` loops for many purposes, including looping. For example, earlier you saw a `for` loop that enables you to process a number of statements 10 times. We can write similar code using a `while` loop by setting the variable to be tested first, and then using an increment operation within the body of the `while` loop:

```
i = 1;
while ( i < 10) {
    statements;
    i++;
}
```

This runs the same as the `for` loop you saw earlier, and in practice there is no real performance advantage to using either a `for` or a `while` loop. The `for` loop is often a little easier to write, but it is primarily a programming style consideration as to which format to use.

The do while Loop

The do while loop is similar to the `while` loop except the condition to be tested for looping is placed at the end of the loop. One major difference between the two types of loops is that the do while loop always executes the statement inside the curly braces at least once (since it doesn't test the condition until afterwards). The `while` loop may never execute the statements inside the curly braces (if the condition is `false`).

> **NOTE**
>
> Flash's do while loop is similar to `until` loops in other programming languages.

The syntax for the do while loop is:

```
do {
    statements;
} while ( condition );
```

The condition can be any valid Flash expression and is placed in parentheses after the while keyword. Note the use of a semicolon after the condition closing parenthesis. A simple example of a do while loop is:

```
do {
    statements;
    if ( condition) {
        num1 = 10;
    }
    statements;
} while ( num1 != 10 );
```

As with the while loop we could rewrite the for loop you saw earlier to loop 10 times using the do while loop:

```
i = 1;
do {
    statements;
    i++;
} while ( i < 10 )
```

The only problem that can occur with the do while loop is usually when you have a condition that is false from the start and you don't want to loop through the statements even once. This is often why you want to use the while statement instead of do while. The do while loop is best used for initializations and other setups.

Any of the loops seen previously can be added to an ActionScript program in the Actions list by selecting the loop from the toolbox. Any parameters that need to be specified can be added in the lower pane in normal mode, or typed directly into the loop command in expert mode.

Controlling Looping

Like many programming languages, Flash uses the break and continue keywords to enable control of loops. The break statement is used to cause the current loop to terminate completely. Whenever the break statement is encountered (usually as part of a condition statement), the loop terminates execution immediately and program flow continues past the closing curly brace.

> **CAUTION**
> The break and continue statements only have meaning inside a loop. Using them outside a loop usually has no effect, although behavior can be unpredictable at times.

An example of using the break statement is shown with the 10-loop program we used earlier, except in this case we want to cause the loop to terminate early if the value of the loop variable is set to 7:

```
for (i = 1; i <= 10; i++){
   statements_1;
   if ( i == 7 ) {
     break;
   }
   statements_2;
}
```

In this program the value of the variable increments normally from 1 to 10 unless the value is explicitly set to 7. When this occurs the if condition is true and the break statement is executed, causing the loop to terminate immediately. Execution proceeds from the closing curly brace of the loop. When the variable is set to seven, the statements called statements_1 are executed (because they are before the break), but the statements called statements_2 are not executed after the break.

> **TIP**
>
> Normally developers don't use the break statement to simply escape from loops, although you could use them to exit infinite loops. Usually, the break statement is reserved for handling error conditions (such as a variable with an illegal value).

The continue statement is used to restart a loop. Any statements below the continue statement to the end of the loop are not executed. When encountered, the continue statement simply sends the program flow back to the start of the loop and causes the condition controlling the loop (except for a do while loop) to be reevaluated.

The continue statement is used often, but it can be used to prevent specific statements from being executed under certain conditions. Normally, continue is used as part of an if condition, such as:

```
for (i = 1; i <= 10; i++){
   statements_1;
   if ( i == 7 ) {
     continue;
   }
   statements_2;
}
```

In this case, the continue statement will prevent the statements in statements_2 from being executed when the variable is set to 7. The loop is not terminated until the variable is set to 10, when the for loop condition fails.

Summary

In this chapter we've looked at the way Flash handles program flow using both conditions and loops. Flash provides four different loop statements, although there are really two variations on two loops. The condition statement is widely used in programs. You also saw the use of the `break` and `continue` statements to control the execution of statements inside a loop.

Sample Questions

1. Which of the following is not a valid Flash keyword?
   A. `else`
   B. `while`
   C. `elif`
   D. `do`

2. What is the primary difference between a `while` and a `do while` loop?
   A. The `break` statement cannot be used with a `do while` loop.
   B. Only one `if` statement can be used in a `while`, but any number can be used in a `do while`.
   C. The statements inside the loop are always executed at least once with the `do while`.
   D. A `continue` statement will terminate the `do while` as the condition is at the end.

3. Which of the following is *not* true?

   A. Functions should be defined in keyframes.
   B. Functions can overwrite primitive Flash functions.
   C. Functions can refer to movie clip events not loaded in the Timeline.
   D. Functions should always have parentheses and curly brace pairs.

CHAPTER 11

Code Reuse

In this last chapter of Part II, "Flash Development," you learn a couple of ways to reuse your code in other projects (or multiple times in one project). The two subjects we deal with specifically are the #include directive and the use of Smart Clips. Both require a little more work the first time they are used, but greatly pay back in time-saving that effort later. Code reuse is an important part of any developer's toolkit because it saves a lot of repeated work!

Includes

The #include directive enables you to import a file, usually containing ActionScript commands. This ability was added to Macromedia Flash 5 primarily to enable developers to create ActionScript programs external to Flash, using favorite editors and debuggers, and then incorporating the external file into a Flash action list. The external file is expected to have a .AS extension. When the FLA file is run (or an SWF file generated from the movie), the .AS files are included automatically through the use of the #include directive.

> **NOTE**
>
> The Flash #include directive is similar to the preprocessor #include directive used by high-level languages like C and C++. When expanded, the #include directive is replaced with the body of the file to be included.

The file to be included does not have to be a self-contained ActionScript program. It can be part of a program, including a custom-assembled library, it could be a set of initializations for variables or a collection of common data, or it could be a set of functions. As long as the statements included in the file are interpretable by ActionScript, they can be included in the action list. Most developers who write a lot of Flash scripts use .AS files to hold reusable code, and simply include it every time they start a new movie.

To include an external .AS file in an action list, use the #include directive anywhere in the list of commands that you want to include the code. It is common practice to place all includes at the top of the code, but this is not strictly necessary. The following is an example of using a #include with a couple of files to be added to the action list:

```
#include "myfunctions.as"
#include "includedata.as"
statements;
```

> **CAUTION**
>
> Note that there is no semicolon at the end of the #include statements. These are technically not ActionScript commands, but preprocessor directives and hence do not take a semicolon. If you do include a semicolon, you will see a malformed statement error when you try to run or test the movie.

The filename to be included is enclosed in quotation marks. The .AS files must be in the same directory as the FLA file; otherwise, it will not be included properly.

> **NOTE**
>
> A #include is only executed when you test or publish a movie. You will not see the .AS file included as part of the action list when writing code.

> **CAUTION**
>
> You cannot upload a .AS file to a Web server to be included in real-time into a Flash movie. If changes are made to the .AS file, the entire SWF file must be regenerated. Therefore, real-time updates using .AS files are not possible.

Smart Clips

Flash 5 added a new type of Library symbol: the Smart Clip. A Smart Clip is a movie clip that has properties or parameters associated with it. These properties are accessed through the Clip Parameter panel. The properties can be associated with any aspect of the clip, including objects that appear on the clip such as buttons.

> **TIP**
>
> Smart Clips are often used when you need to have the same movie clip or clip object several times in the same movie, but with slightly different presentations. Smart Clips enable you to reuse the movie clip, but attach the parameters to suit the needs in each instance. A simple example of a case where a Smart Clip is handy is a button that appears in each instance of a movie clip, but points to a different place in each instance.

Flash has three Smart Clip objects created in the Library and you can create your own custom Smart Clips. For now, let's deal with the existing Smart Clip objects, which are a radio button, a drop-down menu, and a check box. Any of the parameters for these three objects can be customized through the Clip Parameters panel.

Smart Clip Button and Check Box Objects

The two simplest Smart Clip objects are the check box and button. To handle these objects and their associated events in the Smart Clip, you want to set up the parameters to perform the desired actions. Start by creating a Smart Clip (Common Libraries, Smart Clips) and drag an instance of the object (button or check box) to the Stage. Make sure the keyframe to hold the object has been selected in the Timeline.

In the Clip Parameters window (using the context-sensitive menu item) you need to select a variable name, and then replace the value assigned to that variable. In the Value field, use any string you want for the button label, and leave the Type field set to `Default`. The `Default` setting is really the `string` setting; alternatives are `array`, `object`, and user-defined list. Using `Default` enables you to enter the button text in the Clip Parameters panel.

If we are setting a button that rewinds the movie to the start (or any other place for that matter) and stops playback, we can use the Actions panel to create the following function where `label` is a parameter defined in the Clip Parameters panel that tells the function where to jump to (such as a frame number).

```
on(releas(e){
    _root.gotoAndStop(label);
}
```

Smart Clip Menu Objects

The supplied drop-down menu Smart Clip object is a little more complicated than the check box or radio button, so we look at it in more detail. To create a menu object use the Smart Clips Library (Common Libraries, Smart Clips). After choosing the keyframe the Smart Clip resides in (often the first frame of the movie), drag an instance of the menu Smart Clip movie to the Stage. Select the instance on the Stage and open the Clip Parameters panel.

The top item in the panel is `Items: Array[]` and the second is `Style:Auto`. Double-click the `Array[]` entry and the Value dialog opens. Through this window you can create the items that are associated with the menu. There are several default values listed for which you can edit or delete and create new values. (To edit an existing entry double-click the name.) After completing the list of menu items, the window can be closed (use the OK button). If you examine the instance on the Stage, any changes you made through the Values panel do not show up. To see the new menu you need to test the movie (Control, Test movie).

The next step is to assign actions to the different menu items. To do this, again select the menu Smart Clip on the Stage and open the Clip Parameters window. At the bottom of the panel is a Description field with somewhat cryptic notes about using events, but essentially it explains that you have to use the movie-clip event handler to manage the menu selections. You can use the description area to provide instructions about using the Smart Clip you are working on, if you want.

An easy way to add a clip handler is to open the Clip Parameters window (using the context-sensitive menu) and copy the code in the Description area. Then open the Object Actions panel and paste the code there. The code in the Smart Clip looks like this:

```
// Define the following method in the onLoad() handler
// OnMenu() will be invoked whenever you select any items
// in the menu.
onClipEvent(load){
        function onMenu(item, label) {
        // item is a string in the form "itemXX" where "XX"
        //        is the item offset
        // label        - the text string for the item
        // your function's code can then go here
        }
}
```

Alternatively, you could use the Object Actions panel and add the function manually using Expert mode.

Usually, clip handlers have two arguments and you can call them anything you want, although descriptive names are best.

> **TIP**
>
> For debugging purposes, you may want to use trace() functions and remove them later if they are not necessary.

This process may seem a little confusing, so a quick example may help. Suppose you want to have a drop-down menu with four different background colors as items. In the Values window you would list the four colors (such as red, green, blue, yellow). Each is on a line of its own, and when you run the movie in test mode the pop-up menu should show the four menu items. Assuming this is working properly, you can now write the handler for the menu items. For now, a trace() message is displayed indicating your selection so we can cut down the amount of code in the function:

```
onClipEvent ( load ) {
   function onMenu ( choice, color ) {
   trace ("You selected the color " + color);
   }
}
```

When you run this in test mode, you should see messages in the Output window like this:

```
You selected the color red
You selected the color yellow
```

depending on the menu items you choose. If you do see this output, your menu item handler is working properly and you can expand the functions to perform whatever action you want.

> **NOTE**
>
> Most menu item functions have a series of if conditions to test what the user has selected and base the actions on that choice.

Summary

In this chapter we've looked at two ways you can reuse your code segments using #include directives and Smart Clips. Both are handy techniques that can be employed in just about all projects.

Sample Questions

1. Which of the following is true about #include commands?
    A. The included file must be in comma-separated variable format.
    B. A semicolon after the command causes an error.
    C. The included file cannot contain variables.
    D. ActionScript commands can be used in the file, but any loops are ignored.

2. What is the best definition of a Smart Clip?
    A. A movie clip that has other movie clips associated with it.
    B. A movie clip that has functions associated with it.
    C. A class of movie clips that has identical instances.
    D. A movie clip that loops automatically.

3. Which of the following is not a legal Smart Clip object?
    A. A clickable button
    B. A movie clip
    C. A check box
    D. A drop-down menu

PART III

FLASH OBJECTS

12   Using Objects

13   The `MovieClip` Object

14   Arrays

15   Color

16   Key

17   The Mouse Object

18   Sound

19   Other Objects

CHAPTER 12

Using Objects

Macromedia Flash defines objects as items that are placed on the Stage (as opposed to the more generic object-oriented definition of an object). When an object is on the Stage, you can do anything you want with it: modify its properties, drag it around to reshape or move it, copy it, color it, delete it, and so on. Many of these manipulations are performed with the drawing tools, but you can also use the Properties windows to alter the behavior of an object.

In this chapter (and throughout Part III, "Flash Objects") we look at objects in more detail, examining what they are, how you can manipulate each object, and the options and controls you have over them. We not only look at the visible objects such as shapes, buttons, and so on, but also at the more complex objects such as movie clips, sound clips, and others.

What Is an Object?

Without going into great depth about object-oriented programming, we can simply point out that Flash uses objects in much the same way as OO languages do. Every element used in a Flash movie has a particular data type, which simply defines the type of element it is (such as a button, movie clip, and so on). Flash has five data types: MovieClip, number, string, boolean, and object. (A movie clip is an object as well as a data type.) The term "object" can encompass many data types, and all abstract data types are objects in Flash.

Defined simply, an object in Flash is any element that has user-definable properties or actions, which can be set through the use of ActionScript commands. Because movie clips all have parameters and methods that can be set, they are objects and each instance of the movie clip type can have different property values.

Creating Objects

Objects can be created in two ways: using the new operator and using an object initial-izer operator (a pair of curly braces). The two are used for slightly different purposes. If you have an existing object class (either a Flash object or a custom-defined class), you use the new operator. If you are creating an object of the generic Flash Object type, you use the object initializer operator.

The new operator is used with a constructor function. The new operator creates an instance of the object (actually, it instantiates an instance of the object).

> **NOTE**
>
> A constructor function is a function that defines the type of object and the para-meters that are passed to it. They are similar to constructors in C, C++, and other languages although you don't have to specify passed arguments and return values.

For example, to create a new instance of the Sound object, you would use the com-mand:

```
mySound = new Sound();
```

The instance has the name mySound and is of object type Sound. It will inherit all the methods and properties of the Sound object that can be set individually for the instance.

Not all objects need a constructor. For example, the Key object never uses a construc-tor function.

For objects of the generic Object type, you use an object initializer operator. This is done like this:

```
myStuff = {val1: 5,  val2: "hello"};
```

The variables val1 and val2 are properties of the myStuff object and have assigned values in this instance.

After an instance has been created, you can access all the properties and methods of that instance using the instance name. For example, if you created the myStuff instance of a class mentioned earlier, you could access either of the properties using dot nota-tion like this:

```
myStuff.val1;
myStuff.val2;
```

If there were a method associated with the myStuff instance, you would access it the same way. For example, if there were a method called drawCircle that required a radius, you would call it like this to draw a circle of radius 50:

```
myStuff.drawCircle(50);
```

Summary

In this chapter we looked at objects and how Flash uses them. You've seen how to select objects on the Stage, how to create instances of objects, and how to access the properties and methods associated with an instance of an object.

Sample Questions

1. Which of the following will create a new instance of an object called `myDog`?

   A. `myInstance = new myDog;`

   B. `myDog = myInstance;`

   C. `myDog = new myInstance;`

   D. `new myDog myInstance;`

2. Which of the following will call a method called `myMethod` inside the instance `myDog`?

   A. `myMethod.myDog;`

   B. `myDog.myMethod;`

   C. `myDog.myMethod();`

   D. `myMethod(myDog);`

3. If you want to assign the value of the property `mySize` of the `myDog` instance to a variable called `myval`, which command would you use?

   A. `myDog.myval = mySize;`

   B. `mySize = myDog.myval;`

   C. `myval = myDog.mySize;`

   D. `myDog.mySize(myval);`

CHAPTER 13

The MovieClip Object

Macromedia Flash movies can be composed of one or more movie clips. Movie clips are controlled by various actions handled by ActionScript statements, as well as by methods of the MovieClip object. Flash included an object called MovieClip to provide nesting abilities and direct manipulation of movie clips. Many methods are attached to the MovieClip object, and we discuss those methods and how to use them in this chapter.

A movie clip has its own properties and a Timeline separate from other movie clips. To make handling movie clips easier, Flash includes the MovieClip object. The MovieClip object's methods and properties are designed to enable manipulation of movie clips, and handle each instance of a movie clip as a separate entity.

MovieClip Object Methods

The MovieClip object has many methods attached to it. Many of the methods are similar to standard ActionScript statements or other actions available through Flash menus, and some are available only through the use of the MovieClip object (and hence not available through the Actions panel).

The MovieClip object does not need a constructor, as each method is attached to the movie clip by direct reference. For example if you want to use the play method, it is called with the movie clip name that the method refers to. If the movie clip is called dogRunning, the play method is called using dogRunning.play().

The methods included with the MovieClip object are summarized in Table 13.1, along with a brief description of the methods' actions.

Table 13.1 MovieClip *Object Methods*

Method	Description
attachMovie	Attaches a movie from the library
duplicateMovieClip	Makes a duplicate of a movie clip
getBounds	Returns the minimum and maximum coordinates of the movie as x and y values
getBytesLoaded	Returns the loaded size of a movie clip in bytes
getBytesTotal	Returns the total size of a movie clip in bytes
getURL	Loads a document from the given URL
globalToLocal	Converts the object's Stage coordinates to the movie clip's local coordinates
gotoAndPlay	Positions the playhead at a specific frame and plays from that point on
gotoAndStop	Positions the playhead at a specific frame and stops the movie playing
hitTest	Returns a value of true if the bounding box of the movie clip intersects the bounding box of the target movie clip or object
loadMovie	Loads the specified movie
loadVariables	Loads variables from a URL or other location
localToGlobal	Converts a movie clip's local coordinates into the coordinates of the Stage
nextFrame	Positions the playhead at the next frame of the movie
play	Plays the movie
prevFrame	Positions the playhead at the previous frame of the movie
removeMovieClip	Removes the movie clip from the Timeline
startDrag	Indicates a movie clip is draggable and initiates dragging of the movie clip
stop	Stops playing the movie
stopDrag	Stops the dragging of a dragged movie clip
swapDepths	Swaps the depth level of the specific movie with the movie at a specific depth level in the Timeline
unloadMovie	Removes a movie that was loaded with loadMovie

We can take a quick look at some of these methods in more detail to show their use. Many of the methods also take arguments in the method call, so we'll look at the required argument list for those. All of the methods require the movie clip instance name, of course. Some of the methods (such as play and stop) are self-explanatory, so we'll skip those.

The attachMovie Method

The attachMovie method requires three arguments:

- The name of the movie to be attached which must be in the library and match the name in the Symbol Linkage Properties Identifier field

- A unique name for the new instance of the movie clip that is being attached
- The depth level where the new movie clip is to be placed (specified as an integer)

When called, the method creates a new instance of the movie and attaches it to the movie clip instance calling the method. For example, the following command creates a duplicate of the movie `dogJumping` from the library and calls the new instance `mydogJumping`:

```
myDog.attachMovie(dogJumping, "mydogJumping", 2);
```

This is then attached to the `myDog` movie clip at a depth level of 2.

> **NOTE**
>
> To remove a movie that has been attached using the `attachMovie` method, you need to use either `removeMovieClip` action or the `unloadMovie` method. While the `unloadMovie` method can be utilized, it should be avoided because it leaves an empty object reference; the `removeMovieClip` method is a better choice.

The `duplicateMovieClip` Method

The `duplicateMovieClip` method takes two arguments when called: the name of the duplicate movie that is created with this command (the name must be unique), and the depth level at which the movie is to be placed. Unlike the `attachMovie` method, the duplicate movie clip is not attached to an existing movie. An example of duplicating a movie clip using the `duplicateMovieClip` method is:

```
myDog.duplicateMovieClip("myDogCopy", 2);
```

This command creates a duplicate of the `myDog` movie clip, calls it `myDogCopy`, and places it at a depth level of 2.

The `duplicateMovieClip` method creates the duplicate that the movie is playing and positions that duplicate's playhead to the first frame on the Timeline (regardless of where the original movie's playhead is when the method is called).

> **NOTE**
>
> No variables are copied when the `duplicateMovieClip` method is called.

A movie clip that was created with the `duplicateMovieClip` method can be deleted with the `removeMovieClip` method or action of the same name.

> **CAUTION**
>
> If the parent movie clip is deleted, the duplicate movie clip is also deleted automatically.

The getBounds Method

The getBounds method is used to retrieve the minimum and maximum x and y coordinates (and hence define the bounding box) of the movie clip in the coordinate space used by the single argument. The argument is any target path that is to be used as a reference point. For example, the following code retrieves the coordinates of the bounding box for myDog in the main Timeline movie:

```
myDog.getBounds(_root);
```

The coordinates are returned as the properties xMin, xMax, yMin, and yMax, which obviously refer to the minimum and maximum x and y coordinates.

> **TIP**
>
> You can convert the coordinates returned by getBounds by using the localToGlobal and globalToLocal methods.

The getBytesLoaded and getBytesTotal Methods

The getBytesLoaded and getBytesTotal methods return the number of bytes that have been loaded (or streamed) and the total size respectively of a movie clip. The getBytesTotal method actually shows you the size of the SWF file if the movie clip is external. The two methods are used with no arguments. Examples of using these two methods are:

```
myload = myDog.getBytesLoaded();
mytotal = myDog.getBytesTotal();
```

In these two lines, we're storing the results from the method calls into two variables that can be used later. Because internal movie clips are loaded automatically, both the getBytesLoaded and getBytesTotal methods return the same value for internal clips. For non-internal movie clips, the two may be different and a simple calculation can show the percentage of the movie clip that has been loaded. This can be used for a slider display to show the viewer progress of the clip.

> **TIP**
>
> The getBytesLoaded method is used on loaded clips only; otherwise, no value is returned.

The globalToLocal and localToGlobal Methods

The two methods globalToLocal and localToGlobal are used to convert between the coordinate system used on the Stage (global) to the coordinate system used in a movie clip (local). Both methods require a single argument that specifies the name or an identifier of an object created using the object object, which has x and y coordinates.

An example of using the globalToLocal method shows how to store the current x and y coordinates of a cursor on the Stage and convert them to local coordinates for a movie clip:

```
onClipEvent(mouseMove){
    myName = new object();
    myName.xpos = _root._xmouse;
    myName.ypos = _root._ymouse;
    globalToLocal(myName);
}
```

The `localToGlobal` method is used in the same way to convert a movie clip's coordinates (local) to the Stage's coordinates (global):

```
onClipEvent(mouseMove){
    myName = new object();
    myName.xpos =_xmouse;
    myName.ypos =_ymouse;
    localToGlobal(myName);
}
```

You can convert between the local and global coordinate systems as many times as you want in a movie.

The `hitTest` Method

The `hitTest` method is used to determine if a movie clip overlaps or intersects the hit area of another object. This method can be used in two ways. The easiest is to specify a single argument, an object name (usually a button or text field), and `hitTest` returns a value of `true` if the two intersect or overlap. For example, the command:

```
myDog.hitTest(_root.myCat);
```

will return `true` if `myDog` intersects or overlaps the movie clip `myCat`.

The second way to use the `hitTest` method is to specify three arguments, two representing the x and y coordinates of the hit area on the Stage, and the last argument with a value of either `true` or `false`. The last argument is called the `shapeflag` and if `true` means the entire shape of the instance is to be considered, or `false` meaning only the bounding box is to be considered. For example, the following command uses the current x and y mouse properties to see whether the mouse is over the shape of the `myDog` movie clip:

```
myDog.hitTest(_root._xmouse, _root._ymouse, true);
```

You could use the same approach to check whether a movie clip instance is in the proper position on the Stage, for example, or to see if one movie clip obscures another.

> **TIP**
>
> The coordinates used by `hitTest` are relative to the Stage. You can use the `localToGlobal` and `globalToLocal` methods to convert coordinate systems.

The `loadMovie` and `unloadMovie` Methods

The `loadMovie` method (or the action of the same name) is used to play additional movies without closing the Player. This can be a useful method of adding more movies to the playlist without generating new HTML pages. Most developers use this method to simply string multiple movies together, one after another, but it can also be used for some special effects such as running banners (either for advertisements or data displays) and providing navigation controls for a user.

> **TIP**
>
> The `loadMovie` method can also be used to send data (variables and their values) to a CGI script or other external application that can be used to generate an SWF file on the fly.

The `unloadMovie` method is used to remove a movie that was previously loaded using the `loadMovie` method. Use this method to remove movies from the Player stack, to reduce the amount of memory required.

The `startDrag` and `stopDrag` Methods

The `startDrag` and `stopDrag` methods enable viewers to drag a movie clip. After the `startDrag` method has been called, the movie clip is draggable until a `stopDrag` is executed.

The `startDrag` method is called with five parameters, all optional. The first argument is a boolean that indicates whether the movie clip that is about to be made draggable is locked to the center of the mouse position (if `true`) or locked to the where the user first clicks on the movie clip (if `false`). The remaining four parameters are coordinates relative to the movie clip that constrain the dragging rectangle. The coordinates are given as left, right, top, and bottom, respectively. For example, the following command, by itself, means the move clip is draggable anywhere:

```
myDog.startDrag();
```

On the other hand, this command means the clip is draggable within the rectangle coordinates specified and that the dragging is locked to the center of the mouse position:

```
myDog.startDrag(true, 10, 150, 20, 100);
```

> **NOTE**
>
> Only one movie clip is draggable at a time. If another movie clip is made draggable, the current draggable movie clip ceases to be draggable.

The `swapDepths` Method

The `swapDepths` method is used to swap the depth levels (also called the stacking order) of two movies. Both movies must have the same parent clip to be swappable. To use `swapDepths` an argument indicating the second movie has to be specified. For example, the following command swaps the depth levels of the `myDog` and `myCat` movies:

```
myDog.swapDepths(myCat);
```

Using `MovieClip` Methods

Any of the `MovieClip` object methods can be assigned to execute based on the action of buttons on the Stage, entering a frame in the Timeline, or using a movie clip instance. Examples of the ActionScript code for many methods were shown earlier.

When attaching actions to a movie clip you have to use handlers. The `onClipEvent` handler is used for these methods when an event triggers the action (either a Timeline event or a user event). You can use several `onClipEvent` triggers, including `mouseMove`, which results in an action trigger whenever the user moves the mouse.

MovieClip Properties

The `MovieClip` object has several properties attached to it. These are summarized with a description of the property in Table 13.2.

Table 13.2 `MovieClip` Object Properties

Property	Description
_alpha	Sets or returns the alpha transparency of the movie clip
_currentframe	The number of the frame where the playhead is located
_droptarget	The instance name of the movie clip that this movie clip was dropped on after a drag operation
_focusrect	Defines whether a yellow rectangle appears around the button with current focus (if `true` the yellow rectangle appears; if `false` it doesn't)
_framesloaded	The number of frames of a streamed or loaded movie that are currently loaded
_height	The height of the movie in pixels
_highquality	Specifies if antialiasing is applied globally
_name	The name of the instance
_quality	A string indicating the rendering quality to be used globally
_rotation	The rotation of the movie clip in degrees
_soundbuftime	The number of seconds before the streaming of a sound begins.
_target	The path of the movie clip
_totalframes	The total number of frames in the movie
_url	The URL of the SWF file
_visible	Indicates whether the movie is visible (`false` makes them invisible; `true` makes them visible)
_width	Width of the movie in pixels
_x	Sets the x coordinate of the movie relative to the local coordinates of the movie clip
_xmouse	The x coordinate of the mouse position

Table 13.2 **Continued**

Property	Description
_xscale	The horizontal scale of the movie clip from the registration point
_y	The height of the movie in pixels
_ymouse	Sets the y coordinate of the movie relative to the local coordinates of the movie clip
_yscale	The vertical scale of the movie clip from the registration point

Many of the properties attached to the MovieClip object are read-only. Some of the properties are self-explanatory, but a few require a little explanation. These are covered in the following sections.

The _alpha Property

The _alpha property sets or retrieves (depending on how it is used) the alpha transparency of a movie clip. The property is set equal to a value which can range from 0 (full transparency) to 100 (zero transparency), such as:

```
myDog._alpha = 0;
```

The current setting can be retrieved by assigning the value to a variable, such as:

```
myAlpha = myDog._alpha;
```

Any object that has an alpha setting of zero (full transparency) is still active even though it is not visible. This is true for any objects in the movie. For example, you can create an invisible button by setting the alpha to zero, but the button can still be clicked even though it is not visible.

The _quality Property

The _quality property indicates the amount of rendering that should be applied to a movie. The more rendering applied, the better the quality of the movie. The render quality also affects the playback speed; the higher the render quality the slower the playback. There are four possible values for the _quality property, supplied as strings:

- BEST: Very high rendering quality with anitaliasing and smoothed bitmaps
- HIGH: Antialiasing applied with bitmap smoothing if no animation involved
- MEDIUM: Anitaliasing applied, but at a lower level than the higher settings, no bitmap smoothing
- LOW: No antialiasing and no bitmap smoothing

These values can be set using statements like this:

```
_quality = "BEST";
```

> **NOTE**
> The Flash default for the _quality property is HIGH.

Summary

In this chapter we've looked at the MovieClip object's methods and properties. These are used all the time when creating movies in Flash, and many of the properties and methods are useful for controlling the behavior of a clip inside the Flash Player.

Sample Questions

1. Which of these MovieClip methods will create a new instance of a movie currently in the library?

   A. new MovieClip("myDog", 1);

   B. myDog.attachMovie(dogJumping, "myDog", 1);

   C. myDog.createMovie(myDog, 1)

   D. myDog.attachMovie("myDog", 1);

2. Which statement is true about the duplicateMovieClip method?

   A. The depth of the duplicate will be set one lower than the movie it is duplicate from.

   B. The duplicate has no properties.

   C. The _visible property of the duplicate is set to true.

   D. The instance name will have _copy attached.

3. Which property would you set to control the antialiasing and bitmap smoothing of a movie during rendering?

   A. _quality

   B. _highquality

   C. _render

   D. _renderquality

CHAPTER 14

Arrays

Arrays are a construct that often confuses developers who have not programmed in other languages. They are an important facet of Macromedia Flash, though, and should be well understood for those who want to program in ActionScript.

An *array* is a series of variables of the same data type, all referenced by the same name. Arrays in Flash are similar to arrays in other high-level languages. In languages such as C, C++, and others, arrays are subscripted variables of a single data type, such as num[1], num[2], and so on. The number in the square brackets is the index, and refers to the *n*th occurrence of the data type sequence. Flash handles arrays in exactly the same way.

The name before the square brackets identifies the variable itself. Technically, Flash handles arrays by assigning a series of memory locations, all contiguous, for the array values. For example, if you have an array of 10 numbers, there are 10 memory spaces for numbers, one after another. Although the array is referenced by a single name, the index number indicates which particular number in the array is required. Like C, C++, and similar languages, Flash uses a zero-origin numbering scheme where the first array element is [0], the second is [1], and so on. The index is used to calculate the offset from the starting memory location that the variables are stored in.

> **TIP**
>
> For those confused by arrays, the easiest way to think of them is like a set of numbered variables. Instead of having five variables called num1, num2, num3, num4, and num5, an array uses one single name such as num, and a reference to the five variables in sequence. Because the numbering starts at zero, the five variables are num[0], num[1],

> num[2], num[3], and num[4]. The advantage to an array is that all the values are con-
> tiguous in memory, which can be handy for loop programming. Also, arrays can
> be any size, and are much easier to create and define values for than individual
> variables.

The square brackets after the variable name are called array access operators and contain the index of the exact variable wanted.

Where Flash arrays differ from arrays in other high-level languages is that Flash doesn't impose the same type of data type on each element in an array. With C or C++, for example, every element in an array must be of the same type. With Flash, the first element could be a string, the second a number, the third another number, and so on. Mixed data type arrays are no problem with Flash.

Another difference between Flash arrays and other languages is that the length of the array does not have to be fixed in advance. Array length can be increased at any time (or reduced, for that matter). This is similar to the Vector class in the Java programming language.

Creating and Populating Arrays

To create an array you need to first use a constructor function to instantiate the array, and then fill the array with data. The easiest way to create an array is to use the Array object, a predefined object in Flash. Because the constructor is part of the Flash object, it can be called using the new keyword. For example, if you want to create an array called testArray, you would do so like this:

```
testArray = new Array();
```

As with high-level languages you can populate the array at the same time you instantiate it, as you will see in a moment.

The array created in this way can be populated in several ways. Of course, you can assign individual values to array elements using their index, like this:

```
testArray[0] = 10;
testArray[1] = 15;
testArray[2] = 12;
testArray[3] = "end";
```

However, this approach is time-consuming for all but the smallest arrays. (Note the mixing of data types in the previous example; the last element is a string while the others are all numbers.) If you do want to manually assign the values for the array elements, you could do so at the same time as calling the constructor. Using the previous examples, the statement would look like this:

```
testArray = new Array ( 10, 15, 12, "end");
```

Each value is assigned to array elements separated by commas. Flash assigns the elements in order until there are no more arguments. Another way to populate an array is to use a loop, as you will see in the next section.

Array Methods

Array objects in Flash have several methods attached to them. These methods can be called at any time to enable you to add or delete data in the array, move it around by sorting, and concatenate in several ways. The methods for array objects are shown in Table 14.1.

Table 14.1   Array Methods

Method	Description
concat (arr1, arr2,...arrN)	Concatenates the specified array elements into a new array
join(sep)	Concatenates elements of an array inserting sep as a separator between elements, returning a sep-delimited string (the default separator is a comma)
pop()	Removes the last element in the array and returns that element's value
push(elem)	Adds elem to the end of the array and returns the new array length
reverse()	Reverses the order of elements in the array
shift()	Removes the first element of the array and returns that value
slice(arr1, arr2)	Creates a new array from the existing array using elements arr1 through arr2-1, respectively (both counted from zero)
sort()	Sorts the array in alphabetical order
splice(index, count, arr1, arr2)	Inserts elements arr1 through arr2 at the index element number when count = 0; when count > 0 deletes that number of elements starting at index
toString()	Concatenates every element with a comma and returns the resultant string
unshift(elem)	Adds elem to the beginning of the array and returns the new array length

To call any of these methods, they are appended as a dot operator with the array name as usual for calling an object's methods. Some of these methods are very similar. For example, the toString() method is the same as using join() with a comma separator. We can see its operation like this:

```
testArray = new Array (1,2,3,4,5);
str1 = testArray.toString();
str2 = testArray.join(,);
str3 = testArray.join();
```

All these methods result in the string variable having the value "1,2,3,4,5". The join() method can be used with the comma specified or left off to use the default value (which is a comma).

> **TIP**
>
> The concat(), join(), slice(), and toString() methods all result in a new array or a string result. The other array methods do not. It is important to keep in mind which array methods create new arrays or strings.

Methods can be combined in subsequent commands, such as using sort() to create an ascending order array then using reverse() to reverse to a descending order array. For example, the following code orders the elements in testArray in descending order (a temporary array variable was used to hold the sorted array first).

```
tempArray = testArray.sort();
testArray = tempArray.reverse();
```

The pop() and push() operators are similar to those in other programming languages. They add to, or remove, elements from the end of an array and assign the values to variables. For example, the pop() and push() methods have these effects on an array:

```
testArray = new Array (1,2,3,4,5);
num1 = testArray.pop();
num2 = testArray.pop();
```

At this point, testArray has the value of (1,2,3). Note that the pop() method not only changes the array, but also outputs a value, which is the array element's value that was popped. The array can now be added to like this:

```
testArray.push(7);
testArray.push(8);
testArray.push(9);
```

This results in testArray having the value (1,2,3,7,8,9). To add to the beginning of the array, the unshift() method is used:

```
testArray.unshift(6);
```

This results in the value of (6,1,2,3,7,8,9). You can add multiple values at once using the push() and unshift() methods by using a comma separator:

```
testArray.unshift(4,5);
testArray.push(1,2,3);
```

This results in testArray having the value (4,5,6,1,2,3,7,8,9,1,2,3).

The concat() method is used to add a new element to an array and output a new array entirely, which must be assigned like this:

```
testArray = new Array (1,2,3,4,5);
newArray = testArray.concat(1,2,3);
```

This results in the newArray array having the value (1,2,3,4,5,1,2,3).

The splice() method is probably the most complicated method (and the cause of the most confusion among developers). The important thing to remember with splice() is that the value of the second argument determines whether elements are added or deleted. For example:

```
testArray = new Array (1,2,3,4,5);
testArray.splice(1,3);
```

This results in the removal of three elements starting with the number 1 element so the result is a value of (1,5). (Remember zero-origin rules means the 1 element is actually the second element in the array.) To insert elements into the array using splice() you need to specify a second argument as zero and give the elements to be added:

```
testArray = new Array (1,2,3,4,5);
testArray.splice(1,0,6,7,8);
```

This results in the array having the value (1,6,7,8,2,3,4,5).

Loops and Arrays

As mentioned earlier in this chapter, loops are ideal for working with arrays because of the incremental nature of the array access operators. A variable can be used to step through all the elements in the array, either assigning or calculating values.

The simplest way to see a loop used with an array is to populate an array with 10 numbers, from 11 through 20, using this code:

```
testArray = new Array();
for (i=0; i < 10; i++) {
    var myVal = 11;
    testArray[i] = myVal;
    myVal++;
}
```

In this code, a counter called i is used to step through the loop ten times. A local variable called myVal holds a value starting at 11. The first time through, i has a value of 0 and myVal has a value of 11, so testArray[0] is assigned the value 11. The myVal value is incremented by one by the last line in the code block, and then i increments and the loop repeats. This continues until the value of i reaches 10, at which point the for condition fails and the loop terminates. The array testArray has the values from 11 through 20 in the testArray[0] through testArray[9] locations, respectively.

More often you use loops to manipulate the data in an array. For example, suppose the array testArray holds scores in a test, and we want to have the average score from the first 10 values in the array. Assuming testArray is already populated, the code for the average would be:

```
var myAverage = 0;
var mySum = 0;
```

```
var i = 0;
for (i=0; i < 10; i++) {
    mySum = mySum + testArray[I];
}
myAverage = mySum / i;
```

In this program, after initializing two variables to zero, the loop is used to step through the 10 values in the array. In each loop, the variable mySum has the value of the array's element added to it. After the loop terminates, the average is calculated by dividing the sum by the number of loops. We could have written the division by 10 instead, but this enables us to easily change the number of times to loop without checking for other locations that need to be changed. Notice we declared the variable i outside the loop so that it has value outside the loop. Otherwise, the variable would have had an undefined value when we divided for the average.

Flash enables us to calculate the number of elements in an array another way, using the length property. To do this, we would have written the last line of code as:

```
myAverage = mySum / testArray.length;
```

This accomplishes the same result as earlier if the array has been stepped through all the elements, but could cause problems if the array has more than the 10 elements we checked. You have to be aware of limitations like this when working with arrays.

To show how this kind of setup could be used in a movie, we can attach the code for computing the average to a button on the Stage. Using the mouse event handler, the code would be written in ActionScript attaching it to the button click like this:

```
on (releas(e){
    var myAverage = 0;
    var mySum = 0;
    var i = 0;
    for (i=0; i < 10; i++) {
        mySum = mySum + testArray[I];
    }
    myAverage = mySum / i;
}
```

Here, when the mouse event occurs the averaging is performed. Any ActionScript commands can be attached to an event, as you saw earlier, so it is easy to perform array manipulations as part of an event.

Summary

In this chapter we've looked at arrays and how Flash deals with them. You've seen the methods that are provided with the array data type, as well as how you can use array indexing in loops to perform manipulations. Arrays are a powerful data type when dealing with lots of raw data, and are easy to manipulate with ActionScript.

Sample Questions

1. If testArray has the value (1,2,3,4) what is the value of num1 from the command num1 = testArray[3]?
   A. 1
   B. 2
   C. 3
   D. 4

2. If testArray has the value ("dog", "cat", "mouse", "parrot") what is the value of testArray.length?
   A. 3
   B. 4
   C. 5
   D. 6

3. If testArray = (1,2,3,4,5) what is the result of testArray.splice(1,2)?
   A. 1,2,3,4,5,1,2
   B. 1,2,4,5
   C. 1,4,5
   D. 3,4,5

CHAPTER 15

Color

The Color object is used by Macromedia Flash to enable you to set and retrieve the RGB (Red-Green-Blue) color values and transforms of a movie clip. Although this may seem relatively boring, the use of the Color object does offer some interesting effects on the user interface of a movie. For example, you can enable the user to create new color schemes (called "skins") for a Flash movie or choose their own color preferences for interfaces and the player environment. You can also use the Color object methods to perform instant color changes for a movie when key events are reached.

Color Object Methods

The Color Object includes four methods (actually two pairs of get and set methods) that are used to manage the RGB values used in Flash movies. The methods and their purposes are summarized in Table 15.1.

Table 15.1   Color Object Methods

Method	Description
getRGB	Returns the RGB value used in a movie as a number
getTranforms	Returns the transform information used in a movie
setRGB	Sets the RGB value for a Color object as a hexadecimal value
setTransform	Sets the color transform for a Color object

The Color object methods require a constructor when creating a new instance of the Color object prior to calling any of these methods. The constructor is created with the new keyword, like this:

```
myColor = new Color(myDog);
```

myDog is the name of the movie and myColor is the name of the new instance of the Color object. Instances of the Color object are always created with reference to the movie to which they apply.

After an instance of the Color object has been created, the get and set methods for the RGB and transform methods can be used. The setRGB method is used to set the color using a hexadecimal representation of the red, green, and blue components of the color. This method is called as a method in the instance created, like this:

```
myColor.setRGB(0x993355);
```

This sets the RGB value of myColor to 99 for red, 33 for green, and 55 for blue. The preceding "0x" is used to indicate a hexadecimal value and is necessary as part of the argument.

An RGB value can be read from a Color instance using the getRGB method, which returns numeric values. To retrieve the current setting of myColor use the following command, which stores the value in the variable val1:

```
val1 = myColor.getRGB();
```

> **TIP**
>
> Most developers prefer to retrieve the RGB value as a string, which can be accomplished using the toString method to convert the number.

The color transform information is set using the setTranform method and read using getTransform. The parameters in a transform method are in a sequence of values and numbers. The parameters for transforms are shown in Table 15.2.

Table 15.2   *Color Object Transform Parameters*

Parameter	Description
aa	The percentage for alpha (–100 to 100)
ab	The offset for alpha (–255 to 255)
ba	The percentage of blue component (–100 to 100)
bb	The offset for the blue component (–255 to 255)
ga	The percentage of green component (–100 to 100)
gb	The offset for the green component (–255 to 255)
ra	The percentage of red component (–100 to 100)
rb	The offset for the red component (–255 to 255)

> **NOTE**
>
> The parameters involved in a transform refer to either RGB values or offset values. RGB values are percentage-based and range from –100% to 100%. Transform values are offset-based and range from –255 to 255. These values are actually derived from a 24-bit RGB color space using 8-bit color channels (which allows 256 values).

The way to set these transform values is to specify them as hexadecimal values in the argument of the setTransform method in this order:

RRGGBBAA

RGB are the red, green, and blue values and AA is the alpha (transparency) value. The values are set after the parameter names and their values specified as strings, like this:

```
myColor.setTransform( ra: '25', rb: '200', ga: '10', gb: '100', ba: '-12',
➡bb: '30', aa: '25', ab: '100');
```

You can also use the individual parameters and set them individually, like this:

```
myColor.ra = 25;
myColor.rb = 200;
myColor.ga = 10;
myColor.gb = 100;
myColor.ba = -12;
myColor.bb = 30;
myColor.aa = 25;
myColor.ab = 100;
```

The getTransform method returns all this information in the same way:

```
myTransform1 = myColor.getTransform();
```

This assigns the values to the variable myTransform1.

Summary

In this chapter we've looked at the four methods involved in the Color object. These methods enable you to set and retrieve both the RGB value and the transform values for a Color instance. These Color object methods can be used for many effects and customization of a user interface, as well as the appearance of the movie in a Flash player.

Sample Questions

1. If you want to create a new instance of a Color object called myColor to handle the color settings of a movie called myMovie, which ActionScript command accomplishes the task?
   A. myColor = new Color(myMovie);
   B. myColor.myMovie.add Color;
   C. new Color(myMovie, myColor);
   D. myMovie.add Color(myColor);

2. In which order are the parameters for a setTransform command given?
   A. Red, Green, Blue, Alpha
   B. Alpha, Blue, Green, Red
   C. Blue, Green, Red, Alpha
   D. Alpha, Red, Green, Blue

3. Which statement is not true about Color transforms?

   A. Values are set using hexadecimal.
   B. The alpha value indicates the transparency.
   C. Values for offsets range from –255 to 255.
   D. Red offsets and percentages can be specified without reference to the other colors.

CHAPTER 16

Key

Macromedia Flash includes the Key object to help design interface elements controlled through the keyboard. The Key object lets you determine the state of keys pressed by a user and perform actions based on that key's identity. To do this the Key object has a few methods that help you identify the last key pressed, and a number of properties (all of which are constants representing ASCII values). Using simple if statements, you can both detect the last key pressed, as well as perform actions based on the key.

Every key on a Windows or Macintosh keyboard has a value associated with it. These are usually ASCII values, also called key codes. Some keys have more than one value associated with them, especially those special function keys that are now appearing on keyboards.

Key Object Methods

The Key object contains a number of methods that are used for handling keyboard interactions. The Key object methods are summarized in Table 16.1, showing both the method name and a description of the method's purpose.

Table 16.1   Key Object Methods

Method	Description
getAscii	Returns the ASCII value of the last-pressed key
getCode	Returns the virtual key code of the last-pressed key
isDown	Returns true if the key in the argument is the last-pressed key
isToggled	Returns true if the Num Lock or Caps Lock key is active

These four methods can be combined with the Key object properties, as you will see in the next section. This enables you to test for a specific value for a pressed key.

The Key object does not need a constructor function to be used. To use any of the methods, you simply call the method with the object itself, like this:

```
Key.isDown();
```

Most of the time, the Key methods are used with the onClipEvent handler.

Key Object Properties

The Key object has a number of properties associated with it. All of the Key object properties are treated as constants by Flash. The properties are summarized in Table 16.2.

Table 16.2 *Key Object Properties*

Property	Description
BACKSPACE	ASCII value 9; backspace key
CAPSLOCK	ASCII value 20; Caps Lock key
CONTROL	ASCII value 17; Control key
DELETEKEY	ASCII value 46; delete key
DOWN	ASCII value 40; down-arrow key
END	ASCII value 35; end key
ENTER	ASCII value 13; enter key
ESCAPE	ASCII value 27; escape key
HOME	ASCII value 36; home key
INSERT	ASCII value 45; insert key
LEFT	ASCII value 37; left-arrow key
PGDN	ASCII value 34; PgDn key
PGUP	ASCII value 33; PgUp key
RIGHT	ASCII value 39; right-arrow key
SHIFT	ASCII value 16; shift key
SPACE	ASCII value 32; space key
TAB	ASCII value 9; tab key
UP	ASCII value 38; up-arrow key

All of these properties are self-explanatory. You can use these properties with the Key object methods you saw in the previous section. For example, if you want to see if the user has pressed the Up-arrow key on the keyboard, you would use the Key object's isDown method with the constant UP, like this:

```
onClipEvent (enterFrame) {
    if (Key.isDown (Key.UP) {
        statements;
    }
}
```

In this code, the onClipEvent handler is used and triggered when a new frame is entered. Then the Key object's isDown method is called to check whether the key pressed is the same as the UP constant (ASCII 38). If it is, the statements inside the if statement would be executed.

Summary

In this chapter we've looked at the Key object and the methods and properties associated with it. You have seen a simple example of combining the method with the properties to assess the last key pressed by a user. Obviously, using several of these constructs together enables you to create a user interface with many controls and determines the user's requirements either by using a button event or a keyboard press. Providing both mouse and keyboard interfaces is good practice for all movies, as user preferences differ.

Sample Questions

1. Which of the Key methods would you use to tell if a user pressed the CapsLock key?
   A. isDown
   B. isToggled
   C. getAsci
   D. getCode

2. Which statement is true about Key objects?
   A. A constructor is required.
   B. Key methods can be used to detect mouse button clicks.
   C. A Key method can be used to refer to a Key property.
   D. A Key method cannot tell you which key a user last pressed.

3. Which of the following is not a legal Key property?
   A. TAB
   B. ESCAPE
   C. RETURN
   D. LEFT

CHAPTER 17

The Mouse Object

The mouse is usually an integral part of a Macromedia Flash movie, both because it enables the user to interact with elements in the movie (such as buttons and pull-down menus) and because the mouse enables control of the movie Player—resizing the window, closing the Player, and other basic actions. In Flash terms, the mouse can do more, including manipulating the onscreen cursor attached to the mouse. This is done through the Mouse object. Mouse properties are only affected when the user's cursor is on top of a Flash movie. The properties do not affect the mouse when the user has rolled away from the browser window or Flash movie in an HTML page.

In this chapter we look at the Mouse object supplied as part of the Flash ActionScript language. The Mouse object is used to hide and show the cursor.

Mouse Object Methods

The Mouse object has two methods attached to it: hide and show. As the names imply the hide method hides the cursor within a movie and the show method displays the cursor in the movie. No arguments exist for either method.

> **NOTE**
>
> The mouse cursor is always visible by default. It must be hidden using the Mouse.hide method to render the cursor invisible in a movie.

The hide method can be attached to a Timeline and when executed it hides the standard mouse cursor. The easiest way to use the method is to simply call it when a frame is entered on the Timeline. This can be done in many ways, such as with the onClipEvent handler like this:

```
onClipEvent(enterFrame){
    Mouse.hide();
}
```

The Mouse object `hide` method can be used to hide the cursor, while a movie clip can be substituted as a custom cursor. The `hide` method and x/y `customCursor` values are used like this:

```
onClipEvent(enterFrame){
    Mouse.hide();
    customCursorMC_x = _root._xmouse;
    customCursorMC_y = _root._ymouse;
}
```

> **NOTE**
>
> The `root._xmouse` and `root._ymouse` values are the current mouse cursor positions when the mouse is hidden. These are assigned to the `customCursor` x and y positions. Both `xmouse` and `ymouse` are read-only properties.

The Mouse `show` method displays the cursor after it has been invisible. The method call to display the cursor is simple:

```
onClipEvent(enterFrame){
    Mouse.show();
}
```

Summary

In this chapter we've looked at the Mouse object's two methods and seen how to use them to control whether the pointer is visible or not.

Sample Questions

1. If a `show` method is used on a movie that is already visible, what happens?
   A. The cursor blinks.
   B. Nothing visible happens.
   C. The cursor is hidden.
   D. An error is generated by ActionScript.

2. Which statement is true about the mouse cursor?
   A. It is always visible by default.
   B. It inherits the show or hide setting from the parent movie.
   C. If not explicitly set to hide, the cursor inherits the setting from the movie one level up.
   D. The cursor is only visible if a `show` method is in the first frame of the movie.

CHAPTER 18

Sound

The effective use of sound (both sound effects and continuous sounds like music) contributes greatly to the effectiveness and attractiveness of a movie. Macromedia Flash enables you to use sound in a number of ways. You can attach a sound or sound effect to an object in a movie, such as when a button is pressed. You can provide a running background soundtrack as streaming audio. You can synchronize a soundtrack to a movie's events. In short, you can use sounds to enhance your movies and provide a feedback mechanism for the viewer.

Rather than simply enabling you to attach prerecorded sounds to a movie Timeline or objects, Flash goes further and gives you some editing capabilities to tailor the sounds to your needs. You can fade music or sound effects in and out, cross-fade between multiple sounds, or modify sounds to some extent. While Flash is not as complete a sound editing software package as some dedicated sound manipulation tools, you will find Flash has enough power to suit most of your requirements. (You can always use a sound recording, editing, and manipulation software package outside of Flash and import the results.)

In this chapter we discuss how Flash uses sound file objects and how you can incorporate them into your movies. We spend a little time looking at the nature of recorded sound for movies, and how Flash provides editing features for your use. We start with a look at digital sampling rates and how they affect both the quality of the sound produced in a movie, and the file size that is required to store the sound.

Sound Sampling

Flash uses digital audio for sounds and sound effects. (The term digital simply means that the waveforms, whether recorded by analog or digital means, are stored and manipulated as a series of digital values that are converted to analog on playback.) Because sound is stored digitally, the amount of information that is to be stored affects the size of the file. This much is obvious, of course. What is perhaps not so obvious is the amount of information per second's sound is reproduced and how that affects the size of the file, as well as the overall quality of the sound.

In nature we hear sound all around us. All sounds have a frequency (often called pitch) that tells us whether the sound is low or high. The higher the sound pitch, the more cycles per second the sound involves. To give a couple of simple examples, a bass drum on a drum set vibrates relatively slowly producing around 50 cycles per second (Hertz is the proper term, abbreviated Hz, which simply means cycles per second). A violin produces higher-pitched sounds, including some around 2,000Hz. The number of cycles per second is called the frequency of the sound. Violins have a higher frequency than bass drums.

All sounds have a frequency, and related to the frequency is the wavelength (it actually has an inverse relationship). The higher the frequency, the shorter the wavelength. You can think of this like a series of waves in the ocean. With a big rolling swell such as those loved by surfers, the waves come in slowly and have a good amount of distance between the peaks. The distance between the peaks is the wavelength. On the other hand, if you throw a rock in a pond a series of concentric waves appear, with a short distance between peaks. The relationship between wavelength and frequency is a constant, depending on the medium the wave travels through.

> **NOTE**
>
> In air, the constant varies a little depending on altitude and air pressure, but all sounds will have the same relationships between frequency and wavelength at the same place.

Returning to our violin and bass drum, we can see the effects on sound. Because the speed of sound is the same in air for both bass drums and violins, both sounds arrive at your ear at the same time when played simultaneously. The bass drum has a low frequency and hence a long wavelength. The violin has a higher frequency and a shorter wavelength.

Humans can hear sounds in a specific band of frequencies. Most people can hear sounds as low as 20Hz (below this, the sounds are felt more than heard). The only musical instruments that can generate sounds this low are extremely long organ pipes (called diapasons) and electrically generated notes from synthesizers. At the upper end of the frequencies, children can often hear up to 18,000Hz (abbreviated to 18kHz for kilohertz), but we lose hearing in the upper frequencies as we age. By the time a person is 40, upper hearing is in the area of 14kHz, and drops even more as he gets older. This isn't as big a deal as it may sound because even the highest notes produced by an orchestra are well below this range. What we do hear in this range are overtones: naturally occurring multiples of the base frequency. For example, if you hear a violin note played at 2,000Hz, you will also hear an overtone at 4,000Hz, another much fainter at 8,000Hz, and there may be one at very low level at 16,000Hz. It is the overtones in a musical instrument that make it sound distinct and warm, as opposed to an electrically generated tone with no overtones.

All of this is useful to know when we look at storing sounds for Flash movies. While we could theoretically hear sounds from around 20Hz to 15,000Hz, there is no need to store all these frequencies in a sound file. The less we need to store, the less space the file takes up.

> **TIP**
>
> Because the lowest frequencies are seldom produced (most subwoofers in concert halls and movie theatres don't go much below 40Hz). There are few PC speakers that could produce these notes even if they were present, it makes sense to filter those notes too low to be reproduced properly out of the mix. Also, most PC speakers can't produce high frequencies properly, and because overtones are generally so low as to be unnoticed (especially considering the poor quality of most PC speakers), they can also be filtered out. So, we can narrow the band of sounds we need to record.

Sampling Frequency

The next issue is how to record those frequencies digitally, a process called *sampling*. The best way to think of sound sampling is with an analogy to a movie in a theatre. The movies you watch have a series of single frames projected one after another at a rate that fools your brain into thinking there is continual motion on the screen. Movies in a theatre are projected at a rate of 24 frames per second. Most of the movies we produce in Flash are run at 12 frames per second. Because even 12fps looks good on most PCs and fools us into thinking there is motion involved, why do theatres project at 24fps? The quality issue: the most frames per second the less jerky any motion on the screen and the more seamless the image. Essentially, the more frames per second, the better looking the image.

When sampling sounds, the analogy holds. The more samples per second we take of a sound, the better the sound will be. To understand why, we need to consider what happens with a sample. Suppose we are recording a bass drum at 50Hz. In the space of a second, there will be fifty cycles (each wave consists of a full top-to-bottom cycle). If we sampled the sound only twice during the second, the two points we measure could be anywhere on the fifty cycles. From these two points it would be impossible to reconstruct how many cycles there were originally, and hence what the frequency was. If we sampled 2,000 times a second, though, we would have 40 samples from each cycle, and it would be obvious from the 40 points that we were constructing a 50Hz wave. What about the violin tone, though? If the violin is producing a 2kHz tone and we sample

2,000 times, we will have one sample for each cycle, and that is not enough to reconstruct the wave (in fact, if the samples are spaced precisely, we would have a straight
line from the results). To sample a high frequency like the violin we need many more
samples.

If we sample at ten times the rate, meaning 20,000 times a second, the violin would
have ten points for each cycle, which is enough to reproduce the wave properly (our
bass drum tone would have 400 points, which is more than enough to see an almost
perfect wave). But if we now look at an overtone, such as 8,000Hz, we would have only
two points per cycle (rounding off), which isn't enough. So you can see that as the
frequency rises, we need more sampling to reconstruct the waves (and hence the sound)
properly.

CDs are recorded at a rate of 44,100 samples per second. This means that for a 2,000Hz
note (the violin) we would have 20 samples per cycle, which allows the wave to be
reconstructed properly using algorithms. Where CD quality falls down is high
frequencies. Suppose we had a 15kHz note: Only three samples per cycle would be
produced, which is difficult to properly reconstruct. So, CD sound is poor at the higher
ends of the audible spectrum.

> **NOTE**
>
> This is why many people with excellent hearing find that CDs sound harsh and
> brash at high frequencies, while vinyl records, which have no sampling, sound fine.

Sampling at 44.1 samples per second is the same as saying you have a sampling
frequency of 44.1kHz. It also means that for a given second of sound, you need to
record 44,100 data points. If you have a lot of sound duration to record, you can see
that the file needed to hold that much data gets quite large. (This is a simplification at
this point because we're not looking at bit depth yet.)

There are other sampling frequencies in common use. FM radio, for example, uses a
sampling rate equivalent to 22.05kHz. FM radio doesn't have a lot of high-frequency
sound (it is filtered out). At lower sampling frequencies, you can record a talking voice
at around 5kHz and obtain listenable audio, but music sounds terrible at this rate. (For
the record, studios recording music record at sampling rates of 48kHz or 96kHz, with
even higher multiples now in use.)

This all relates to the PC in a simple way: All audio cards for PCs handle sounds in
multiples of 44.1kHz. When you record or play back a sound through a PC, the
frequencies should be a multiple of 44.1kHz (such as 22.05kHz or 11.025kHz). Any
non-multiple can cause real problems for playback on a PC. As mentioned earlier,
22.05kHz is a quality similar to FM radio and is acceptable to most people. 11.025kHz
sounds flatter and has less life than higher frequencies, but is fine for voice and sound
effects. For music, it is barely acceptable.

Flash works in multiples of 11.025kHz. If you import a sound file that has a multiple of this frequency, the sound is imported with no change. However, if you import a sound with a different sampling frequency, Flash resamples to a multiple of 11.025kHz, which affects the way the sound is heard. Usually, the imported file is down-sampled, meaning resampled to the next lowest multiple of 11.025kHz.

TIP

For best results, always import files with a multiple of this fundamental 11.025kHz sampling frequency.

Bit Depth

When you sample a sound digitally, each sample records a point on the waves in the music. The sample shows not only which frequency is being sampled, but also how loud the sound is. The loudness of each sound is important when reproducing the original signal through an analog conversion. This brings up the issue of dynamic range, or the difference between the quietest and the loudest volumes that are recorded. When there is a lot of difference between the two extremes, you need to have a way of storing that data in a file. The larger the difference in extremes, the more bits you need to store the difference.

Bit resolution deals with the number of bits that are allocated to describe each sound's volume. Digital audio uses an 8-bit multiple for this. The simplest digital recording process uses 8 bits to describe the sound (this is called an 8-bit depth). Using 8 bits is only enough to describe a few levels of sound (256 to be precise), and so the difference between the softest sound (usually a background hiss) and the loudest sound (the music) is small, making the recording sound hissy and compressed.

NOTE

When the analog signal is re-created by the digital algorithms, only the 256 levels of sound can be used (as that is all the digital file recorded), so the original and reconstructed signals sound very different.

Bit depth increases in 8 bit increments. Using 16 bits to record means more difference between the loudest and softest levels (65,536 levels), so the hiss is more suppressed and music sounds more natural instead of compressed. Going to even more bit depth gives more levels. CDs are recorded at a bit depth of 16 bits.

NOTE

Newer CD and DVD standards are using 24-bit depths to give millions of levels of difference in sound between the softest and loudest levels, but this is overkill for a PC sound file.

File Sizes

The file size of a sound file thus depends on both the sampling frequency (how many samples per second and the bit depth [how many bits are used to describe each sample]). The math is quite simple: A file recorded in 16-bit depth will be twice the size as the same file recorded at 8-bit depth. A sound recorded at 44.1kHz requires twice as much space as a sound recorded at 22.05kHz. Keep in mind that this applies to a single channel or a mono sound. If you want to record in stereo, you need to have two channels, or double the amount of information in the file. (If you go to surround sound, there are five or six channels of data to record!)

> **TIP**
>
> Combining the bit depth and sampling frequencies enables you to figure out file sizes. 8 bits is a byte; 22.05kHz is going to mean 22,000 bytes per second; 10 seconds of sound at 22.05kHz; and 8-bit depth is going to require 220,000 bytes or approximately 220kb disk space, ignoring headers, checksums, and other additional material in the sound file. If it is a stereo signal, double the file size to half a megabyte.

Which combination of bit depth and sampling frequencies should you use? Let's deal with a few issues before we look at a concrete answer. First, although many developers think 8-bit depth is suitable, in actuality it isn't. The first issue with 8-bit depth is that many recording codecs (for compression-decompression, the algorithm that samples and rebuilds the analog sound can't work at 8-bit depth. Most use 16-bit; a few will produce an 8-bit depth, but it may not be a true 8 bit signal, but a compressed 16 bit, saving no space. The more important issue is quality of the sound. Simply put, an 8-bit sound is awful. True, 8-bit could be used for a simple sound effect such as a button being pushed, but you should use 16-bit sounds as a bare minimum for all your work. Going beyond 16 bits is silly for most Flash applications on a PC.

Sampling frequency is a harder issue, because there is no single answer. If you are recording simple voice, sound effects, or limited frequency tones, a lower sampling frequency of 11.025kHz may be acceptable, but you should consider 22.05kHz as a minimum. For music, you will easily notice the difference between 22.05kHz and 44.1kHz, and so will your viewers. File size does come into the equation, and this is where the compromise to a mono channel or 22.05kHz is sometimes necessary. A better approach is to forget about a stereo signal and record a single channel at 44.1kHz. (Most PC cards and speakers can't reproduce the stereo effect properly, anyway.)

> **TIP**
>
> Not sure about which bit depth and sampling frequency to use? The recommended defaults are 16-bit, 22.05kHz mono. This produces a good compromise between quality of sound and file size. If you have complex music, double the sampling rate to 44.1kHz.

Working with Flash sound files you quickly realize two things:

- Sound files tend to be large and require a lot of disk space.
- Managing sound files is a slow and cumbersome task.

Keep in mind download times for all the music files you work with. Your long Flash movie without sound is often a smaller download than a short movie with background music. Balance the requirements based on your viewers.

> **TIP**
>
> To reduce file sizes make sure you edit any silent or very low-level audio at the start and end of the clip. If you want to use background music with your movie, consider making a short loop.

Supported Sound File Formats

Flash supports a number of popular file formats for importing sounds. (The most important aspect of Flash 5 from a sound perspective was the addition of MP3 file support.) The standard three file formats are:

- AIFF (Audio Interchange File Format): The .AIFF and .AIF file formats were developed for use with the Macintosh and many sound applications (such as ProTools, Acid, and many others) that support .AIFF. A PC requires QuickTime 4 to be installed to support .AIFF files.
- MP3 (MPEG-1 Audio Layer 3): MP3 files are the most popular format for distributing music on both Windows and Macintosh platforms. MP3 uses an efficient compression scheme and remarkable quality playback for the file size.
- WAV (Windows Wave): Until MP3 emerged, .WAV files were the standard file format for sound under Windows. Many sound applications support .WAV files as their basic export format. (Flash under the Macintosh supports .WAV files only when QuickTime 4 is installed.)

> **NOTE**
>
> QuickTime audio files (.MOV or .QTA) are not directly supported by Flash 5. However, QuickTime Pro 4 can save these files as .AIFF or .WAV files, enabling Flash 5 to import them.

For exporting audio, Flash 5 can provide a number of different sound compression codecs (compression-decompression algorithms), including MP3. The formats available for export, and a brief description, are:

- ADPCM (Adaptive Differential Pulse-Code Modulation): Was the Flash standard until version 5; provides compression similar (but not as efficient) as MP3. ADPCM should be used when compatibility with old Flash players is required.
- MP3 (MPEG-1 Audio Layer 3): MP3 is supported only by Flash players version 4 and above.

- RAW: The RAW format is an uncompressed audio file, but useful when working with some other applications for editing or creating movies and sound files. RAW produces very large files due to the lack of any compression techniques.

The exporting of sound files is discussed later in this chapter.

Flash and Sound

We can think of Flash as handling two different kinds of sounds: sounds tied to an event and streamed sounds. The two are treated differently by Flash, so we can deal with them as two kinds of sounds. Streamed sounds start to play as soon as the first few frames have been loaded and continue to play as long as the stream is available. Streamed sounds are always synchronized to the Timeline. Event sounds are loaded in their entirety before they begin to play and the sound continues playing until it is stopped by some mechanism.

Importing Sound Files

To import sound files into a Flash movie you use the File, Import command. Depending on whether QuickTime 4 or above is available on the system, the supported file formats will differ, as we mentioned earlier in this chapter.

When you import a sound file it is stored in the Library as with any other object. If you are going to reuse a sound (such as a button sound effect) you only need one object in the Library, as you can drag multiple instances of the object on the Timeline. You can launch the sound either by dragging it to the Stage, associating it with an object or event, or by using ActionScript commands.

> **TIP**
>
> If you want to use an imported sound in a shared library you need to provide an identifier string for the sound file using the Symbol Linkage Properties window. This identifier can then be used by ActionScript commands.

Using Sounds in a Movie

Once a sound file resides in the Library it can be used in the Timeline. To add sound to a movie it is best to create a layer just for each sound. The parameters for the sound clips are then set using the Sound panel.

Sounds can be placed anywhere on a layer, including on a layer with other non-sound objects on it. You can also place as many sound objects on a single layer as you want. Macromedia recommends using one sound per layer. When you generate a movie, all the sounds on all the layers are combined. Until the movie is generated, though, each layer of sound acts like a separate channel.

> **NOTE**
>
> If you use the recommended one sound per dedicated layer, you have better control over the sound in your movie. However, when working with multiple sounds you have many layers of which to keep track. To reduce the number of layers, you could decide to use a single layer for certain sound effects, another layer for music, and so on. Most developers try to keep the sound layers grouped for convenience.

Because there is no way to organize sound layers in Flash, many developers create a mask or Guide layer with all the sound layers below it. For example, create a mask layer called Sounds and drag all the sound layers below it. Flash indents each masked layer below the mask layer, making it easier to see the sound layers.

To add a sound effect or music clip to a movie, import the sound into the Library if not already there. Then, create a new layer for the sound using Insert, Layer. Select the sound in the Library and drag it to the Stage (the sound automatically appears in the current layer). To set the properties for the sound, open the Sound panel using Windows, Panels, Sound.

The Sound panel has several options you can use. The first field enables you to choose the sound file from the pop-up menu (if the file is not already shown). The bottom three fields are for special processing of effects, synchronization to the Timeline, and looping the sounds. You can use several effects choices for a sound. These are summarized in Table 18.1.

Table 18.1 Effects Available from the Sound Panel

Effect	Description
None	No effect applied to the sound (or removes all applied sounds)
Left Channel	Plays the sound only in the left channel
Right Channel	Plays the sound only in the right channel
Fade In	Slowly increases the volume
Fade Out	Slowly decreases the volume
Custom	Enables you to use the Edit Envelope to set In and Out points

The Synchronization field is used to determine if the sound is synchronized to an event. This field has several settings, shown in Table 18.2.

Table 18.2 Synchronization Options from the Sound Panel

Setting	Description
Event	Synchronizes the sound to the start of the event; the sound starts playing when the keyframe is displayed and plays through independently of the Timeline (even if the movie is paused).
Start	Same as Event except a new instance of the sound is started even if the sound is already playin.

Table 18.2   Continued

Setting	Description
Stop	Stops playback of the sound
Stream	Synchronizes playback for Web movies; animation is forced to keep up with streamed sounds or frames are skipped. If the movie stops so does the sound.

The Stream setting enables you to play a sound clip through without any hesitation, whether the video components can keep up or not. Flash drops frames in a movie to maintain synchronization with the sound, based on the length of the frames on the Timeline. The other settings in the Synchronization field are for non-streaming sounds. Both Event and Start have a sound file play through to the end even if the movie is paused or stopped.

The Loop field in the Sounds panel is used to indicate how many times the sound should loop. If you want a sound to loop three times, you would enter 3 in the field. For continually looping sounds, use a large number. When looping streamed sounds be aware that Flash will add frames to the movie to show the looping repetitions, and the exported filesize is considerably larger because the loops are expanded on export. This is not the case for non-streamed sounds.

The most common requirement for a sound file is to start it and stop it at particular points in the Timeline. This is done to synchronize the sound with animation frames, and uses keyframes. To start or stop a sound at a keyframe, add the sound to the movie in a layer of its own as usual. Make sure the sound keyframes line up with the event keyframes in another layer. The sound plays when the event keyframes are reached in both the event and sound layers. To stop the playback at a keyframe, use the Sound panel and choose the Stop option from the Synchronization field. When the keyframe is reached, the sound stops playing (even if the sound file has not played through completely).

Sounds and Buttons

Apart from background music or narration, the most common use of sounds is to provide audible feedback of button use. To do this, you need to associate a sound with each of the states of the buttons. Because sounds are stored with the symbol in the Library, the sounds you attach appear for each instance of the button, unless you override them specifically on the Stage.

To add a sound to a button select the button object in the Library and use the Edit item from the Library Options menu. In the button Timeline create a new layer for the sound (Insert, Layer). To associate a sound with a particular button state (such as Hit or Down), create a keyframe in the sound layer that corresponds to the button event keyframe. Select the keyframe and open the Sounds panel (Window, Panels, Sound). Choose the sound file from the drop-down list and choose Event in the Synchronization field. Repeat the procedure for each button state that you want a sound for (you could have four different sounds for the four states, although you usually don't associate a sound with the Up event).

> **TIP**
>
> Most developers add sound effects only for the Over and Down states of a button.

Background Music

Instead of assigning sound clips to events, you can also place a sound file on the Timeline to be used as background music. The simplest way to provide a music score for a movie is to place the sound slip on the Timeline in a layer of its own. Make sure the start of the sound clip is at the proper place in the movie, and use a keyframe to trigger the sound.

The process for adding background music is to create a new layer in the Timeline, and then create a keyframe to indicate the starting frame for the music. Place the sound on the Timeline or choose the sound from the Sound panel after selecting the keyframe. In the Sound panel, set the parameters however you want, and provide a looping number if you want the sounds to loop.

> **TIP**
>
> When trying to synchronize music and frames in a movie, it helps to expand the Timeline layers for the sounds so you can see the waveforms on the Timeline. You can increase the layer display by up to three times for a layer to see the waveform more easily. (Use the Layer Properties, Modify option to expand the layers.)

Linking Sounds

To use a sound in one library with multiple movies, you need to assign a linkage for the sound and store the sound in a shared library. To use a sound in multiple movies it must be in a shared library. Sounds in a shared library need an identifying string that can be used to reference the sound. When in a shared library, you can use ActionScript to call the sound as well as to control the sound file.

To assign the identifier string use the Symbol Linkage window. Select the sound in the Library window and choose Linkage from the Library Options menu (or use the pop-up menu and choose Linkage). In the Symbol Linkage Properties window that appears, under Linkage select the Export This Symbol box and enter the identifier string you will use in the text field, and then click OK. The string is now associated with the sound and can be used by ActionScript.

Sound Editing Controls

Flash provides a rudimentary sound editor that enables you to tailor sound files to your needs. The abilities of the sound editor are limited, so if you need to perform special editing and effects you should consider using a third-party application. Many excellent sound tools are available for Windows and Macintosh. After editing on those tools, you can import the sound and perform any final adjustments in the Flash sound editing panel, if necessary.

The sound editing control in Flash enables you to set the starting and ending points of a sound, as well as control the volume and any fade effects (fade in or fade out). You can also use the sound editor for setting a loop point, which is where the sound starts from when looping (which does not have to be the start of the file).

To use the sound editing controls, select a sound and display the Sound panel (Window, Panels, Sound), and then click the Edit button. This displays the Edit Envelope window. This window has the sound waves displayed on the panel with a time control strip down the middle. The bottom left has stop and play buttons for the playhead, and the bottom right has zoom buttons, and a toggle for either seconds or frames counter on the strip.

To change the starting or ending points of the sound, use the Time In and Time Out bars in the middle strip. Simply drag the bars to correspond to the starting and ending points. (Normally you use the Time In and Time Out adjustments to remove dead air or noise from the beginning and ending of the clip.)

To change the volume of the clip at any point, use the envelope line, which is the line imposed over the sound wave. This line has a number of handles that can be attached, which show up as square hollow boxes. The line from box to box shows the relative volume of the sound in that area. You can create new handles at any point by clicking the envelope line, and then dragging the handle to the appropriate volume.

> **NOTE**
>
> The maximum number of possible handles on the sound envelope is eight.

To produce a fade-in effect, the first handle at the start of the clip should be at the bottom of the window, and the next handle should be where the volume reaches maximum a little further on. The amount of time you take for the fade-in is up to you. The increase in volume is linear, following the straight line between handles. Repeat the same process for fade-outs, with the envelope at zero volume when the sound finished. You can place volume adjustments anywhere in the sound clip, including reducing the volume during the clip playback to enable another sound clip to be heard.

Exporting Sounds

To export sounds you use the Export Settings in the Sound Properties dialog. This is displayed either by double-clicking the sound in the Library or by using the pop-up menus when the sound object is selected. The export options enable you to set compression methods as well as sample frequency and bit depth rates.

> **TIP**
>
> The Test button on the Sound Properties window is useful for testing the effect of the choices you make and ensuring the quality of the sound is not degraded excessively. This is handy for previewing the effects of your selections.

For the Compression, choose Default, ADPCM, MP3, or RAW. The Default setting chooses whatever default values were set in the Publish Settings dialog; when using Default all the parameters are set for you. (You can change the defaults at any time, of course.) A number of different settings become available, depending on the compression choice (except Default). From these options, choose the sample rate, preprocessing (which enables you to choose mono or stereo), and the bit depth. Not all these options are available for all compression schemes.

> **CAUTION**
>
> You cannot export a sound at a higher sampling frequency than that used when the file was imported. In other words, no up-sampling is allowed.

Using Sounds Effectively

Because sound effects and music occupy a huge amount of space in a published file use them carefully. It may be tempting to leave sound out of a movie entirely, but audible feedback is an important aspect to a viewer's experience with your movie. For this reason, you should provide at least basic sound effects for buttons and other standard actions in a movie.

Earlier in this chapter you saw the effects of sampling frequency and bit depth on the file size, and these considerations should be taken into account. Obviously, if you intend your movie for a LAN with high bandwidth you have a little more latitude with sound effects and music than a movie to be viewed over an analog modem.

As a general rule, you can use just a few sound clips, but creatively use the fade-in and fade-out points to make the sounds a little different for different events or objects. Some developers have a single sound file with a few sounds incorporated on them, and simply select the fade-in and fade-out points to select each different sound in the sample.

Looping can also be an effective way of providing background music or longer-duration effects. Third-party loop packages such as Acid are ideal for creating short, seamless effects, and music that seems much longer than it really is. These can be easily imported into Flash, although Flash does not have the editing capability to create fancy loops itself.

When working with sound files, make sure you trim the quiet parts of the file from the start and end (and sometimes during the sound itself). This reduces the overall file size and ensures the sound appears on cue when synchronized to an event.

> **TIP**
>
> When using the Stream option for a sound file, make sure you test the published movie on multiple platforms as they may behave differently depending on processor speed.

Summary

In this chapter we've looked at how you can employ sounds in your movies, both for music and sound effect purposes. The overriding concern with most sound usage in a Flash movie is the additional file size required to publish the movie, but judicious use of sound can be managed within reasonable file size limits. Although Flash's sound editing capabilities are basic, they do enable simple trimming of sound files as well as managing volume. Sounds add dramatically to a movie's impact and should be used in most movies.

Sample Questions

1. Which of the following sound formats cannot be used for exporting a sound?
   A. ADPCM
   B. AIFF
   C. MP3
   D. RAW

2. How many handles are allowed in a volume envelope?
   A. Two
   B. Four
   C. Eight
   D. Any number

3. Which Synchronization setting forces an animation to synch with sound?
   A. Stream
   B. Event
   C. Start
   D. Stop

CHAPTER 19

Other Objects

Flash includes several objects that are used frequently in ActionScript programming. These are the Math, Date, and String objects. We look at each of these three objects, and more importantly the methods that are attached to those objects, in this chapter. We show some examples of the methods these objects contain to demonstrate their use. Although these examples are simple, they can easily be extended to complex application use.

Math

The Math object has been seen in previous chapters. It enables you to perform a variety of basic mathematical and trigonometric functions on numbers. The Math object also includes the logarithmic functions for base 10 and base e (natural) logs. A generator of random numbers is also included (which replaces a standalone action in previous releases of Flash).

The methods included with the Math object are shown in Table 19.1. Most of these methods involve arguments and many involve uppercase letters as part of the method name. Ensure that the proper case is preserved with these Math object methods.

Table 19.1 Math Object Methods

Method	Description
abs(num)	Returns the absolute value of num
acos(num)	Returns the arccosine of num
asin(num)	Returns the arcsine of num
atan(num)	Returns the arctangent of num
atan2(y,x)	Returns the angle in radians from the x axis to the y point
ceil(num)	Rounds num up to the next highest integer

Table 19.1 Continued

Method	Description
cos(num)	Returns the cosine of num
exp(num)	Returns the exponent of e
floor(num)	Rounds num down to the next lowest integer
log(num)	Returns the natural logarithm of num
max(x,y)	Returns the larger of x or y
min(x,y)	Returns the smaller of x or y
power(x,y)	Returns x to the exponent y
random()	Returns a random number between 0.0 and 1.0
round(num)	Rounds num to the nearest integer
sin(num)	Returns the sine of num
sqrt(num)	Returns the square root of num
tan(num)	Returns the tangent of num
E	Base of natural logarithms (e or Euler's constant)
LN2	Natural logarithm of 2
LOG2E	Base 3 logarithm of 2
LN10	Natural logarithm of 10
LOG10E	Base 10 logarithm of e
PI	Value of pi
SQRT1_2	Square root of 0.5
SQRT2	Square root of 2

Most of these methods are self-explanatory. You can combine methods to produce any effect you need. While most of the time you use the methods for direct mathematical manipulation, you also find them useful for other circumstances, such as creating a clock hand that can be dragged to a new position.

One common call to the Math methods is for random numbers. The random function produces a number between 0.0 and 1.0, so this needs to be moved into the range that is required. For example, if you want to generate a random number between 1 and 25, you would write code like this:

```
num1 = Math.random() * 24 + 1;
```

The multiplication by 24 results in a number between 0 and 24 and the addition of one moves it to between 1 and 25.

Date and Time

Using the Flash-supplied Date object you can obtain and manipulate both time and date values. Flash can work with local or GMT (UTC) time and date values. Using a set of methods associated with the Date object, you can determine any of the date specifics (such as current year, month, day, hour, minutes, seconds, and milliseconds). By assigning these to variables you can determine elapsed time, or you can create date objects that enable specific date manipulations, which have nothing to do with the current date to be performed.

> **TIP**
>
> The GMT (Greenwich Mean Time) designation has been replaced by UTC (Universal Coordinated Time; and no, the acronym does not match—that's just the way it is) by all standards bodies. While the designation GMT is still in wide use, the correct way to indicate time from the prime meridian is to specify UTC. They both mean the same thing.

To work with the Date object you need to instantiate a new Date with a constructor function, and then use that instantiated variable's methods to extract the hours, minutes, day of the week, and other parameters that you want to use. You can also use a timer function to count elapsed time, as you see later.

Date Methods

The Date object has several methods built in that can be used to return all or part of the current date and time. The Date methods are shown in Table 19.2. If not specified as UTC, all the date methods are referenced to the local time as established by the computer's clock functions.

Table 19.2 The Date Methods

Method	Description
getDate()	Returns the day of the month as a number (1 through 31)
getDay()	Returns the day of the week as a number with Sunday = 0 and Saturday = 6
getFullYear()	Returns the year as a four-digit number
getHours()	Returns the hour of the day as a number (0 through 23)
getMilliseconds()	Returns the number of milliseconds in the current time (0 through 999)
getMinutes()	Returns the number of minutes as a number (0 through 59)
getMonth()	Returns the month as a number with January = 0 and December = 11
getSeconds()	Returns the number of seconds as a number (0 through 59)
getTime()	Returns the number of milliseconds since January 1, 1970 UTC
getTimezoneOffset()	Returns the number of minutes between local time and UTC according to the host computer
getUTCDate	Returns the day of the month according to UTC (1 through 31)
getUTCDay	Returns the day of the week according to UCT (0 through 6)
getUTCFullYear()	Returns the UTC full year as a four-digit number
getUTCHours()	Returns the hour according to UTC (0 through 23)
getUTC Milliseconds()	Returns the number of milliseconds in the current time according to UTC (0 through 999)
getUTCMinutes()	Returns the number of minutes according to UTC as a number (0 through 59)

Table 19.2 *Continued*

Method	Description
getMonth()	Returns the month UTC as a number with January = 0 and December = 11
getSeconds()	Returns the number of seconds UTC as a number (0 through 59)
getYear()	Returns the year
setDate()	Sets the full year for the Date object
setFullYear()	Sets the full year for the Date object
setHours()	Sets the hours for the Date object
setMilliseconds()	Sets the milliseconds for the Date object
setMinutes()	Sets the minutes for the Date object
setMonth()	Sets the month for the Date object
setSeconds()	Sets the seconds for the Date object
setTime()	Sets the date in milliseconds since January 1, 1970 for the Date object
setUTCDate()	Sets the full year for the Date object using UTC
setUTCFullYear()	Sets the full year for the Date object using UTC
setUTCHours()	Sets the hours for the Date object using UTC
setUTCMilliseconds()	Sets the milliseconds for the Date object using UTC
setUTCMinutes()	Sets the minutes for the Date object using UTC
setUTCMonth()	Sets the month for the Date object using UTC
setUTCSeconds()	Sets the seconds for the Date object using UTC
setUTCTime()	Sets the date in milliseconds since January 1, 1970 for the Date object using UTC
setYear()	Sets the year for the Date object
toString()	Returns a string for the date and time
Date.UTC	Returns the number of milliseconds since January 1, 1970 UTC

The list of methods may seem long, but there are really duplicates for each function in both UTC and local time. On top of that, there are matching set and get functions, so there really are eight basic functions in total, modified only by get or set, UTC or local.

Creating and Using a Date Variable

To work with date and time, you need to instantiate a Date object first. This is done in the usual way using the new method:

```
myDate = new Date();
```

The instantiated object can then be used with any of the Date functions. If you want to provide a value for the new instance, you can give the date and time components as a comma-separated list in this order:

- Year
- Month
- Day
- Hour
- Minute
- Second
- Milliseconds

For example, to set the new date object to have a date of 5:10 p.m. local time on May 31, 2002, you would use the command:

```
myDate = new Date(2002, 05, 31, 17, 10, 0, 0);
```

Here we have assumed zero seconds and milliseconds. Note also the use of the 24-hour clock to indicate 5:00 p.m. This has set the time locally. If we were to assign this value to a string (using the toString method it would look like this:

```
Fri May 31 17:10:00 GMT-0500 2002
```

Assuming we were in the Eastern Standard Time zone (hence GMT minus 5 hours) when the command was entered.

> **NOTE**
>
> The toString method does not display milliseconds, the year is appended to the end of the string, and the timezone display is a constant set by the local time setting on your computer.

If you do not specify a time setting when instantiating a Date object, the system's local time and date are used. For example, the following command shows the current hour setting (using the 24-hour clock) established by your computer's clock functions:

```
myDate = new Date();
num1 = myDate.getHours();
```

You can override the entire date setting as shown previously, or you can use the system date and modify it using the get functions. For example, to set a date variable to one hour later than the current system hour, you could write:

```
myDate = new Date();
num1 = myDate.getHours();
myDate.setHours(num1+1);
```

When you change any portion of the date or time, only the individual item you change is affected; the rest is left to their previous settings.

To show the use of the date and time methods, the easiest approach is to create a display of the values in a movie. If you want to assign the date and time values to variables, you can do so using a series of method calls. For example, the following code creates a new date variable and uses the methods to store the day of the month, month, and year in variables and assigns all three combined into a string:

```
myDate = new Date();
myDay = myDate.getdate();
myMonth = myDate.getMonth();
myYear = myDate.getFullYear();
showDate = myMonth + " " + myDay + ", " + myYear;
```

As is, this displays the date, September 24, 2001, in a format like this:

```
9 24, 2001
```

This is acceptable for many uses, but would look better with an expanded month description (September instead of 9). Because there is no Date method to expand the month to its full descriptive, we have to find another way to do so. Fortunately, it's relatively simple to do by setting up an array with the month names in them, and then using an index to the actual month to expand the name. This can be done by modifying the previous code to create an array and use the getMonth method to get the index in that array:

```
myDate = new Date();
myDay = myDate.getdate();
myMonth - myDate.getMonth();
myYear = myDate.getFullYear();
monthArray = new Array ("January", "February", "March", "April",
➥"May", "June", "July", "August", "September", "October",
➥"November", "December");
showDate = monthArray[myMonth] + " " + myDay + ", " + myYear;
```

This now results in the string having the value:

```
September 24, 2001
```

This is a lot friendlier. You could do the same with the day of the week, setting up an array with the expanded names of the days and using the index from the getDay method to find the correct expansion.

The same can be done for time, but here we have to decide if we're going to update the time continually, and if so, how often. To begin we can retrieve the current local time like this:

```
myDate = new Date();
myHours = myDate.getHours();
myMinutes = myDate.getMinutes();
mySeconds = myDate.getSeconds();
showTime = myHours + ":" + myMinutes + ":" + mySeconds;
```

Using the 24-hour clock for 2:02 p.m., this results in a display like this:

```
14:2:47
```

The use of a single digit for minutes is unsettling, so we need to add a leading zero if the minutes are less than 10. This is done like this:

```
myDate = new Date();
myHours = myDate.getHours();
myMinutes = myDate.getMinutes();
mySeconds = myDate.getSeconds();
if (myMinutes < 10) {
    myMinutes = "0"+"myMinutes;
}
showTime = myHours + ":" + myMinutes + ":" + mySeconds;
```

This changes the output to look like this:

```
12:02:47
```

You have to do the same to handle seconds (and hours, if you want to). If you want to use a 12-hour clock, you can use an `if` condition to check if the hours are greater than 12 and deduct 12 from them if they are, as well as tag "PM" at the end:

```
myHours = myDate.getHours();
myMinutes = myDate.getMinutes();
mySeconds = myDate.getSeconds();
if (myMinutes < 10) {
    myMinutes = "0"+"myMinutes;
}
if (myMSeconds < 10) {
    mySeconds = "0"+"mySeconds;
}
if (myHours > 12 ) {
    myHours = myHours - 12;
    myAmpm = "PM";
}
else{
    myAmpm = "AM";
}
showTime = myHours + ":" + myMinutes + ":" + mySeconds + " " + myAmpm;
```

You can see how you can manipulate the date methods to display time and date any way you want. We did the previous time methods using local time, but we could have used UTC as well.

All these actions can be attached to a movie, either by using an object on the Stage like a dynamic text field, or by using a display variable. A dynamic display makes sure the time is continually updated to reflect the current time.

Using a Timer

Flash includes the `getTimer` function. (It is a function and not a Date method.) This enables you to obtain the number of milliseconds that have elapsed because the movie started to play. For differences in times, you simply use the method twice and subtract the two.

Elapsed timers are useful not only for direct feedback to a viewer, but also for timing activities in a movie. For example, you might have a trivia question movie, and time the amount of time it takes the viewer to respond (or enables them to run out of time).

Because `getTimer` is a function and not a method, it doesn't need a constructor. You can assign the results from the function to a variable easily like this:

```
startTime = getTimer();
```

And by sampling a second time, such as:

```
endTime = getTimer();
```

You can then calculate an elapsed time like this:

```
elapsedTime = Math.round( (endTime - startTim(e)/ 1000);
```

The difference between the two times is determined by subtraction, and the result is divided by 1,000 to convert from milliseconds to seconds (note the use of parentheses to ensure the correct order of operations). The `Math.round` function is used to round the result to the nearest second, instead of keeping it as a fraction. This result could then be displayed on the Stage.

> **TIP**
>
> You can also create an elapsed timer by using the Timeline and counting the number of frames that have played. If you know the number of frames per second displayed, you can calculate the elapsed time from the start of the movie using the `_currentframe` property.

String Object

The String object contains many string methods and properties. Technically, the String object is a wrapper for a data type, which enables any object to be converted to a string. This means that most of the String methods can work on any data type, not just strings, because they call the `toString()` function first (hence converting whatever the data type is to the string data type).

It is important not to confuse the String object with literal strings. Literal strings are defined using quotation marks to indicate a literal character string. String objects are more complex and often exhibit behaviors different than you would expect from a string.

The String methods are summarized in Table 19.3. In addition, there is one property for the String object, called `length`. The `length` property returns the length of the string as a number.

Table 19.3   *String Object Methods*

Method	Description
charAt(s)	Returns a number indicating the placement of s in the string
charCodeAt(s)	Returns the integer value of the character at position s
concat (s1, s2...sn)	Concatenates the specified strings into a new string
fromCharCode (x1, x2...xn)	Returns the specified characters into a string
indexOf(s)	Returns a number specifying the index of substring s occurring first inside the string
lastIndexOf(s)	Returns a number specifying the index of substring s occurring last inside the string
slice(x,y)	Extracts a substring of the string starting at x index and ending at the y-1 index and returns a new string
split(delim)	Breaks the string into substrings in an array using delim as the character at which to break
substr(x,y)	Returns the substring in the string starting at x and running for y characters
substring(x,y)	Returns the substring in the string between the x and y indexes.
toLowerCase()	Converts the string characters to lowercase
toUpperCase()	Converts the string characters to uppercase

A few simple examples help clear up some of the more confusing methods.

Several String object methods appear to do very similar work, such as substr(), substring(), and slice(). The slice() method creates a new string without modifying the original string at all. The following code causes the slice() method to extract a substring starting at the third index (counting from zero) and up to, but not including, the seventh index:

```
myStr1 = "abcdefghijk";
myStr2 = String.slice(3,7);
```

The resultant string stored in myStr2 is "defg". The original string is untouched.

The substr() method uses the two arguments to specify the starting location and the length of the substring. For example:

```
myStr1 = "abcdefghijk";
myStr2 = String.substr(3,3);
```

This results in myStr2 having the characters from the third index and running for three characters, so it is equal to "def". If no length is specified, the rest of the string is taken. If a negative number is used for the starting index, the first character is found by starting at the last character and moving backward from the number of indexes specified (so –4 would mean move back four characters from the end, which is treated as –1). The substring() method is similar to substr(), but it specifies the starting and ending indexes, like slice() did.

The indexOf() and charOf() methods are opposites of each other. The charOf() method returns the character that occupies the specified location, so the following code returns "d".:

```
myStr1 = "abcdefghijk";
myStr2 = String.charOf(3);
```

The indexOf() method tells you where a character or substring occurs in the string, so the following code returns the number 3:

```
myStr1 = "abcdefghijk";
myStr2 = String.indexOf(d);
```

The other methods attached to the String object are self-explanatory.

Summary

In this chapter we've looked at three of the complex objects provided with Flash: the Math, Date, and String objects. These should not be confused with data types, as they are complex objects with attached methods and properties. Using these three complex objects, along with the MovieClip object, enables you to perform all the manipulations you need for a Flash movie.

Sample Questions

1. Given the a variable with the value 3.14159, what would the result of the ceil() method be?
   A. 3
   B. 1
   C. 4
   D. 3.2

2. Which of these objects has to have an instance created using new to work with it?
   A. Math
   B. Date
   C. String
   D. string

3. Given the string myStr = "a b f j w", what would be the result from myStr.indexOf();?
   A. 0
   B. 1
   C. 2
   D. 3

PART IV

BUILDING APPLICATIONS

20   External Data

21   Data-Driven Movies

22   Debugging

23   Error Handling

24   Profiling

CHAPTER 20

External Data

Macromedia Flash movies don't exist in a vacuum. They interact with their host environment, whether it is an operating system (for the stand-alone Flash player) or a Web scripting language (for the Web-based player). Communicating with the environment is an important aspect of designing complex Flash movies, and many times you want to send commands to (or receive commands from) the environment.

You can also send to, and retrieve data from, the environment. This enables you to use Flash to send specific information to JavaScript programs, for example, or use JavaScript to send data collected in a Web page to the movie player. This chapter shows you how to perform these basic interactions.

Sending Messages

Messages can be sent from a Flash movie being played in a Flash Player to the environment that is hosting it (such as a Web browser). To send messages from a movie use the fscommand command. The primary reason for passing messages from a Flash movie is to enable auxiliary material to be displayed next to the movie. For example, a Flash movie can use fscommand to send JavaScript instructions to a browser to open a new browser instance and display information or controls for the movie being played.

> **NOTE**
>
> Because most of the interaction between Flash and the environment is through a Web browser, we'll concentrate on the Web for the most part in this chapter. A movie can send fscommand commands to a stand-alone Flash player, and these are interpreted by the player itself and not the operating system.

Flash player methods are used to send commands to scripting languages such as JavaScript and VBScript. Any Web language that can accept incoming requests can be used with Flash player.

The `fscommand` command is the most common interface between Flash movies and scripting languages. The syntax for `fscommand` is:

```
fscommand(command, args);
```

where `command` is the command to be sent and `args` are any arguments that need to be passed with the command. The commands that are sent must, of course, be understood by the receiving application.

Standalone Flash Player

The standalone Flash player can receive and understand only specific commands from `fscommand`. These are shown in Table 20.1 with the possible arguments and a description.

Table 20.1 Standalone Flash Player Commands

Command	Arguments	Description
allowscale	true/false	Enables viewer to be scaled when `true`, prohibits scaling when `false`
exec	path	Executes the application given by path within the player
fullscreen	true/false	Expands to fullscreen when `true`, normal viewing size when `false`
quit	none	Closes the player
showmenu	true/false	Enables the context menu commands when `true`, dims them when `false`

A simple example of using `fscommand` for a stand-alone Flash player is to employ a button on the movie that enables a viewer to expand the player to full-screen or reduce the size. You saw the code for this action in an earlier chapter. For a standalone Flash player, the incoming `fscommand` must be one of the predefined commands enabled. The `fullscreen` property accepts either `true` or `false` arguments, so the ActionScript code to send an instruction to zoom to full screen based on a mouse click a button would look like this:

```
on (release) {
    fscommand ("fullscreen", "true");
}
```

In this case, we are passing the `fullscreen` command with the `true` argument. Both parameters are enclosed in quotation marks, which are stripped when they are sent by `fscommand`.

Using Web-based Flash Players

When playing a Flash movie inside a Web browser, you can use the fscommand command to send instructions to the Flash player itself or to the hosting language. If you want to communicate with the Flash player only, the process is the same as you saw in the previous code. For the hosting language to get involved, more steps are required.

Web-based Flash players (those used by browsers) can communicate with the operating environment using fscommand. The commands must have meaning to the language that interprets them, such as JavaScript. For the command to be interpreted by JavaScript, for example, a handler has to be enabled to intercept and understand the incoming command. In JavaScript, for example, the function name_DoFSCommand (where name is the name of the Flash movie) is used in the HTML page that embeds the Flash movie.

To show what this means for JavaScript, the most widely used hosting language for fscommand, we can use a simple example. If we want a Flash movie to be played through an HTML page, and the movie name is dogRunning, we would embed the following JavaScript code as part of the HTML instructions:

```
function dogRunning_DoFSCommand(command, args) {
    if (command == ...) {
        statements...;
    }
    if (command == ...) {
        statements...;
    }
    etc...
}
```

Inside the JavaScript function dogRunning_DoFSCommand is a series of if conditions that check to see what the incoming command is, and the statements for each of those commands is enclosed in the code block after the condition. You need to code a condition for each command that can be passed. (The parameter names command and args are local variables that can have any name; these are simply the convention.)

When you publish a movie using the HTML Publish Settings menu item, this code is automatically added to your movie with the appropriate movie name and ID parameters. For this reason, you want to be consistent with the command names throughout all your movies. You must use the FSCommand template in your movie, or the FSCommands do not work. Special parameters are embedded in the HTML code to enable the FSCommands to be used.

If we wanted to be able to pass the instruction to open a message box from the Flash movie, one of the if conditions inside the DoFSCommand function would be:

```
if (command == "messagebox") {
    alert(args);
}
```

This tells JavaScript to run the alert function (which is similar to Flash's trace function) with the specified arguments. The fscommand call would be like this:

```
fscommand("messagebox", "Thanks for watching our movie!");
```

This approach works not just for JavaScript, although the procedure is slightly different for other Web languages. For example, if you want to send fscommand commands to a program designed with Microsoft's Visual Studio series (such as Visual InterDev, Visual C++, or Visual Basic), you can use the ActiveX controls that these products support to send VB events.

Sending and Receiving Data

Flash usually communicates with server-side scripts through the loadVariables, getURL, and loadMovie actions. Each action uses HTTP to send the request along with any variables used in the movie that are required by the server-side script.

The getURL command is used to send a URL request to the browser window. The loadMovie command tells the Flash Player to load a particular movie, and the loadVariables command loads a variable into the Timeline of the movie currently on the Flash Player.

Using loadVariables

You use loadVariables to obtain data from a location, usually a script or bin file that has the handles to receive a data request and the methods to send the data. The data must be in application/x-www-urlformencoded MIME format. (This is not as awkward as it may sound because this is the standard format for all CGI and similar scripts.) The data sent from the remote application comes back in pairs of variable name and value. For example, a typical reply from a CGI script to a Flash loadVariables request (ignoring extraneous data) looks like this:

```
intro_unix=100&adv_unix=64&intro_c=145&adv_c=24&request1=intro+ada...
```

Each pair has the variable name followed by an equal sign and the current value and is separated from the next by an ampersand.

To use loadVariables specify where the data is obtained, as well as either the GET or POST methods used by HTTP. For example, if an item description is loaded from a location, the command would look like this:

```
loadVariables(http://www.tpci.com/cgi-bin/itemdesc.php, _root.myMovie, GET);
```

In this command, the URL is expanded and the PHP script called itemdesc.php sends the necessary variables using the HTTP GET method. The variables are loaded in the current movie, which is myMovie.

> **NOTE**
>
> As a security feature, all requests for server-side data from a Flash movie being played in a Web browser must be targeted at the same domain that the Flash SWF movie is hosted on. This prevents access to other domains through a Flash movie request, which can be a potential security problem.

Flash and XML

Flash can communicate using XML (eXtensible Markup Language) in the same way as JavaScript and other Web languages. (It is important to remember that XML is not a programming language, but a markup language.) Unlike HTML that simply uses tags to indicate the way text or images are to be displayed on a page, XML tags are used to identify each chunk of text. This is the approach taken by SGML (Structured Generalized Markup Language), which was the basis of both HTML and XML. By identifying the text or other objects, XML enables reuse of the objects much more easily. The primary benefit of XML over HTML is that it enables a separation of content and design.

XML tags (or nodes, as they are called) are used a little differently than HTML tags. All XML documents have a container node, which is simply a name for the entire document or section of the document. All XML nodes have a type and may have attributes and children that inherit the attributes.

> **TIP**
>
> The tree-structure that all XML objects are part of is called the DOM (Document Object Model), and is very similar to JavaScript's DOM.

An example of a simple chunk of XML code may help. In this code fragment, we define two items:

```
<SHIRTS>
    <TSHIRT_R
        COST="12"
        COLOR="RED"
        SIZE="XL"
        CODE="154367"
    />
    <TSHIRT_B
        COST="12"
        COLOR="BLUE"
        SIZE="XL"
        CODE="154368"
    />
</SHIRTS>
```

As with HTML tags, XML nodes use angle brackets around keywords, and the slash to indicate the end. This code defines the container node SHIRTS. This node has two child nodes called TSHIRT followed by a letter color code. Each TSHIRT has four attributes or properties, each with a value defined. No text is defined in this code, but it would appear between tags.

Flash XML Object

Without going into too much detail about XML, we can look at how Flash and XML can communicate. To communicate with XML, Flash uses an XML object. You can create an instance of the object in the usual way:

```
myXMLStuff = new XML();
```

We need to use some methods from the Flash XML object to handle Flash-XML communications. The Flash XML object methods of use are:

- load: Downloads XML and places it in an ActionScript XML object
- send: Sends a Flash XML object to a URL, which may result in information returned to the browser window
- sendAndLoad: Sends a Flash XML object to a URL, which may result in information placed in an ActionScript XML object

These methods can be used to structure information to be passed between the Flash movie (through the Flash XML object) and XML itself. For example, to click a button in a movie and order one of the red T-shirts mentioned earlier, you would attach the code to the button to format the order as an XML document, which is then sent to the server-side script that interprets XML. After the server-side processing is completed, an XML document is sent from the server application to the Flash movie as an XML document, which is then converted and handled by ActionScript. For XML to send data to Flash the POST method used by HTTP is called.

To use the load method you need to specify an external data location. For example, to call the file shirts.xml that holds the code you saw earlier, you would write:

```
myXMLStuff.load("shirts.xml");
```

assuming the XML file was in the same directory as the SWF file. Otherwise, you would have to provide a full URL to the file.

The Flash XML object has a method designed to trigger another function after a load. This is called onLoad and all it does is define a function to be executed when the XML document has been received.

TIP

A common misconception is that this function executes the target function when the onLoad command is processed. It doesn't: It waits for the XML document to be completely received before triggering the function.

To use the `onLoad` function, you need to specify the function to be run after the load, like this:

```
myXMLStuff.load("shirts.xml");
myXMLStuff.onLoad = runthisfunction;
```

The function should be defined in the ActionScript code, of course. If arguments are passed to the function, they are specified in the function definition, not the `onLoad` method call.

When you need to pass information to an application that is processing XML, you need to format the XML document. For example, to send an order for a T-shirt mentioned earlier, the ActionScript code for the ordering depends on creating an instance of the XML object then using the `createElement` method to construct an XML document containing the order info. The individual properties of the element are defined using the `attribute` keyword:

```
orderXML = new XML();
orderElement = orderXML.createElement("Order");
orderElement.attributes.code = "154367";
orderElement.attributes.qty = "1";
orderXML.appendChild(orderElement);
```

This code creates an XML document that looks like this:

```
<Order code="154367" qty="1" />
```

The document contains the element name (order) and the attributes and values defined for that element.

Flash XMLSocket Object

If you need to establish a continuous connection to a server-side application you can do so using a socket. (A *socket* is a combination of an IP address and a port number, and uses TCP to maintain a persistent connection.) The Flash XMLSocket object is used to enable such a connection. Because this is an XML object, all communications using XMLSockets are in XML document format.

> **TIP**
>
> A persistent connection is not necessary for all movie to server-side application communications. Normally, these can be handled using HTTP. A persistent connection is used for sending and receiving information continually and as soon as possible (almost real-time). Network overhead is involved, so persistent connections should be used only when necessary.

For Flash to communicate with the XMLSocket object, a server-side application that knows to wait for a connection request must be running. When Flash sends the request for a connection, the server-side application confirms the request and establishes the connection.

The XMLSocket object has both connect and send methods to establish the socket with a server-side application and to send XML documents. When a connection has been established, the onConnect method is called to launch a function (much like onLoad with the XML object). A close object terminates the connection. The general approach to coding an XMLSocket ActionScript is like this:

```
mySocket = new XMLSocket();
// establishes an instance of XMLSocket
mySocket.connect(http://www.tpci.com/cgi-bin/sockserv.exe, 1024);
// requests a connection to a server-side application using port 1024
mySocket.onConnect = myDataTransfer;
// run a script when connected
```

Most developers expand the code to handle connection refusals or failures.

Summary

In this chapter we've examined the way Flash movies can communicate with the environment or server-side applications using either Flash Player commands or integration with JavaScript and XML. We didn't go into great detail about the ActionScript necessary for these interactions because the details are dependent on your applications. You need to understand the basic processes and those we've shown here with their attendant methods.

Sample Questions

1. Which command or method is necessary for the operating system or other host application to communicate with a stand-alone Flash player?
   A. fscommand
   B. onLoad
   C. connect
   D. XMLSocket

2. What format is necessary to transfer data using loadVariable?
   A. XML document
   B. comma-separated variable
   C. raw ASCII
   D. application/x-www-urlformencoded MIME

3. Which of the following descriptions best explains the command "myXMLStuff.onLoad = myXMLStuffLoad"?
   A. When data loading is complete run myXMLStuffLoad.
   B. When data loading has started run myXMLStuffLoad.
   C. Set the method onLoad in myXMLStuff to have the value stored in myXMLStuffLoad.
   D. Load data from myXMLStuffLoad into myXMLStuff.

CHAPTER 21

Data-Driven Movies

One of the features available to Macromedia Flash developers is integration with external data sources. In Chapter 20, "External Data," you read how data can be passed in or out of a Flash movie by using functions and methods. Until lately, though, you couldn't find any descriptions of how to drive a Flash movie dynamically using incoming data to control the way the movie appears, runs, or the controls a user has over the movie. This is possible using interactions between databases and Flash.

Flash and Middleware

Flash cannot have a movie communicate directly with any database or external data source, such as an SQL server or a B-tree data manager. What can be accomplished, though, is to have Flash communicate with a server-side application as you saw in Chapter 20. Server-side applications are often called middleware because they reside between the data source and the application with which the user interacts. The software is in the middle acting as a funnel and data formatter.

Although Flash movies cannot directly talk to data sources such as databases, the middleware can and in fact is designed to do exactly that. Flash can talk to the middleware, leaving the possibility of a data-driven movie through the interaction with the middleware. The middleware can be any server-side application that has interfaces to the outside, such as CGI (Common Gateway Interface), ASP (Active Server Pages), and others.

To create a data-driven movie, you have to not only know how to write the ActionScript commands to talk to the middleware, but also know how to write the code for the middleware to data source interaction. For the purposes of this chapter we consider using an SQL (Structured Query Language) database as the source of the data, and any of the commercial middleware packages on the market, or custom written middleware written for CGI or other server-side applications.

SQL databases are widely used, and the most popular. Oracle, Informix, Microsoft Access, Microsoft SQL Server, Sybase, DB2, mySQL, FileMaker, and others all have the ability to interact with middleware. To do this, the middleware usually has to create an SQL query and pass it to the database engine, which then returns the result of the query. Most RDBMS (Relational DataBase Management System) engines also have their own scripting language which can also be used, but using standard SQL ensures portability.

On the Flash movie side, you need to design a movie that requests and processes information from middleware, which is much the same as designing a form for user input. Forms are an integral part of creating a data-driven movie, so knowledge of Flash forms is important.

> **TIP**
>
> One of the advantages to using middleware to query a database for data is the ability to constantly formulate queries and extract up-to-date information, which can then be passed back to Flash movies in near real-time for display on the interface.

Data Interaction with Middleware

Data-driven movies can be used in many ways, whether receiving the data from the database via middleware, or passing data from the user through the middleware to the database. The latter is the easiest to look at, so we can start there.

To accept user data in a movie and pass it to a database, you can use editable text fields in a form or simple interface layout, and accept the user's data in the usual way. Then, to pass the data to the middleware you can use a `getURL` or a `loadVariables` action to send the data using either a `GET` or `POST` method to the middleware. The middleware can then create the correct SQL query or database language statement to send the data received to the database itself. You can also use the `XML.send` and `XML.sendAndLoad` methods to accomplish the same tasks.

To receive data automatically from an SQL database, you need to have the middleware formulate the SQL query to extract the data from the database, and then pass that to Flash movies using `loadVariables`, `XML.sendAndLoad`, or another action. The Flash movie should have the routines to accept incoming data built in, and be able to handle no data reception as well as an overabundance. Timing routines in the middleware software can control the rate at which data is retrieved from the database and fed to Flash.

The more complex approach to data-driven movies is to combine the two methods mentioned previously. In this approach, the user provides some parameters that are passed to the middleware, which then formulates a query and passes it to the SQL database. The results of that query are passed back to the middleware, reformatted, and passed through to the Flash movie that then displays it as necessary for the user. This process can be done entirely through SQL in the middleware, or a SQL query string can be generated by the Flash movie itself and passed through the middleware without change.

Summary

In this chapter we've briefly looked at the ability to integrate data from an SQL engine (or any other form of data storage, for that matter), and pass it through middleware to a Flash movie. Flash can interact with the middleware in several ways, and data can be passed from the database to the movie, from the movie to the database, or both in turn. Writing this type of interaction is not trivial and requires a good mastery of not only Flash, but also the middleware and database systems.

Sample Questions

1. Which method can Flash use to extract data from an external application such as an SQL database?
   A. Use getURL to leave data in the SQL database engine queue.
   B. Use loadVariables to read data from the SQL database.
   C. Use the GET and POST methods to pass SQL queries.
   D. Use middleware as an intermediary.

2. How can you dynamically retrieve data from an external source such as a Web site CGI application into a Flash movie as it loads?
   A. Append the data in a URL calling the movie.
   B. Use the #include directive.
   C. Use the loadVariable action.
   D. Data cannot be dynamically set when a movie loads.

3. Which of the following will let you dynamically load a JPEG file from an external source when a movie is loading?
   A. JavaScript
   B. Macromedia Director
   C. Middleware
   D. Generator

CHAPTER 22

Debugging

Debugging Macromedia Flash programs involves the process of running and testing your movies, as well as correcting any problems that crop up with your ActionScript coding. For ActionScript errors, Flash includes a debugger that helps you decode problems in a movie as they occur, and usually to change the values of variables and object properties in a recursive process of changing values until the movie runs properly. In this chapter we look at the built-in Flash debugger as well as the use of the Output window (part of the Flash 5 developer environment) and the `trace` command. The `trace` command is useful for displaying current conditions and values.

NOTE

You don't have to use the Flash debugger to correct ActionScript errors. If you are used to working with external tools, they too can be used for debugging and making changes to ActionScript code, but they do not interact with the movie in Flash as it is tested. For this reason, many developers prefer to use the Flash debugger even if external editors are used to code ActionScript.

The Output Window

When you are running a movie in Test mode (Control, Test Movie), the Output window shows you any information about syntax errors and other problems. The Output window display is generated automatically whenever Test mode is used, but usually only the syntax errors are displayed. To display other information you need to use the `List Objects` and `List Variables` commands.

> **TIP**
>
> If you use the `trace` command as part of your debugging process you can send specific information (such as the value of a specific variable) to the Output window while a movie is running in Test mode.

The Output window may not be open when you run a movie in Test mode, but if any syntax errors are encountered, the Output window is automatically opened and the errors listed. You can always display the Output window using the Window, Output menu item.

After the Output window is open, you can use the Options menu to copy any of the highlighted contents of the window to the clipboard (Copy option), clear the window (Clear option), save the window's contents to a file for later use (Save to File option), or route the contents of the window to a printer (Print option).

The `List Objects` and `List Variables` commands enable you to change what is displayed in the Output window. The `List Objects` command (Debug, List Objects) displays each object type (whether it is a button, movie clip, or a drawn shape), the level and frame the object occupies, and the path of the movie clip instance. When hierarchies exist, such as with movie clips, a hierarchical display is used automatically.

> **NOTE**
>
> It is important to remember that the `List Objects` command is not a real-time selection: as a movie clip plays the objects displayed by the command are not automatically updated if changes occur. To refresh the display you must issue a `List Objects` command each time.

The `List Variables` command displays all the variables in the movie, in much the same manner as the Debug window. When active (Debug, List Variables) the variables are listed with their name and target path, as well as their value.

> **TIP**
>
> Unlike the Debug window, the Output `List Variables` command is not updated automatically. As with `List Objects`, you have to manually refresh the variable list in the window.

Using the `trace` Command

The `trace` command can be used in ActionScript programs to display information in the Output window. This is handy for displaying variable values or messages when an event is triggered. You can use the `trace` command as many times as you want in your code to display values or messages.

> **NOTE**
>
> Those familiar with the JavaScript `alert` statement will find Flash's `trace` command very similar.

When writing a statement using `trace`, you can use expressions as arguments. When the `trace` statement is expanded in the Output window, all expressions are resolved to a value. For example, you can have a statement like this:

```
trace("x position is " + root.xmouse);
trace("y position is " + root.ymouse);
```

The display in the Output window has the properties substituted, like this:

```
x position is 35
y position is 134
```

You can use the `trace` command within loops and conditional statements to show values of variables as they change. This is a handy way of debugging problems in an ActionScript program.

Examining the Debugger

The Flash debugger is a part of a special version of the Flash Player, called the Flash Debug Player. When you installed Flash, the Flash Debug Player was also installed. It is used automatically when you are authoring movies. Of course, the Debug version is not used when you are playing movies with the Flash Player external to the Flash environment unless the movie author has turned on the Debug option.

> **TIP**
>
> You can export a Flash movie with the debugger mode active by setting File, Publish Settings, Flash, Debugging Permitted. If you do not specifically enable debugging mode, there will be no debug information shown.

> **TIP**
>
> You can attach a password to the debugger mode. Without this password, a viewer cannot enable the Debugger. This is a handy way of preventing variables and properties from being viewed; set a password that only you know.

To use the Debugger, the Debugger window should be open in Flash (Window, Debugger). You can also launch the Debugger from inside a movie running in a Web browser (assuming the Debug option is active) by using the pop-up menu and selecting Debugger from the menu. If it is grayed out, the Debug option is not set in the published movie.

The top of the window is a status bar that tells you the type of Flash Player that is running the current movie as well as the URL or path to the movie being played. Four playback environment values usually appear in the status bar:

- ActiveX: When Internet Explorer is used under Windows using ActiveX to show a movie
- Netscape plug-in: When Netscape Navigator (Windows) or Internet Explorer (Macintosh) is playing a movie using the Netscape plug-in
- Standalone player: When the Flash Player (with no debug capabilities) is used for the movie
- Test movie: Uses an embedded player in the Flash environment

The top pane of the Debugger window is the Display list that shows a real-time view of the movie clip display list. When there are subsections involved in the list, expansion and contraction icons are next to the items. As movie clips are added to (or removed from) the movie, the Debugger Display list updates automatically to show the changes.

The lower pane of the Debugger window shows three tabs: Properties, Variables, and Watch list. The Properties tab enables you to display the property values of any movie clip loaded on the Stage. You can also see the current value of any property and change it immediately (although some properties are read-only and cannot be changed). The variables tab displays the name and any values assigned to variables in the movie. Any variable can have a value changed in the Debugger window and the change is immediately seen in the movie playback. The Watch list is a set of variables displayed in this window pane with their complete path and their current values. The Watch list enables you to narrow the variables that you are interested in from the Variables tab, and simply displays those variables you need to observe. Variables can be added to or removed from the Watch list easily at any time.

> **CAUTION**
>
> Watch list variables are not the same as breakpoints or watchpoints that have a trigger value and action in other high-level languages. In Flash, a Watch list is simply a selected list of variables and their values.

> **NOTE**
>
> When you add a variable to the Watch list, a blue dot appears next to the variable name in the Variables tab.

You can resize the Display list and the Variables tab by either dragging the horizontal divider between the two panes to reflect the proportional sizes of each pane, or expand the entire window by dragging a corner.

Using the Debugger

When the Debugger is used with a movie, you can examine properties or variables at any time. For example, to examine a variable's values (and perhaps to change the value), make sure the Debugger window is open and the movie is loaded. The movie does not have to be playing for you to work with the variable and property values.

Select the movie clip containing the property or variable from the Display list. If working with a variable, click the Variables tab. Of course, if you are looking at a property, click the Properties tab. All the variables or properties that are active at the location of the playhead in the Timeline are shown. If you are working with an object or array variable type, expansion and contraction are icons next to the name to enable you to see all the values that type has. As the movie plays, variables and properties may be added or removed (especially if subclips are involved).

To modify a property or variable value, select the name from the tab. The name and value are highlighted. After a name has been selected, enter a new value in the value column. The new values must be consistent with the variable type (number or string, for example). For properties, you cannot use an expression for a value, only a constant (string or number). Strings should be entered with quotation marks around them. Booleans can be used for either variables or properties, but are limited to the values true or false.

> **CAUTION**
>
> You cannot update object or array values using the Debugger Variable value column. Only single-value variables can be updated in this manner.

To add a variable to the Watch list, find the variable in the Variables list. Use the pop-up menu (right-click [Windows], Control+click [Macintosh]) and select the Watch option from the menu. The variable appears in the Watch list. Alternatively, you can be viewing the Watch list already and choose Add from the pop-up context menu, and then select the variable name. To remove a variable from the Watch list, display the pop-up context menu and select Remove.

> **NOTE**
>
> Properties cannot be added to the Watch list, only variables.

Summary

In this chapter we've looked at the tools available to help you debug your Flash ActionScripts and movies in general. The use of the trace command enables you to see variables and messages in the Output window as a movie plays. For more careful debugging, the Debug window is useful. These debugging tools are easy to use and can help solve most ActionScript problems when used correctly.

Sample Questions

1. The List Objects option shows what in the Output window?
   A. Buttons, movie clips, shapes, and text
   B. Links to URLs used by the current movie
   C. A hierarchical display of the current movie clip's properties
   D. All variables attached to objects in the movie

2. What is the best way to enable debugging of a movie from a remote location?
   A. Embed `trace` statements in the code.
   B. Set the debugging option in the Publish Settings option.
   C. Use Generator to display the movie as it runs.
   D. Use a Control+D keyboard shortcut when the movie plays.

3. Which statement is true about the `trace` command when properly used in ActionScript code?
   A. It enables you to see when an event has occurred.
   B. It enables you to change a variable's value while the movie is playing.
   C. It shows every line of code executed in the Output window.
   D. It shows the line numbers of each ActionScript code line executed.

CHAPTER 23

Error Handling

Programming errors are an unfortunate side effect of most coding, either because a typographic error was made or some unforeseen circumstance was not handled properly. Although the types of errors that are encountered in Macromedia Flash are limited compared to the number and type of errors found with most high-level programming languages, errors do exist.

Most Flash errors fall into two categories: problems with ActionScript logic, and problems with variable values, either as a result of coding problems (syntax errors) or due to user inputs. Both of these types of problems can be handled by ActionScript code corrections or routines. There are other problems that occur, of course, when a Flash Player is playing a movie. The most common is a problem with the HTML calls to the Flash Player, or a problem finding the proper file. Again, a little careful coding can handle all these errors.

ActionScript Error Handling

By far the most common problems with ActionScript programs are due to coding errors or the inability to handle specific variable values. Coding errors tend to be easy to spot and correct because the Flash Action window shows syntax errors as you type statements into the window. (Syntax errors occur much more often with Expert mode than Normal mode, primarily because Normal mode fills in most of the statements for you. Still, there are syntax errors due to variable misnaming, amongst others.) When using an external editor to write ActionScript programs, syntax errors can be checked by using the Check Syntax option in the Actions panel pop-up menu.

The syntax checking routines built into the Actions panel check only for common syntax problems, such as misspelled keynames. Misspelled variable names are beyond the scope of the syntax checker, so make sure you are using the proper variable names and that case is correct. To help spot these kinds of errors, use the Debugger window and the Output panel, discussed in Chapter 22, "Debugging."

> **TIP**
>
> Misplaced or misused parentheses and curly brace pairs are a common error. Make sure all parentheses and curly braces are paired and there are no nesting errors. Each function should have parentheses following the function name and curly braces are used after the parentheses.

The ActionScript error that is harder to see when writing code is due to variable values. For example, a number may be used instead of a string, or a zero used in a variable value that may result in a divide by zero error. Variable name collision is also common, resulting from a global variable being overridden by a local (or vice versa inside a function). There is no easy way to find these errors ahead of time other than to test your movie thoroughly.

> **TIP**
>
> Data type errors are very common. Take the time to carefully check the data types of each variable used in your ActionScript program and make sure only legal values can be entered in that variable.

You can embed instructions inside your ActionScript programs to handle common user errors. These usually require an `if` conditional to test for an error condition. Ideally, you code error handlers for any input required from the user, because users cannot usually be relied on to enter the correct type of data. This is especially a problem with ActionScript because the language lacks type enforcement or boundary value checking within the language. (Of course, the lack of all this extra checking makes ActionScript easier to work with!)

A typical example of embedding error handling code in your ActionScript programs is a common source of problems. If a user is to enter a number in an input field, entering a character or string can often cause problems within the ActionScript code resulting in errors or undefined data values. To check an entry field to see if a number has been entered by the user, you can use code like this:

```
on(release){
    if (isNaN(quantity){
          quantity = 0;
          msg="Use numbers only";
    }
    statements...
}
```

In this program, the isNaN (is not a number) function is used to check the field into which a user entered a value. In this case it is a field called quantity. If quantity is not a number, the condition is true and the statements inside the conditional curly braces are executed, setting the quantity to zero (to prevent undefined value errors) and entering a string into a variable that can be displayed by another statement later in the code. If a number was entered, the condition is false and the code proceeds as usual. (An else statement could have been included to provide number processing statements, if desired, when a number was entered.)

Although it may seem tedious to code a lot of error handling routines in your ActionScript programs, you can usually copy and paste the basic codes wherever needed. An alternative is to code a function that checks for allowed values and simply calls the function when a user enters a value.

Other common errors relate to button hit areas. Make sure all stages of a button are defined (unless they are hidden). Also, make sure the hit area of a button is properly defined around the button shape.

Showing HTML Errors

One of the abilities of a Flash movie is alerting viewers and other users to problems with HTML. This is accomplished through the Publish ability. The Publish function is used to create an HTML document with embedded instructions telling a Web browser to display the files Flash has created.

To alert users to problems with HTML, select the Show Warning Message option. This shows error messages when an error has been encountered.

> **TIP**
>
> A common error for a Flash Player is an inability to find a movie because of an incorrect path. Double-check all paths for movie clips, objects, and variables prior to publishing a movie.
>
> A useful trick is placing a Stop action in the first keyframe of a movie to prevent looping or automatic starting, unless this effect is desired.

Summary

In this chapter we've examined error handling for ActionScript and HTML problems. A little careful testing and debugging prior to publishing a movie are helpful at finding these kinds of errors, but this doesn't negate the need for careful coding of data entry routines to account for strange user entries. Remember that there is no such thing as a foolproof program: Some users are better fools than we give them credit for!

Sample Questions

1. What error occurs with this code: `function snafu{ z = 12%5;}`?
   A. The variable z is not defined.
   B. The function lacks parentheses.
   C. The function doesn't return a value.
   D. The result of `12%5` is of the wrong data type for z.

2. To catch number-specific data entry type errors, what is the best approach?
   A. Restrict the data type to allow only certain values.
   B. Check the values with `isNaN`.
   C. Force the user to use a pull-down menu for all data entry possibilities.
   D. Use the `if` statement to check the user's entry against an array of valid values.

CHAPTER 24

Profiling

After you have developed a movie, preview it not only to make sure the movie flows the way you want it to, but also to make sure the users get to see the movie the way you intended them to. This is a function of the speed with which the Macromedia Flash Player receives data, especially over the World Wide Web. To help you preview movies at a particular rate of transfer, Macromedia Flash includes a utility called the *Bandwidth Profiler*.

> **NOTE**
>
> It is important to remember that previewing a movie in the Flash development environment does not give you a true feel for how a Web surfer will see the movie, usually because of connection speed issues. Previewing a movie with the Bandwidth Profiler lets you see your movie how a Web surfer will see it.

Previewing Movies

To see how a movie or a scene plays in a Flash Player, you need to create a test movie (use Control, Test Movie, or Scene command). This opens a Flash Player that shows your movie. While the Player is open, you can perform several different steps to preview the movie, as well as examine its behavior under different transfer rates.

The View menu in the Flash Player or Flash environment can be used to control the Player holding your test movie. Two commands enable you to enlarge or shrink the movie (Zoom In and Zoom Out). These zoom options can be handy for examining any artifact problems that occur, as well as ensuring that details of a movie can be seen properly. The Magnification submenu enables you to change the zoom factor of the test movie, but this option also enables you to compensate for pixel size effects. (All of these menu commands are also available in the context menu displayed using the right-click.)

The Bandwidth Profiler is used to examine the behavior of a movie at different transfer rates. This is an important subject for movies that are transferred over slow connections, such as analog asynchronous modems.

The Bandwidth Profiler

The Bandwidth Profiler is a tool that enables you to simulate any download speed for your Flash movies and scenes. This enables you to see how your movie runs at 56kbps, for example, or over a 400kbps cable modem. The Bandwidth Profiler is used after you have created a test movie.

> **TIP**
>
> As a general rule when using a 28.8kbps modem, any transfer rate above 200 bytes per frame at 12 frames per second can cause problems. The relationship between bytes per frame and transfer rate is constant, so at 24 frames per second, 100 bytes per frame is the practical limit. Doubling the transfer speed of the modem allows double the number of bytes per frame. (Do not assume a 56kbps modem is twice as fast as a 28.8bps modem—it isn't.)

To view the Bandwidth Profiler, use the View, Bandwidth Profiler menu option (or Control+B [Windows], Command+B [Macintosh]). When launched the SWF movie shrinks in size to accommodate the Bandwidth Profiler window.

The Bandwidth Profiler window has two parts. The left side shows three separate sections of information: Movie, Settings, and State. The Movie section shows:

- The dimensions of the movie in pixels
- The frame rate used to show the movie
- The size of the movie (in both kilobytes and bytes)
- The duration of the movie
- The preload (in both number of frames and number of seconds)

The Settings section displays the current speed used to display the movie to emulate different connection speeds. These are all set in the Debug menu of the Bandwidth Profiler window. Finally, the State section shows the current frame number being played and its byte requirements, as well as the percentage of the movie loaded.

The right side of the Bandwidth Profiler window shows the Timeline header and a graph displaying several pieces of information. A red line running beneath the Timeline header shows whether each frame streams in real-time (this may change depending on the connection speed selected).

The Flash Player's Show Streaming menu item is used with the Bandwidth Profiler and shows the download progress of the movie through the use of a green bar in the Timeline header. A running total of the number of bytes downloaded is shown in the State section of the Bandwidth Profiler window.

The Debug menu in the Bandwidth Profiler window is used to set the download rates to 14.4kbps, 28.8kbps, or 56kbps (preset values) or any of three custom settings that you can save and use repeatedly. You can also use the Customize option to select any transfer rate specifically.

> **NOTE**
>
> Frame's Bandwidth Profiler does not take the rates provided in the Debug menu literally. For example, a transfer speed of 28.8kbps should theoretically enable 3.5kbps to be downloaded. This is never achieved in practice. Frame uses a more realistic rate around 2.3kbps for this setting, and adjusts all the other speeds for more realistic speeds as well.

Two additional commands are available when the Bandwidth Profiler is loaded: the Streaming Graph and Frame-by-Frame Graph. The Streaming Graph mode is the default when the Bandwidth Profiler loads. Streaming Graph mode shows how the Flash movie streams at the selected transfer rate, and how the movie appears in a browser window, for example. In the right side of the Bandwidth Profiler window, alternating light and dark blocks are used to represent each frame. The size of each block indicates its size relative to the other blocks.

The Frame-by-Frame Graph option is a second mode in the Bandwidth Profiler that shows each frame side by side under the Timeline header. The appearance of the Bandwidth Profiler window is similar to the Streaming Graph option, but the blocks mean different things. If any of the frame blocks are shown beyond the red line in the display (which changes location depending on the connection speed used), the play-back halts until the entire frame has been downloaded. This enables you to pinpoint any frames that are causing repetitive delays.

Summary

In this chapter we've examined the bandwidth profiler and how you can use it to show test movies at different transfer rates. In a movie this can help you isolate frames that are causing bottlenecks, as well as making sure the movie flows the way you want it to without stuttering or streaming delays. The Bandwidth Profiler is a useful tool to this end and should be used for all movies intended for distribution over the Web.

Sample Questions

1. What does the red line in the Bandwidth Profiler mean?
   A. The frames beyond the red line do not stream in real time at the selected transfer rate.
   B. The frames beyond the red line have ActionScript errors in them.
   C. The frames beyond the red line are too large for transfer at the current transfer rate.
   D. The frame rate changes at the red line.

2. Where would you find information about both the size of each frame and the total size of a movie as it is played in the Flash Player?

   A. The Object panel
   B. The Bandwidth Profiler
   C. The Debug panel
   D. The Publish Settings dialog

PART V

APPENDIX

A   Answers

APPENDIX A

Answers

Chapter 1

1. B. The Flash ActiveX control is required by Microsoft Office to play a Flash movie.
2. A. The Movie Explorer is the only panel or window listed that allows a find and replace operation to be performed.
3. A. The SWF file format contains a compressed version of the bytecode for a movie and can be interpreted by Flash Player.

Chapter 2

1. B. The Magnet option of the Arrow tool applies a grid over the Stage. Any items moved on the Stage snap to the grid.
2. B. A hollow box is used to indicate an anchor point for the pen tool.
3. B. A pressure-sensitive tablet allows you to change the size of the brush stroke by varying your pressure on the tablet.

Chapter 3

1. D. Symbols can be of many different types, not just movie clips.
2. B. A mask contains only a single element which is used to render parts of lower layers visible or opaque.
3. B. Most Web-based animations run at 12fps.

Chapter 4

1. D. The Hit state defines where the button can be triggered. This state is invisible and is never seen by a viewer.
2. B. A Roll Out event occurs when a cursor has moved over a button's hit area, but then moves off the hit area without being clicked.
3. D. Invisible buttons need to have a Hit event defined, but do not have to have an Up, Over, or Down event.

Chapter 5

1. A. A variable that has no value assigned to it is an undefined data type and hence has an undefined value.
2. C. The var keyword defines a variable as local.
3. D. Flash does not contain a function that tells you whether a variable is a local or not.

Chapter 6

1. B. Methods are functions that are attached to an object
2. C. A Smart Clip is a movie clip that has some parameters associated with it that a user can configure as needed for each instance.
3. B. The class1.class2.var1 syntax indicates an object with a variable var1 associated with a class called class2, which itself is an instance of a class called class1.

Chapter 7

1. A. The letter "a" appears in the frame when a frame event is placed on the Timeline.
2. D. The Toggle High Quality event is used to turn antialiasing on or off. When on, the image is of higher quality but requires more CPU cycles.
3. A. The word "this" is used as a prefix when referring to the current Timeline.

Chapter 8

1. C. Flash treats Object as an object not a primitive data type.
2. A. The string data type can use the + operator to concatenate strings.
3. B. The value of undefined is returned when you reference a variable that is not in the current Timeline.

Chapter 9

1. A. Any variables that do not have assigned values in a function call are assigned an undefined value by Flash.
2. C. Missing a return statement at the end of a function will result in an undefined value returned from the function call.
3. C. Functions can refer only to movie clip events that are loaded in the current Timeline.

Chapter 10

1. C. The `elif` keyword is not used by Flash.
2. C. A `do while` loop always executes the statements inside the curly braces at least once.
3. C. Functions cannot refer to movie clip events that are not loaded in the Timeline.

Chapter 11

1. A. Flash requires all included files to be in comma-separated variable format.
2. B. Smart Clips are movie clips that have functions or properties associated with them.
3. A. Buttons (clickable objects defined in a user interface) are not legal Smart Clip objects.

Chapter 12

1. A. An instance of an object is created with the new operator before the object name.
2. C. A method of an instance is called using the dot notation followed by the name of the method and a pair of parentheses (which may contain values).
3. C. To assign a property value to a variable, call the property using the dot notation after the instance name and use the assignment operation of an equal sign after the variable name.

Chapter 13

1. B. To crate a new instance of a movie already in the library, use the `attachMovie` method.
2. C. When the `duplicateMovieClip` method is used, the `_visible` property of the duplicate is set to `true`.
3. A. The quality setting of a movie is used to control the amount of antialiasing and bitmap smoothing applied during rendering.

Chapter 14

1. D. Because of zero origin numbering, array element number 3 is actually the fourth element in the array.
2. B. There are four values in the array even though they are numbered zero through three. The length is the number of values, hence four.
3. C. The splice method will remove elements starting at the number 1 element and removes 2 elements total, hence array elements 1 and 2 are removed.

Chapter 15

1. A. The command `myColor = new Color(myMovie);` will create a new instance of a Color object called `myColor`.
2. A. The `setTransform` command uses parameters in the order Red, Green, Blue, Alpha.
3. D. Red offsets and percentages (or any color and alpha values, for that matter) cannot be specified alone.

Chapter 16

1. B. The `isToggled` method is used to tell when a user presses the Caps Lock key.
2. C. `Key` methods can be used to refer to `Key` properties to determine which keys have been pressed and the state of keys.
3. C. The `RETURN` is not a legal `Key` property. `ENTER` is a legal property.

Chapter 17

1. B. When a `show` method is used on an already visible cursor, nothing new happens.
2. A. A mouse cursor is always visible by default.

Chapter 18

1. B. The AIFF file format cannot be used for exported sounds with Flash.
2. D. A maximum of eight handles are allowed in a volume envelope.
3. A. The Stream setting for Synchronization forces animation in a movie to synch with the sound.

Chapter 19

1. C. The `ceil()` method run against the value 3.14159 will round up to 4.
2. B. The Date object must be used with a constructor, and hence the `new` keyword is used to create an instance.
3. B. Because no argument was provided for the `indexOf` method, the value of 1 will be returned.

Chapter 20

1. A. `fscommand` is used to communicate between the operating system and a standalone player.
2. D. When using `loadVariable`, the `application/x-www-urlformencoded` MIME format is used.
3. A. The `onLoad` method is used to load data and then start running a function.

Chapter 21

1. D. Flash uses middleware as an intermediary to extract data from external applications.
2. A. Data can be passed to Flash through a URL that specifies the movie and the data being passed.
3. D. Generator lets you load a JPEG from an external source when a movie is loading.

Chapter 22

1. A. The List Objects option will show all buttons, movie clips, shapes, and text.
2. B. The Debugging option should be set in the Publish Settings panel to enable debugging of a movie from a remote location.
3. A. The `trace` command lets you see when an event has occurred.

Chapter 23

1. B. Every method or function needs parentheses.
2. B. The use of `isNaN` lets you check number-specific data entries to make sure they are numbers.

Chapter 24

1. A. Beyond the red line in the Bandwidth Profiler shows which frames will not stream in real time at the selected transfer rate.
2. B. The Bandwidth Profiler shows the size of each frame and the total size of the movie.

INDEX

Symbols

(&&) and condition, 109
-- (autodecrement) operator, 96
++ (autoincrement) operator, 96
{} (braces), 126
<EMBED> tag (HTML), 98
.FLA extension, 10
#include directive, 117-118
% (modulus) operator, 95
(!) not condition, 109
(||) or condition, 109
_parent (dot syntax), 76
_root (dot syntax), 76
.SWF extension, 11

A

abs(num) method (Math object), 171
acos(num) method (Math object), 171
actions. *See also* events
 assigning to objects, 80
 buttons, 52-54
  ActionScript, 53-55
 clip actions, 86-87
 defined, 76
 loadVariables, 186
 mouse actions, 80-81
 movie actions, 81
  assigning, 81
  FSCommand, 81, 84
  Get URL, 81, 84
  Go To, 81-82

If Frame Is Loaded, 82, 86
Load Movie, 81, 85
Play, 81-83
Print, 82
Stop, 81-83
Stop All Sounds, 81-83
Tell Target, 82, 85-86
Toggle High Quality, 81-83
Unload Movie, 82, 85
testing, 80
ActionScript, 9
arguments, 74
curly braces, 74
parentheses, 74
button commands, 53-55
comments, 73-74
errors, 201-203
functions, 61, 67-68
keywords, 73
programs, 70
building, 70-71
editing, 72
expert mode, 70-72
normal mode, 70-72
syntax highlighting, 72
statements, 74
semicolons, 74
terminology, 76-77
variables, scopes, 61-63
ActionScripts, writing scripts, 73
activating. *See* **turning on/off**
ActiveX, 198
**Adaptive Differential Pulse-Code
Modulation (ADPCM), 163**
adding
actions to buttons, 52-54
ActionScript, 53-55
frames, 43
**ADPCM (Adaptive Differential Pulse-
Code Modulation), 163**
**AIFF (Audio Interchange File
Format), 163**

**allowscale command (stand alone
Flash player), 184**
**alpha property (MovieClip object),
135-136**
alpha transparency (movie clips), 136
animated masks, 39
animating, buttons, 55
**animation sequences, converting to
movie clip symbols, 35**
animations, frame-by-frame, 44
creating, 44
testing, 45
antialiasing settings, turning on/off, 83
arguments
ActionScript, 74
curly braces, 74
parentheses, 74
defined, 76
arithmetic operations
assignment operator, 96
bitwise operators, 96
comparison operators, 96
logical operators, 96
numeric operators, 95-96
order of precedence, 95
arrays, 139-140
adding elements to, 141
array access operators, 140
concatenating, 141
creating, 140-141
defined, 139
joining, 141
loops, 143-144
methods, 141-143
concat(), 141-142
join(), 141-142
pop(), 141-142
push(), 141-142
reverse(), 141-142
shift(), 141
slice(), 141
sort(), 141-142

splice(), 141, 143
toString(), 141
unshift(), 141-142
populating, 140-141
removing first element of, 141
removing last element of, 141
reversing order of, 141
sorting, 141
splicing, 141
Arrow tools, 19-21
resizing items, 21
rotating items, 20
AS files, 118
asin(num) method (Math object), 171
assets, 16
assigning actions to objects, 80-81
assignment operator, 96
variables, 60
atan(num) method (Math object), 171
atan2(y, x) method (Math object), 171
attaching
functions to classes, 104
movies, 130-131
attachMovie method, 130-131
**Audio Interchange File Format
(AIFF), 163**
audio. *See* **sound; sound files**
autodecrement operator, 96
autoincrement operator, 96

B

background music, 167
**BACKSPACE property (Key object),
152**
Bandwidth Profiler, 205-206
Bandwidth Profiler window, 206-207
bit depth (sounds), 161
Bitmap Properties window, 56
bitmaps
converting to vector graphics, 57
importing, 56-57
modifying, 57

bitwise operators, 96
block scope, 102
boolean function, 100
booleans, 92
braces ({}), 126
break statements, 114-115
Brush tool, 27
mode modifiers, 28-29
building ActionScript programs, 70-71
button symbols, 34
buttons, 49. *See also* **symbols**
actions, 52-54
ActionScript, 53-55
animating, 55
creating, 49-50
invisible, 55
defining, 56
functions, 56
Modify Onion Markers, 41
mouse buttons, events, 80-81
movies, 51-52
shapes, 52
Smart Clips, 119
sounds, 166
states, 49
setting, 50-51
Test, 57
buttons symbols, 16

C

calling functions, 101
**CAPSLOCK property (Key object),
152**
ceil(num) method (Math object), 171
charAt(s) method (String object), 179
**charCodeAt(s) method (String object),
179**
checkbox objects, 119
classes, 68
creating, 104-105
defined, 76
functions, attaching, 104

methods, 68-70
newframe, 104
properties, 68-70
clip events, 86-87
clips
alpha transparency, 136
coordinates
converting, 132-133
finding, 132
copying, duplicateMovieClip
method, 131
depth levels, swapping, 134
dragging, 134
events, 86-87
loading, 134
movie clip data type, 93-94
MovieClip object, 129
methods, 129-135
properties, 135-136
multiple, 44
nested, 44
rendering quality, 136
size, finding, 132
Smart Clips, 118-119
buttons, 119
checkboxes, 119
menu objects, 119-121
when to use, 118
unloading, 134
code reuse, 117
#include directive, 117-118
Smart Clips, 118-119
buttons, 119
checkboxes, 119
menu objects, 119-121
when to use, 118
coding errors, 201
ActionScript logic, 201-203
HTML, 203
variable values, 201
color, Highlight, 20
Color object, 147
methods, 147-148
transform parameters, 148-149

Color section (Toolbox), 22
**color values, RGB (Red-Green-Blue),
147**
commands
ActionScript, buttons, 53-55
getURL, 98
List Objects, 195-196
List Variables, 195-196
loadVariables, 97
movie actions
FSCommand, 81, 84
Get URL, 81, 84
Go To, 81-82
If Frame Is Loaded, 82, 86
Load Movie, 81, 85
Play, 81-83
Print, 82
Stop, 81-83
Stop All Sounds, 81-83
Tell Target, 82, 85-86
Toggle High Quality, 81-83
Unload Movie, 82, 85
stand-alone Flash player, 184
trace, 195-197
Zoom In, 205
Zoom Out, 205
comments, 103
ActionScript, 73-74
comparing
instances and symbols, 34
motion and shape tweening, 45
comparison operators, 96
**compatibility, SWF files and applica-
tions, 11**
concat method (String object), 179
concat() method, 141-142
concatenating
arrays, 141
strings, 90
conditional statements, 108
conditions
and (&&), 109
not (!), 109
or (||), 109

connect method, 190

constants, 90

constructor functions, defined, 126

constructors

Color object methods, 148

defined, 76

continue statements, 114-115

CONTROL property (Key object), 152

controlling loops, 114

break statements, 114-115

continue statements, 114-115

converting

bitmaps to vector graphics, 57

keyframes, 42

movie clip coordinates, 132-133

objects into symbols, 34-35

strings

to lowercase, 91

to numbers, 91

to uppercase, 91

convertToKilometers function, 102

coordinates, movie clip coordinates

converting, 132-133

finding, 132

copying movies, duplicateMovieClip method, 131

cos(num) method (Math object), 172

createElement method, 189

creating

arrays, 140-141

buttons, 49-50

classes, 104-105

data-driven movies, 191

frame-by-frame animations, 44

functions, 101-103

keyframes, 42

motion tweening, 46

objects, 126

new operator, 126

object initializer operator, 126

shape tweening, 46-47

symbols, 34-35

test movies, 205

variables, 60, 89, 95

curly braces, ActionScript arguments, 74

currentframe property (MovieClip object), 135

custom classes, creating, 104-105

Custom effect (Sound panel), 165

custom functions, creating, 101-103

customizing

classes, 104-105

functions, 101-103

Pen tool, 25-26

stroke styles, 23-24

D

data event, 86

data type errors, ActionScript, 202

data types, 89

booleans, 92

defined, 76

determining, 94

movie clip, 93-94

numbers, 92

converting strings to, 91

double precision floating-point format, 92

objects, 93

primitive, 89

reference, 89

strings, 90-92

concatenating, 90

converting to lowercase, 91

converting to uppercase, 91

declaring, 90

escape characters, 91

extracting substrings from, 92

finding characters in, 91

variables, 60-61

data-driven movies, 191

creating, 191

middleware, 191-193

Date object, 172-173
    instantiating, 174-177
    methods, 173-174
        Date.UTC(), 174
        getDate(), 173
        getDay(), 173
        getFullYear(), 173
        getHours(), 173
        getMilliseconds(), 173
        getMinutes(), 173
        getMonth(), 173-174
        getSeconds(), 173-174
        getTime(), 173
        getTimezoneOffset(), 173
        getUTCDate(), 173
        getUTCDay(), 173
        getUTCFullYear(), 173
        getUTCHours(), 173
        getUTCMilliseconds(), 173
        getUTCMinutes(), 173
        getYear(), 174
        setDate(), 174
        setFullYear(), 174
        setHours(), 174
        setMilliseconds(), 174
        setMinutes(), 174
        setMonth(), 174
        setSeconds(), 174
        setTime(), 174
        setUTCDate(), 174
        setUTCFullYear(), 174
        setUTCHours(), 174
        setUTCMilliseconds(), 174
        setUTCMinutes(), 174
        setUTCMonth(), 174
        setUTCSeconds(), 174
        setUTCTime(), 174
        setYear(), 174
        toString(), 174
    Timer function, 178
Date variables, creating, 174-177
Date.UTC() method (Date object), 174
deactivating. *See* **turning on/off**

Debugger window, 197-198
    Properties tab, 198
    properties, modifying, 199
    status bar, 197
    variables
        adding to Watch list, 199
        modifying, 199
    Variables tab, 198
    Watch list tab, 198-199
debugging Macromedia Flash programs, 195
declaring strings, 90
default window, 10
defining
    classes, 104-105
    functions, 101-103
    mask layers, 39
definitions, ActionScript terminology, 76-77
DELETEKEY property (Key object), 152
depth levels (movie clips), swapping, 134
dialog boxes
    Fill color, 22
    Line Style, 23
    Movie Explorer, 12
    swatches, 22
digital audio. *See* **sound files**
directives, #include, 117-118
disabling. *See* **turning on/off**
Display List (Movie Explorer), 12-13
do, while loop, 110-114
DoFSCommand function, 185
dot syntax, 75
    _parent, 76
    _root, 76
double precision floating-point format, 92
DOWN property (Key object), 152
Down state (buttons), 49-50
Drag Out event, 81
Drag Over event, 81

dragging movie clips, 134
drawing tools, 24
    Brush tool, 27-29
    Line tool, 24
    Oval and Rectangle tool, 27
    Pen tool, 25-26
    Pencil tool, 24-25
        Ink modifier, 24-25
        Smooth modifier, 24-25
        Straighten modifier, 24-25
Dropper tool, 29
droptarget property (MovieClip object), 135
duplicateMovieClip method, 130-131

E

editing
    ActionScript programs, 72
    Onion Skin mode, 41
    Sort window, 16
    sounds, 167-168
enabling. *See* **turning on/off**
END property (Key object), 152
ENTER property (Key object), 152
enterFrame event, 86-87
Eraser mode modifier, 30-31
Eraser tool, 30-31
error handling, coding, 201
    ActionScript logic, 201-203
    HTML, 203
    variable values, 201
escape characters, 91
escape function, 100
ESCAPE property (Key object), 152
Euler's constant (E) method (Math object), 172
eval function, 100
event handlers, 79
Event option (sound synchronization), 165
events, 79. *See also* **actions**
    clip events, 86-87
    defined, 76, 79

    event handlers, 79
    frame events, 81
        assigning, 81
        FSCommand, 81, 84
        Get URL, 81, 84
        Go To, 81-82
        If Frame Is Loaded, 82, 86
        Load Movie, 81
        Play, 81-83
        Print, 82
        Stop, 81-83
        Stop All Sounds, 81, 83
        Tell Target, 82, 85-86
        Toggle High Quality, 81, 83
        Unload Movie, 82, 85
    mouse, Objects Action panel, 54
    mouse events, 80-81
    programming, 80
    testing, 80
exec command (stand alone Flash player), 184
exp(num) method (Math object), 172
expert mode, ActionScript programs, 70-72
exporting sound files, 168-169
expressions, defined, 76
eXtensible Markup Language. *See* **XML**
extensions
    .FLA, 10
    .SWF, 11
extracting substrings, 92

F

Fade In effect (Sound panel), 165
Fade Out effect (Sound panel), 165
false function, 100
files
    .AS files, 118
    FLA, 10
    importing
        #include directive, 117-118
        into movies, 56

loading from URLs, 84
sound files, 157
   adding to buttons, 166
   adding to movies, 164-166
   background music, 167
   bit depth, 161
   exporting, 168-169
   file formats, 163-164
   importing, 164
   linking, 167
   looping, 169
   sampling, 159-161
   size of, 162-163
   sound editing controls,
     167-168
   sound frequency, 158-159
   Sound panel options, 165-166
   synchronization, 165-167
   tips and guidelines, 169
SWF, 11
Fill color dialog box, 22
Fill tab, 24
finding
characters in strings, 91
frames, Go To action, 82
movie clip coordinates, 132
movie clip size, 132
FLA files, 10
Flash
launching, 10
movies, 9-10
overview, 9
Flash Action window, 201
Flash Debug Player, 197
Flash debugger, 195
Flash default window, 10
Flash players
stand alone Flash player
   commands, 184
     sending messages to, 184
Web-based Flash players, sending
   messages to, 185-186
floor(num) method (Math object), 172

**focusrect property (MovieClip object),
  135**
for loop, 110-112
for, in loop, 110-112
formats, sound files, 163-164
frame labels, 42-43
frame rates, 43
Frame View menu, 40
frame-by-frame animations, 44
creating, 44
testing, 45
FrameRate variable, 60
frames, 9
events, 81
   assigning, 81
   FSCommand, 81, 84
   Get URL, 81, 84
   Go To, 81-82
   If Frame Is Loaded, 82, 86
   Load Movie, 81, 85
   Play, 81-83
   Print, 82
   Stop, 81-83
   Stop All Sounds, 81, 83
   Tell Target, 82, 85-86
   Toggle High Quality, 81, 83
   Unload Movie, 82, 85
finding, Go To action, 82
in-between, 43
keyframe, 9
keywords, 42
static, 9
targets, 85-86
Timeline, 41
**framesloaded property (MovieClip
  object), 135**
frequency (sound), 158-159
**fromCharCode method (String
  object), 179**
FSCommand action (movies), 81, 84
fscommand() function, 183-184
**fullscreen command (stand alone Flash
  player), 184**

function calls, ActionScript, 74-75
function keyword, 102
function literals, 103-104
functions, 99-100. *See also* **methods**
   ActionScript, 61, 67-68
   attaching to classes, 104
   boolean, 100
   calling, 101
   constructor functions, defined, 126
   convertToKilometers, 102
   creating, 101-103
   defined, 77, 99
   DoFSCommand, 185
   escape, 100
   eval, 100
   false, 100
   fscommand(), 183-184
   function literals, 103-104
   getProperty, 100
   getTimer, 100
   getURL, 186
   getVersion, 100
   globalToLocal, 100
   hitTest, 100
   indexOf(), 91-92
   int, 100
   invisible buttons, 56
   isFinite, 100
   isNaN, 100
   localToGlobal, 100
   maxscroll, 100
   naming conventions, 102
   newline, 100
   number, 100
   Number(), 91
   overwriting, 102
   parameters, 102
   parseFloat, 100
   parseInt, 100
   predefined functions, 100-101
   Publish, 203
   random, 100
   scroll, 101

   setframeSize, 104
   slice(), 92
   sqrt(), 93
   string, 101
   TargetPath, 101
   Timer (Date method), 178
   toLowerCase(), 91
   trace(), 120
   true, 101
   typeof(), 94
   unescape, 101
   variables, 59

G

Get URL action (movies), 81, 84
getAscii method, 151
getBounds method, 130, 132
getBytesLoaded method, 130, 132
getBytesTotal method, 130, 132
getCode method, 151
getDate() method (Date object), 173-174
getDay() method (Date object), 173
getFullYear() method (Date object), 173
getHours() method (Date object), 173
getMilliseconds() method (Date object), 173
getMinutes() method (Date object), 173
getMonth() method (Date object), 173-174
getProperty function, 100
getRGB method, 147
getSeconds() method (Date object), 173-174
getTime() method (Date object), 173
getTimer function, 100
getTimezoneOffset() method (Date object), 173
getTransform method, 147
getURL command, 98

getURL function, 186

getURL method, 130

getUTCDate() method (Date object), 173

getUTCDay() method (Date object), 173

getUTCFullYear() method (Date object), 173

getUTCHours() method (Date object), 173

getUTCMilliseconds() method (Date object), 173

getUTCMinutes() method (Date object), 173

getVersion function, 100

getYear() method (Date object), 174

global variables, scopes, 61-62

globalToLocal function, 100

globalToLocal method, 130, 132-133

GMT (Greenwich Mean Time), 173

Go To action (movies), 81-82

gotoAndPlay method, 130

graphic symbols, 34

graphics, importing, 56

graphics symbols, 16

Greenwich Mean Time. *See* GMT

guide layers, 38

    mask, 39

    motion, 38

H

handlers, defined, 77

handlers (event), 79

height property (MovieClip object), 135

hide method, 155-156

Highlight color, 20

highlighting syntax, ActionScripts programs, 72

highquality property (MovieClip object), 135

Hit state (buttons), 49-50

hitTest function, 100

hitTest method, 130, 133

HOME property (Key object), 152

HTML errors, 203

HTML (Hypertext Markup Language) tags, <EMBED> tag, 98

I

icons

    Magic Wand Properties, 21

    Magnet, 20

    Movie Explorer, 11

    Onion Skin, 40

    Paint Bucket, 30

    Pen, 27

    Swap Colors, 22

    Timeline, 40

identifiers, defined, 77

If Frame Is Loaded action (movies), 82, 86

if statement, 107-110

if-else statement, 107-108

importing

    bitmaps, 56-57

    files, #include directive, 117-118

    files into movies, 56

    graphics, 56

    sound files, 164

in-between frames, 43

indexOf() function, 91-92

indexOf(s) method (String object), 179

Ink Bottle tool, 29

Ink modifier, 24-25

INSERT property (Key object), 152

inserting frames into Timeline, 41

instance names, defined, 77

instances

    defined, 77

    symbols, 33-34

instantiating

    Date object, 174-177

    objects, 126

int function, 100
invisible buttons, 55
defining, 56
functions, 56
isDown method, 151
isFinite function, 100
isNaN function, 100
isToggled method, 151

J-K

join() method, 141-142
joining arrays, 141

Key object, 151
methods, 151-152
properties, 152-153
Key Press event, 80
keyDown event, 86-87
keyframes, 9, 40, 42
converting, 42
creating, 42
keys, Key object, 151
methods, 151-152
properties, 152-153
keyUp event, 86-87
keywords
ActionScript, 73
defined, 77
function, 102
new, 104
return, 103

L

Lasso tools, 19, 21
lastIndexOf(s) method (String object), 179
launching Flash, 10
Layer Properties window, 36
Layer window, 36
adding layers, 37
deleting layers, 38
editing layers, 38

layers, 35
adding to Layer window, 37
deleting, 38
editing, 38
guide, 38
mask, 39
motion, 38
locked, 36
Timeline window, 35-36
Left Channel effect (Sound panel), 165
LEFT property (Key object), 152
Library, 14
Library Sort pane, 14
Library window, 14-16
Line Style dialog box, 23
Line tool, 24
linking sound files, 167
List Objects command, 195-196
List Variables command, 195-196
literals, function literals, 103-104
LN10 method (Math object), 172
LN10E method (Math object), 172
LN2 method (Math object), 172
load event, 87
load method, 188
Load Movie action (movies), 81, 85
loading
files from URLs, 84
movies
Load action, 85
loadMovie method, 134
verifying loaded files, 86
variables, 89, 97-98, 186
loadMovie, 11
loadMovie method, 130, 134
loadVariables action, 186
loadVariables command, 97
loadVariables method, 130
local variables, scopes, 62
localToGlobal function, 100
localToGlobal method, 130, 132-133
locked layer, 36
log(num) method (Math object), 172
LOG2E method (Math object), 172

logical operators, 96
looping, 114
>   break statements, 114-115
>   continue statements, 114-115
>   sound files, 169
loops, 110
>   arrays, 143-144
>   controlling, 114
>>   break statements, 114-115
>>   continue statements, 114-115
>   do, while, 110, 113-114
>   for, 110-112
>   for, in, 110, 112
>   while, 110, 112-113
lowercase, converting strings to, 91

M

Macromedia Flash 5. *See* Flash
Magic Wand Properties icon, 21
Magnet icon, 20
mask guide layers, 39
masks
>   animated, 39
>   static, 39
Math object, 171
>   methods, 171-172
>>   abs(num), 171
>>   acos(num), 171
>>   asin(num), 171
>>   atan(num), 171
>>   atan2(y, x), 171
>>   ceil(num), 171
>>   cos(num), 172
>>   Euler's constant (E), 172
>>   exp(num), 172
>>   floor(num), 172
>>   LN10, 172
>>   LN10E, 172
>>   LN2, 172
>>   log(num), 172
>>   LOG2E, 172
>>   max (x, y), 172

min (x, y), 172
PI, 172
power(x, y), 172
random(), 172
round(num), 172
sin(num), 172
sqrt(num), 172
SQRT1 2, 172
SQRT2, 172
tan(num), 172
math operations
>   assignment operator, 96
>   bitwise operators, 96
>   comparison operators, 96
>   logical operators, 96
>   numeric operators, 95-96
>   order of precedence, 95
max (x, y) method (Math object), 172
maxscroll function, 100
menus
>   Frame View, 40
>   Library window, 15-16
>   Movie Explorer, 12-13
>   Smart Clips, 119-121
messages, sending
>   fscommand() function, 183-184
>   stand alone Flash player, 184
>   Web-based Flash players, 185-186
methods. *See also* functions
>   attachMovie, 130-131
>   classes, 68-70
>   Color object, 147-148
>>   constructors, 148
>>   transform parameters, 148-149
>   concat(), 141-142
>   connect, 190
>   createElement, 189
>   Date object, 173-174
>   Date objects
>>   Date.UTC(), 174
>>   getDate(), 173
>>   getDay(), 173
>>   getFullYear(), 173

getHours(), 173
getMilliseconds(), 173
getMinutes(), 173
getMonth(), 173-174
getSeconds(), 173-174
getTime(), 173
getTimezoneOffset(), 173
getUTCDate(), 173
getUTCDay(), 173
getUTCFullYear(), 173
getUTCHours(), 173
getUTCMilliseconds(), 173
getUTCMinutes(), 173
getYear(), 174
setDate(), 174
setFullYear(), 174
setHours(), 174
setMilliseconds(), 174
setMinutes(), 174
setMonth(), 174
setSeconds(), 174
setTime(), 174
setUTCDate(), 174
setUTCFullYear(), 174
setUTCHours(), 174
setUTCMilliseconds(), 174
setUTCMinutes(), 174
setUTCMonth(), 174
setUTCSeconds(), 174
setUTCTime(), 174
setYear(), 174
toString(), 174
defined, 77
duplicateMovieClip, 130-131
getAscii, 151
getBounds, 130, 132
getBytesLoaded, 130, 132
getBytesTotal, 130, 132
getCode, 151
getRGB, 147
getTransforms, 147
getURL, 130
globalToLocal, 130, 132-133

gotoAndPlay, 130
gotoAndStop, 130
hide, 155-156
hitTest, 130, 133
isDown, 151
isToggled, 151
join(), 141-142
load, 188
loadMovie, 130, 134
loadVariables, 130
localToGlobal, 130, 132-133
Math object, 171-172
Math objects
    abs(num), 171
    acos(num), 171
    asin(num), 171
    atan(num), 171
    atan2(num), 171
    ceil(num), 171
    cos(num), 172
    Euler's constant (E), 172
    exp(num), 172
    floor(num), 172
    LN10, 172
    LN10E, 172
    LN2, 172
    log(num), 172
    LOG2E, 172
    max (x, y), 172
    min (x, y), 172
    PI, 172
    power(x, y), 172
    random(), 172
    round(num), 172
    sin(num), 172
    sqrt(num), 172
    SQRT1 2, 172
    SQRT2, 172
    tan(num), 172
Mouse object, 155-156
nextFrame, 130
onLoad, 189
play, 130

pop(), 141-142
prevFrame, 130
push(), 141-142
removeMovieClip, 130
reverse(), 141-142
send, 188, 190
sendAndLoad, 188
setRGB, 147
setTransform, 147
shift(), 141
slice(), 141
sort(), 141-142
splice(), 141, 143
startDrag, 130, 134
stop, 130
stopDrag, 130, 134
String object, 178, 180
    charAt(s), 179
    charCodeAt(s), 179
    concat, 179
    fromCharCode, 179
    indexOf(s), 179
    lastIndexOf(s), 179
    slice(x, y), 179
    split(delim), 179
    substr(x, y), 179
    sunstring(x, y), 179
    toLowerCase(), 179
    toUpperCase(), 179
swapDepths, 130, 134
toggleHighQuality(), 83
toString(), 141
unloadMovie, 130, 134
unshift(), 141-142
middleware
    advantages, 192
    data-driven movies, 191-193
min (x, y) method (Math object), 172
modifiers
    Brush Mode, 28-29
    Eraser mode, 30-31
    Ink, 24-25
    Smooth, 24-25
    Straighten, 24-25

Modify Onion Markers button, 41
modifying
    bitmaps, 57
    button shapes, 52
modulus operator, 95
motion guide layers, 38
motion tweening, 45
    creating, 46
    shape tweening, comparing, 45
mouse events, 80-81
    Objects Action panel, 54
Mouse object, 155-156
mouseDown event, 87
mouseMove event, 87
mouseUp event, 87
movie clip data type, 93-94
movie clip symbols, 34-35
movie clips symbols, 16
movie clips. *See* **clips**
Movie Editing mode, 51
Movie Explorer, 11-13
    menu options, 12-13
Movie Explorer dialog box, 12
Movie Explorer Display List, 12-13
Movie Explorer icon, 11
MovieClip object, 129. *See also* **clips**
    methods, 129-130
        attachMovie, 130-131
        duplicateMovieClip, 130-131
        event handlers, 135
        getBounds, 130, 132
        getBytesLoaded, 130, 132
        getBytesTotal, 130, 132
        getURL, 130
        globalToLocal, 130, 132-133
        gotoAndPlay, 130
        gotoAndStop, 130
        hitTest, 130, 133
        loadMovie, 130, 134
        loadVariables, 130
        localToGlobal, 130, 132-133
        nextFrame, 130
        play, 130

prevFrame, 130
removeMovieClip, 130
startDrag, 130, 134
stop, 130
stopDrag, 130, 134
swapDepths, 130, 134
unloadMovie, 130, 134
properties, 135
alpha, 135-136
currentframe, 135
droptarget, 135
focusrect, 135
framesloaded, 135
height, 135
highquality, 135
name, 135
quality, 135-136
rotation, 135
soundbuftime, 135
target, 135
totalframes, 135
url, 135
visible, 135
width, 135
x, 135
xmouse, 135
xscale, 136
y, 136
ymouse, 136
yscale, 136
movies
actions, 81
assigning, 81
FSCommand, 81, 84
Get URL, 81, 84
Go To, 81-82
If Frame Is Loaded, 82, 86
Load Movie, 81, 85
Play, 81-83
Print, 82
Stop, 81-83
Stop All Sounds, 81, 83
Tell Target, 82, 85-86

Toggle High Quality, 81, 83
Unload Movie, 82, 85
antialiasing settings, turning on/off, 83
attaching, 130-131
buttons, 51-52
clips, Smart Clips, 118-121
copying duplicateMovieClip
method, 131
data-driven movies, 191
creating, 191
middleware, 191-193
depth levels, swapping, 134
files, importing, 56
Flash, 9-10
frames, finding, 82
loading
Load action, 85
loadMovie method, 134
verifying loaded files, 86
movie clips. *See* clips
playing, Play action, 82-83
previewing, 205-206
sound files, 157
adding to movies, 164-166
bit depth, 161
file formats, 163-164
importing, 164
sampling, 159-161
size of, 162-163
sound frequency, 158-159
stopping, 82-83
targets, 85-86
test movies, creating, 205
unloading
Unload action, 85
unloadMovie method, 134
**MP3 (MPEG-1 Audio Layer 3) files,
163**
multiple clips, 44
multiple timelines, 43-44
music. *See* **sound files**

N

name property (MovieClip object), 135
naming conventions
functions, 102
variables, 94
nested clips, 44
nested timelines, 43-44
Netscape plug-in, 198
new keyword, 104
new operator, 104, 126
newframe class, 104
newline function, 100
nextFrame method, 130
nodes (XML), 187-188
normal mode, ActionScript programs, 70-72
number function, 100
Number() function, 91
numbers, 92
converting strings to, 91
numeric operators, 95-96

O

object data type, 93
object initializer operator, 126
objects, 68, 125
arrays, 139-140
adding elements to, 141
array access operators, 140
concatenating, 141
creating, 140-141
defined, 139
joining, 141
loops, 143-144
methods, 141-143
populating, 140-141
removing first element of, 141
removing last element of, 141
reversing order of, 141
sorting, 141
splicing, 141
assigning actions to, 80

Color, 147
methods, 147-148
transform parameters, 148-149
creating, 126
new operator, 126
object initializer operator, 126
Date, 172-173
instantiating, 174-177
methods, 173-174
Timer function, 178
defined, 77, 125
instantiating, 126
Key, 151
methods, 151-152
properties, 152-153
Math, 171-172
Mouse, 155-156
MovieClip, 129. *See also* clips
methods, 129-135
properties, 135-136
Smart Clips, 118-119
buttons, 119
checkboxes, 119
menu objects, 119-121
when to use, 118
sound files, 157
adding to buttons, 166
adding to movies, 164-166
background music, 167
bit depth, 161
exporting, 168-169
file formats, 163-164
importing, 164
linking, 167
looping, 169
sampling, 159-161
size of, 162-163
sound editing controls, 167-168
sound frequency, 158-159
Sound panel options, 165-166
synchronization, 165-167
tips and guidelines, 169

String, 178
  methods, 178-180
XML, 188-189
XMLSocket, 189-190
Objects Action panel, 53
  mouse events, 54
On Mouse Event command, 53
Onion Skin icon, 40
onion skinning, 40
  edits, 41
onLoad method, 189
operators
  assignment, variables, 60
  assignment operator, 96
  bitwise operators, 96
  comparison operators, 96
  defined, 77
  logical operators, 96
  new, 104, 126
  numeric operators, 95-96
  object initializer, 126
  order of precedence, 95
order of precedence, arithmetic operations, 95
Output window, 195-196
Oval and Rectangle tool, 27
Over state (buttons), 49-50
overwriting functions, 102

P

Paint Bucket icon, 30
Paint Bucket tool, 29-30
painting tools, 29
  Dropper tool, 29
  Ink Bottle tool, 29
  Paint Bucket tool, 29-30
panels
  Object Actions, 53-54
  Sound panel
    sound editing controls,
      167-168
    sound effects, 165-166
    synchronization options, 165
  Stroke, 22

panes, Library Sort, 14
parameters
  function parameters, 102
  transforms, Color object, 148-149
**parentheses, ActionScript arguments,
  74**
parseFloat function, 100
parseInt function, 100
Pen icons, 27
Pen tool, 25-26
Pencil tool, 24-25
  Ink modifier, 24-25
  Smooth modifier, 24-25
  Straighten modifier, 24-25
percent sign (%), 95
persistent connections, 189
PGDN property (Key object), 152
PGUP property (Key object), 152
PI method (Math object), 172
Play action (movies), 81-83
play method, 130
players
  stand alone Flash player
    commands, 184
    sending messages to, 184
  Web-based Flash players, sending
    messages to, 185-186
Playhead, 39-40
playing movies, Play action, 82-83
pop() method, 141-142
populating arrays, 140-141
power(x, y) method (Math object), 172
precedence, arithmetic operations, 95
predefined functions, 100-101
Press event, 80
prevFrame method, 130
previewing movies, 205-206
primitive data types, 89
  booleans, 92
  double precision floating-point format, 92
  numbers, 91-92
  objects, 93

strings, 90-92
    concatenating, 90
    converting to lowercase, 91
    converting to numbers, 91
    converting to uppercase, 91
    declaring, 90
    escape characters, 91
    extracting substrings from, 92
    finding characters in, 91
Print action (movies), 82
programming errors, 201
    ActionScript logic, 201-203
    HTML, 203
    variable values, 201
programs
    ActionScript, 70
        building, 70-71
        editing, 72
        expert mode, 70-72
        normal mode, 70-72
        syntax highlighting, 72
    debugging Macromedia Flash, 195
properties
    classes, 68-70
    Debugger window, 199
    defined, 77
    Key object, 152-153
    MovieClip object, 135
        alpha, 135-136
        currentframe, 135
        droptarget, 135
        focusrect, 135
        framesloaded, 135
        height, 135
        highquality, 135
        name, 135
        quality, 135-136
        rotation, 135
        soundbuftime, 135
        target, 135
        totalframes, 135
        url, 135
        visible, 135

        width, 135
        x, 135
        xmouse, 135
        xscale, 136
        y, 136
        ymouse, 136
        yscale, 136
    prototype, 104
prototype property, 104
Publish function, 203
push() method, 141-142

Q

quality property (MovieClip object), 135-136
QuickTime audio files, 163
quit command (stand alone Flash player), 184

R

random function, 100
random() method (Math object), 172
rates, frames, 43
RAW format, 164
Red-Green-Blue (RGB), 147
reference data types, 89
    movie clip, 93-94
Release event, 80
Release Outside event, 80
removeMovieClip method, 130
removing array elements, 141
rendering quality (movie clips), 136
resizing, Arrow tools, 21
return keyword, 103
reusing code, 117
    #include directive, 117-118
    Smart Clips, 118-119
        buttons, 119
        checkboxes, 119
        menu objects, 119-121
        when to use, 118

reverse() method, 141-142
reversing array order, 141
RGB (Red-Green-Blue), 147
Right Channel effect (Sound panel), 165
RIGHT property (Key object), 152
Roll Out event, 81
Roll Over event, 80
rotating, Arrow tools, 20
rotation property (MovieClip object), 135
round(num) method (Math object), 172

S

sampling sound files, 159-161
scopes, 61-63
    block scope, 102
    global variables, 61-62
    local variables, 62
scripts, 73
scroll function, 101
semicolons, ActionScript statements, 74
send method, 188, 190
sendAndLoad method, 188
sending
    messages
        fscommand() function, 183-184
        stand alone Flash player, 184
        Web-based Flash players, 185-186
    variables to Flash movies, 97-98
setDate() method (Date object), 174
setframeSize function, 104
setFullYear() method (Date object), 174
setHours() method (Date object), 174
setMilliseconds() method (Date object), 174
setMinutes() method (Date object), 174

setMonth() method (Date object), 174
setRGB method, 147
setSeconds() method (Date object), 174
setTime() method (Date object), 174
setting button states, 50-51
settings, Stroke and Fill, 22-24
setTransform method, 147
setUTCDate() method (Date object), 174
setUTCHours() method (Date object), 174
setUTCMilliseconds() method (Date object), 174
setUTCMinutes() method (Date object), 174
setUTCMonth() method (Date object), 174
setUTCSeconds() method (Date object), 174
setUTCTime() method (Date object), 174
setYear() method (Date object), 174
shape hints, 47
shape tweening, 45
    creating, 46-47
    motion tweening, comparing, 45
shapes, buttons, 52
SHIFT property (Key object), 152
shift() method, 141
Shockwave Flash Movie File, 11
showmenu command (stand alone Flash player), 184
sin(num) method (Math object), 172
size
    movie clips, finding, 132
    sound files, 162-163
skins (color), 147
slash syntax, 76
slice() function, 92
slice() method, 141
slice(x, y) method (String object), 179
Smart Clips, 118-119
    buttons, 119
    checkboxes, 119

menu objects, 119-121
when to use, 118
Smooth modifier, 24-25
software, middleware
advantages, 192
data-driven movies, 191-193
Sort window, 14-15
editing, 16
sort() method, 141-142
sorting arrays, 141
sound, turning off (Stop All Sounds command), 83
sound editing controls, 167-168
sound files, 157
adding to buttons, 166
adding to movies, 164-166
background music, 167
bit depth, 161
exporting, 168-169
file formats, 163-164
importing, 164
linking, 167
looping, 169
sampling, 159-161
size of, 162-163
sound editing controls, 167-168
sound frequency, 158-159
Sound panel options, 165-166
synchronization, 165-167
tips and guidelines, 169
Sound panel
sound editing controls, 167-168
sound effects, 165-166
synchronization options, 165
soundbuftime property (MovieClip object), 135
SPACE property (Key object), 152
splice() method, 141, 143
splicing arrays, 141
split(delim) method (String object), 179
sqrt() function, 93
sqrt(num) method (Math object), 172

SQRT1 2 method (Math object), 172
SQRT2 method (Math object), 172
Stage, 10
stand alone Flash player
commands, 184
sending messages to, 184
Stand alone player, 198
Start option (sound synchronization), 165
startDrag method, 130, 134
statements. *See also* **keywords**
ActionScript, 74
break, 114-115
continue, 114-115
if, 107-110
if-else, 107-108
static frames, 9
static masks, 39
status bar, Debugger window, 197
Stop action (movies), 81-83
Stop All Sounds action (movies), 81, 83
stop method, 130
Stop option (sound synchronization), 166
stopDrag method, 130, 134
stopping movie playback, 82-83
storage, variables, 60
Straighten modifier, 24-25
Stream option (sound synchronization), 166
string function, 101
String object, 178
methods, 178, 180
charAt(s), 179
charCodeAt(s), 179
concat, 179
fromCharCode, 179
indexOf(s), 179
lastIndexOf(s), 179
slice(x, y), 179
split(delim), 179
substr(x, y), 179
substring(x, y), 179

toLowerCase(), 179
toUpperCase(), 179
strings, 90-92
concatenating, 90
converting to lowercase, 91
converting to numbers, 91
converting to uppercase, 91
declaring, 90
escape characters, 91
extracting substrings from, 92
finding characters in, 91
Stroke and Fill settings, 22-24
Stroke and Fill tabs, 22
Stroke panel, 22
Stroke tab, 22
Subselect tools, 19, 21
substr(x, y) method (String object), 179
substring(x, y) method (String object), 179
substrings, extracting from strings, 92
Swap Colors icon, 22
swapDepths method, 130, 134
swatches dialog box, 22
SWF files, 11
application compatibility, 11
symbols, 33. *See also* **buttons**
button, 34
buttons, 16
creating, 34-35
graphics, 16, 34
instances, 33-34
movie clips, 16, 34
synchronizing sound files, 165-167
syntax
dot, 75
_parent, 76
_root, 76
highlighting, ActionScript programs, 72
if statement, 107
slash, 76
syntax errors, ActionScript, 201

T

TAB property (Key object), 152
tabs
Fill, 24
Properties (Debugger window), 198
Stroke, 22
Stroke and Fill, 22
Variables (Debugger window), 198
Watch list (Debugger window), 198-199
tags (XML), 187-188
tan(num) method (Math object), 172
target paths, defined, 77
target property (MovieClip object), 135
TargetPath function, 101
targets, 85-86
Tell Target action (movies), 82, 85-86
terminology, ActionScript, 76-77
Test button, 57
test movies, creating, 205
testing
actions, 80
frame-by-frame animations, 45
Timeline, 10, 39
buttons, 49
frames, 41
icons, 40
Timeline window, 39
layers, 35-36
timelines
multiple, 43-44
nested, 43-44
Timer function (Date object), 178
Toggle High Quality action (movies), 81, 83
toggleHighQuality() method, 83
toggling, antialiasing settings, 83
toLowerCase() function, 91
toLowerCase() method (String object), 179

Toolbox, 10
Color section, 22
Stroke and Fill settings, 22-24
tools, 19
Arrow, 19-21
resizing items, 21
rotating items, 20
drawing, 24
Brush tool, 27-29
Line tool, 24
Oval and Rectangle tool, 27
Pen tool, 25-26
Pencil tool, 24-25
Eraser, 30-31
Lasso, 19, 21
painting, 29
Dropper tool, 29
Ink Bottle tool, 29
Paint Bucket tool, 29-30
Subselect, 19, 21
View, 10
toString() method, 141
toString() method (Date object), 174
totalframes property (MovieClip object), 135
toUpperCase() method (String object), 179
trace command, 195-197
trace() function, 120
transforms, parameters (Color object), 148-149
true function, 101
turning on/off
antialiasing settings, 83
sounds, Stop All Sounds command, 83
tweening, 45
motion, 45-46
motion tweening, 45
shape, 45
creating, 46-47
motion tweening, comparing, 45

typeof() function, 94
types of data. *See* **data types**

U

unescape function, 101
Uniform Resource Locators (URLs), loading files from, 84
unload event, 87
Unload Movie action (movies), 82, 85
unloading movies
Unload action, 85
unloadMovie method, 134
unloadMovie method, 130, 134
unshift() method, 141-142
UP property (Key object), 152
Up state (buttons), 49-50
uppercase, converting strings to, 91
url property (MovieClip object), 135
URLs (Uniform Resource Locators), loading files from, 84

V

variables, 59
ActionScript functions, 61
arrays, 139-140
adding elements to, 141
array access operators, 140
concatenating, 141
creating, 140-141
defined, 139
joining, 141
loops, 143-144
methods, 141-143
populating, 140-141
removing first element of, 141
removing last element of, 141
reversing order of, 141
sorting, 141
splicing, 141
assignments operators, 60
constants, 90

creating, 60, 89, 95
data types, 60-61, 89
    booleans, 92
    determining, 94
    movie clip, 93-94
    numbers, 92
    objects, 93
    primitive, 89
    reference, 89
    strings, 90-92
Debugger window
    adding to Watch list, 199
    modifying, 199
defined, 77
FrameRate, 60
functions, 59
global, scopes, 61-62
loading, 89, 97-98, 186
local, scopes, 62
naming conventions, 94
operators
    assignment operator, 96
    bitwise operators, 96
    comparison operators, 96
    logical operators, 96
    numeric operators, 95-96
    order of precedence, 95
scopes, 61-63
sending to Flash movies, 97-98
storage, 60
verifying loaded files, 86
View tool, 10
**visible property (MovieClip object),
  135**

W

WAV (Windows Wave) files, 163
**Web-based Flash players, sending
  messages to, 185-186**
while loop, 110-113
**width property (MovieClip object),
  135**

windows
Bandwidth Profiler, 206-207
Bitmap Properties, 56
Debugger, 197-198
    Properties tab, 198
    properties, modifying, 199
    status bar, 197
    Variables tab, 198
    variables, adding to Watch list,
      199
    variables, modifying, 199
    Watch list tab, 198-199
default, 10
Flash Action, 201
Layer, 36
    adding layers, 37
    deleting layers, 38
    editing layers, 38
Layer Properties, 36
Library, 14
Output, 195-196
Sort, 14-16
Timeline, 39
    layers, 35-36
Windows Wave (WAV) files, 163
writing ActionScript scripts, 73. *See
  also* **creating**

X

x coordinates (move clips)
  converting, 132-133
  finding, 132
x property (MovieClip object), 135
**XML (eXtensible Markup Language),
  187-188**
  tags, 187-188
  XML object, 188-189
  XMLSocket object, 189-190
XML object, 188-189
XMLSocket object, 189-190
**xmouse property (MovieClip object),
  135**

xscale property (MovieClip object),
136

Y-Z

y coordinates (move clips)
 converting, 132-133
 finding, 132
y property (MovieClip object), 136
ymouse property (MovieClip object),
 136
yscale property (MovieClip object),
 136

Zoom In command, 205
Zoom Out command, 205